Emerging Security Threats in the Middle East

Emerging Security Threats in the Middle East

The Impact of Climate Change and Globalization

Ashok Swain and Anders Jägerskog

ROWMAN & LITTLEFIELD
Lanham • Boulder • New York • London

Published by Rowman & Littlefield
A wholly owned subsidiary of The Rowman & Littlefield Publishing Group, Inc.
4501 Forbes Boulevard, Suite 200, Lanham, Maryland 20706
www.rowman.com

Unit A, Whitacre Mews, 26-34 Stannary Street, London SE11 4AB

British Library Cataloguing in Publication Information Available

Library of Congress Cataloging-in-Publication Data
ISBN 978-1-4422-4763-5 (cloth : alk. paper)
ISBN 978-1-4422-4764-2 (pbk. : alk. paper)
ISBN 978-1-4422-4765-9 (electronic)

♾™ The paper used in this publication meets the minimum requirements of American National Standard for Information Sciences—Permanence of Paper for Printed Library Materials, ANSI/NISO Z39.48-1992.

Printed in the United States of America

Contents

List of Tables

Preface

The Middle East was the global hub of knowledge, trade, and religion for ancient civilizations. In more recent times, oil, trade routes, geographical location, religion, and ideology all contribute to the strategic importance of this region. The Middle East has been a region of geopolitical and economic significance and it critically "matters" for global peace and development. The region has never been a trouble-free one, yet at present, it is especially turbulent. The effects of Islamic extremism, volatile oil prices, political instability, and sectarian violence are being felt worldwide.

Thus, the Middle East is, perhaps as much as ever, in the limelight of international attention and action. The developments resulting from the Arab Spring and the Syria crisis manifest themselves in the region as well as have major international repercussions. The Israeli-Palestinian conflict continues to simmer and negatively affects the prospects for positive developments in the region. The situation in the region can be broadly defined by the parameters of regional and global security. However, there are a number of undercurrent trends in the region affecting the security situation, and these are arguably not receiving enough attention in the region. Even so they are bound to affect the region in major ways in the decades to come.

It is understandable that both research and international attention are focused on the current ongoing conflicts, but if attention is not paid to the *vulnerabilities* that are currently developing into security threats, it will be a major omission. In this book, we have tried to focus on what we see as some of the major developments that are, already today, and even more so in the future, bound to further affect the security situation in the region. The aim is to go beyond the traditional focus on military or state security and take into account nontraditional security challenges. Food security, water scarcity, energy development, and large population migration are all challenges that are set to increase in importance over the years to come. The threat of climate change and processes of globalization further add to regional complexities and challenges. By including human security considerations in the analysis of the book, the linkages between the security developments in the region and the new development agenda, with the new Sustainable Development Goals (SDGs) that were adopted in the United Nations in September 2015, are also made clearer. In the end, an attempt has been made to outline pathways for how to successfully address emerging threats to achieve regional peace and stability.

Ashok Swain and Anders Jägerskog
Uppsala and Amman, October 2015.

Acknowledgments

This book is the culmination of one year of focused research but many years of following developments relating to security, and in particular, new and emerging security challenges, in the Middle East. To write this book, we have received support from many individuals and institutions. The Department for Peace and Conflict at Uppsala University and the Stockholm International Water Institute (SIWI) have provided us inspiring environments for research.

The book seeks to assist researchers, students, professionals, and all those interested in the security architecture in the Middle East by approaching the region with a broader and more inclusive lens than is commonly done. The need for a broader perspective on security issues is warranted as a counter to complement the general focus on "hard security," which is more commonly applied. While much has been written on the different subjects dealt with in this book, it was felt that few have tried to approach them by systematically analyzing linkages between them and the broader security architecture in the region. We hope that this book provides a readily accessible *vade mecum* to the new and emerging security challenges in the Middle East. Moreover, it is our hope that it will provide researchers as well as policy makers with an improved understanding of the complexity and linkages between water, food, energy, and migration in the region and the challenges that they pose from both a security and a development perspective.

Part of the research for this book was funded by the Swedish Research Council through the grants for the projects: "Changing parameters for Hydropolitics in light of Global Climate Change: The Governance of Trans-boundary Waters," 2011–2015 and "Intergroup Trust after War: The Effects of Migration," 2015–2017. For this support the authors are grateful. We are also grateful to the anonymous reviewers of the book proposal who provided many insightful comments and pointers to our approach. The book has also been influenced heavily by the report *Security in the Middle East-Increasingly Multidimensional and Challenging*, which Ashok wrote together with Joakim Öjendal and Michael Schulz for the Swedish Armed Forces in 2009.

Many individuals have been sources of encouragement and support throughout our research careers and have provided, either directly or indirectly, support to the endeavor of writing this book. We would like to offer our sincere gratitude to Aaron Salzberg, Ana Cascao, Anders Frankenberg, Anton Earle, Bahar Baser, Carol Chouchani Cherfane, Cecilia Albin, Charlotta Sparre, Clovis Maksoud, Emil Sandström, Florian Krampe, Fuad Bateh, Gidon Bromberg, Håkan Tropp, Hazem el-Naser, Helena Rietz, Itay Fischhendler, Jan Lundqvist, Jim Lee, Joakim Öjendal, Johan Schaar, Jonathan Hall, Kyungmee Kim, Malin Falkenmark, Mark Zeitoun, Martin Keulertz, Mats Hårsmar, Michael Talhami, Munqeth Mehyar, Munther Haddadin, Nader Khateeb, Peter Wallensteen, Ram Aviram, Riad Khouri, Roland Kostic, Roula Majdalani, Shaddad Attili, Shafiqul Islam, T. V. Paul, Terje Ostigaard, Therese Sjömander-Magnusson, Tony Allan, Torgny Holmgren, and Yana Abu Taleb. In various ways, they have been sources of inspiration for our continued work. We are indebted for the research assistance provided by Maisa Young to write chapter 4 and chapter 5. Our special thanks go to Andreea-Denis Pavel for her skilled research assistance to prepare the final manuscript. Deep appreciation also goes to Marie-Claire Antoine, Senior Acquisitions Editor of Rowman & Littlefield, for her encouragement and support to us throughout the process.

A deep and very special thanks goes to our respective families. From Anders a deep thanks to Elin, wife, supporter, and best friend. You are always there and together with you life has become even better than what I could dream of. Many thanks also to my children Agnes, Hedda, Edith, and Nils for being so loving and caring. You help me see what is important in life. One day you may even read the book and understand what I did in front of the computer all those hours. I would also like to thank my parents who have always provided support, love, and encouragement.

From Ashok—Special thanks to my family for showing patience with me for having taken yet another challenge that reduces the amount of time I can spend with them. Loving gratitude to my wife, Ranjula, for her unvarying love, understanding, and support and for being my inspiration and motivation for my continuous quest to improve my knowledge. I would also like to thank my children Kabir and Simran, who are just about the best kids a dad could hope for.

Finally, we would like to note that any errors or omissions remain the responsibility of the authors alone.

Chapter 1

Introduction

Middle East and Its New Sources of Insecurity

The Middle East is a highly securitized part of the world with composite security threats on several levels in the regional structure.[1] The region also experiences several more or less discernable conflicts with violent outbreaks and risks for future escalation. The violent conflicts have, moreover, deep historical roots, sectarian divides, disparities in natural resource distribution, and overwhelming vested major power interests. As no other region in the world, the violent conflicts seem to be both resilient and able to cause political tumult far beyond the borders of the region itself.[2] Undoubtedly, the security concerns in this part of the world are of major significance to the region and to the outside world as well, but there are also no straightforward or short-term solutions to the security dilemmas at hand.

Furthermore, the region itself contains contentious underlying security liabilities such as religious radicalism, an ethnic assortment, widespread terrorism, unfinished state-building projects, democratic deficits, repressive gender relations, and major power patrons, which all accompany the "traditional" security problems as typically seen between states and acted out through diplomacy (at best) or violence (at worst). Moreover, the region also suffers from a strained resource base (water, arable land, and forest), highly attractive natural resources (oil and gas), and growing poverty problems and large-scale human migration. Historically, the region gives evidence of limited ability to solve its "internal" security problems. In combination, this creates a highly complex and fragile configuration, where several of the above-mentioned security issues are interrelated and have system-wide, regional, and international implications.[3]

Given the above, this book is an attempt to be comprehensive and inclusive, tries to apply a broadened security concept as well as a theoretical frame, which will include the emerging security challenges with regional

1

dynamics at play in the region. It will, moreover, as a key aspect, draw the
tenants from the national and regional security issues into the wider global
security analysis that this perspective obviously calls for. The book will,
furthermore, outline some exploratory scenarios, particularly in the context
of globalization and climate change, as to where the emerging security issues
are evolving in this region and subsequently indulge in a discussion on possible policy responses.

UNDERSTANDING SECURITY IN THE MIDDLE EAST

The term "security" originates from the Latin word *securitas*, which comes
from *sine* (without) *cura* (troubling), and basically refers to a situation or
condition of being free from the threat of harm. Conflicts and peace, military
threats and war strategy, and even population and health issues have occupied
the minds of philosophers and writers for centuries; however, the security
study as an academic field came into being after the end of the Second World
War.[4] Security is often equated with peace as political and academic discourses usually relate these concepts to order and stability.[5] Though the peace
research discipline considers itself as a parallel discipline to security studies,
it is more of a school being developed in empirical rather than theoretical
works, positivist in its method and epistemology, and focused on attempting
at a critical analysis of the traditional concept of security. However, its influence has been to a large extent responsible in bringing changes to the way
security has been traditionally studied and practiced.[6]

These days, security refers to the absence of a threat to the order and stability of the international or regional system, to countries, or to individuals. For
much of the second half of the twentieth century, "security" has been defined
in terms of "national security" and has typically been pursued by states with
the aim of guaranteeing the state's survival based on the idea of sovereignty
and territory, assigning to the neighbor the status of a potential enemy and
applying military means to achieve these ends.[7] "Neo-Realism"—holding
these ideas—has also been the dominant approach to the study of security
and international relations since the Second World War. Certainly, most of
the available studies on security in the Middle East have applied these rationalities in trying to understand the key actors and their primary strategies.[8]
However, for nearly three decades, the security concept has been subject to
revision, both broadening and deepening its scope.

Since the 1980s, several scholars[9] have argued that the concept of security
needed to be opened up in two directions. First, the idea of security should
no longer be confined to the military domain. Nowadays, security concerns a
set of issues that affects the strong states as much as it does the weaker ones.

Security is not as easy to define, as this was the case at the time of the Cold War. Its ambiguities and contested nature are now unavoidable. The world and its problems have become too complex and too divisive, thus demanding a more exhaustive approach to deal with its security issues.[10] For security analysts, finding an inclusive approach has become a necessity as the security through military deterrence has lost some of its significance. This is also evidenced by what peace researchers have been questioning for some time—a limited concept of security that has focused almost exclusively on the military. As Åsberg and Wallensteen[11] argue, "ecological, economic, political and sociocultural factors are gaining importance at the expense of purely military aspects of security." Second, the referent object of "security," that which needs to be secured, should not be conceptualized solely in terms of the state, but should also embrace the individual below the state and the international system above it.[12] As Helga Haftendorn[13] says, "There is no one-concept of security; national security, international security and global security refer to different sets of issues and have their origins in different historical and philosophical contexts." Therefore, the question of how security is defined and framed is extremely important for our understanding and analysis of the security dynamics in the Middle East. Since this book aims at both a comprehensive and inclusive approach, we outline below how we theoretically approach the task of analyzing security in the Middle East.

With its roots in accelerating globalization and the diminishing preeminence of the state as the sole actor on the international scene, the core dynamics of "the state" has changed considerably.[14] Hence, this book takes the two major paradigmatic changes within the field of security seriously: First, rooted in the idea of "order" within international politics,[15] epitomized by the writing of Buzan[16] and later developed within the "Copenhagen School," driven by increasing international interdependence, and in particular, under the perception of structurally increased significance of world regions, "regional security complex" theory has by now become an important and established addition to "traditional" security analysis.[17] The regional security complex is normally conceived of as an interstate system defined "in terms of the patterns of amity and enmity substantially confined within some geographical area."[18] The idea differs from the "billiard balls" metaphor, following in the tradition of Hedley Bull,[19] assuming that states have "relations" beyond their respective power and that there exists some sort of "order" even though the system at large is "anarchic."

This security perception challenges the dominant neorealist approach to international affairs on two grounds: First, it left the previous absolute focus on the state level, and second, it introduced "soft" issues such as patterns of amity and enmity into "high politics." The regional approach is defended through the fact that "most political and military threats travel more easily over short distances than over long ones, insecurity is often associated with proximity."[20] Or in other words, neighbors have more frequent issues with each other than with countries outside the region. Hence, the amity/enmity dimension takes away the sole focus from power and interest and introduces intangibles possibly as wide reaching as cultural like-mindedness, social integration, and historical relations.

The security perceptions and concerns of neighboring states are so closely linked that national security cannot be evaluated apart from one another. Thus, the regional security complex approach helps to investigate the indigenous pattern of security interdependence.[21] In other words, the approach allows for a more integrated and qualitative security analysis. In its later versions, it also moves beyond a state-centric view in that it introduces the idea of "heterogeneous complexes." Moreover, the security complex theory explicitly works with "levels," putting the regional level at the center but referring up and down in the system. State rationalities constitute the complex, and external forces often feed it with its content and impact on its actors' key strategic choices, so do subnational dynamics. In a normative tradition, this opens up for discussions on "security community" in the tradition of Deutsch et al.[22]

Several security challenges tend to take shape regionally. Many have argued that security dynamics have increasingly become regionalized since the 1980s.[23] Civil wars and social movements are increasingly taking a regional character. Many aspects of poverty, environment, food and water availability, and population migration usually encompass the whole of a region. Moreover, different regions have developed different degrees of conflict management mechanism as well. This has a bearing on the security thinking of the Middle East, but it should be noted right from the beginning that the focus on the regional level does not imply that there necessarily are dynamics of regional cooperation, or even less regional integration at work, but it does imply that there are significant regional dynamics in motion.

Second, the development of the concept of "human security" launched by UNDP,[24] and further developed within and outside the UN system, now constitutes a norm of sorts, implies the widening of the security agenda away from states' security to a more people-centered approach. Once the iron grip of the Cold War was released, the hitherto-dominating realist security concept invented during the Westphalian Era and thriving during the Cold War was put under pressure. In a globalizing world in a post–Cold War era, the state as the sole referent object and ultimate supplier of security became increasingly unrealistic. Thus, in introducing the concept in "hoping to increase attention and resources on development and to assist vulnerable people," the political objective of the United Nations was "to shift financial and human resources away from the traditional security agenda on win-win grounds that this was good for people in the South and good for the security of the North."[25]

With the introduction of the concept of human security by UNDP, a vast field of security studies has opened up. This followed a critical analysis of the traditional security concept. In particular, it was seen as inadequate on four different grounds: First, its basic weakness is the creation of a "security dilemma" where one's security is the other's insecurity, creating a perpetual systemic insecurity, arms race, and eventually outbreak of violence. Or as Mary Kaldor[26] argues, the classic security paradigm with its total reliance on military means, sovereignty, territories, and boundaries is exactly what creates insecurity. Second, the sole focus on the state as the security provider is increasingly out of sync with reality as overall regional and global interdependence has been fast emerging.[27] Third, it was focused on physical violence as the only feature of insecurity and (threats of) violence as the means to restore and keep up security. Fourth, and finally, it was the military—or the "security apparatus" at large—which was the primary and only actor in guaranteeing security. In the post–Cold War era, and with the birth of the human security concept, all these cornerstones of the neorealist assumptions of security were called into question.

Thus, the emergence of the human security concept is considered much more than the absence of military threat, since at a minimum, it requires that basic needs are met, acknowledging that sustained economic development, human rights and fundamental freedoms, the rule of law, good governance, and social equity are as important to global peace as are arms control and disarmament.[28] The primary premise of this concept is that "the world can never be at peace unless people have security in their daily lives." The concept identifies seven core elements, namely, economic security, food security, personal security, community security, health security, environmental security, and political security. As such, the concept was supposed to be "people centered," "multidimensional," "interconnected," and "universal";[29] or in other words, it is not only the state that shall be secured; it is not only physical violence that is considered; it is not only particular interests and/or claims to sovereignty that are regarded; and it is not only particular areas or country that are relevant for this wider security conception. In doing the above, human security stretched into the development realm, or as Gaspers[30] puts it, "It is proposed as a partner, rather than component, of "human development"; or sometimes even as its container, perhaps the biggest Russian doll of all."

Slowly but steadily it has become a widely applied concept, and it has become a standard procedure to work this concept into national human development reports, de facto merging the ideas of security and development.[31] Undoubtedly, "human security" has become a widely accepted prominent term in international affairs. However, as Keynes once said, quoted in Des Gaspers, about shifting paradigms, "The (new) ideas . . . are extremely simple and should be obvious. The difficulty lies in, not the new ideas, but escaping from the old ones, which ramify, for those brought up as most of us have been, into every corner of our minds."[32] Furthermore, Chandler stated, in a critique of the human security concept, that the discourse of human security has become "dominant in international policy circles," while at the same time "it has had so little impact on policy outcome."[33] Hence, although discursively, the "human security" concept has been established, in many ways a realist security concept still de facto dominates international affairs.

Both "freedom from fear" and "freedom from want" are needed for human security, and these hold the key to achieving security and stability for any political unit. "Freedom from fear" indicates the protection of human beings, which only includes violent and easily identifiable threats that are directed toward the individual safety, like armed conflict, terrorism, ethnic expulsion, and political and criminal violence. However, the objective of "freedom from want," which emphasizes on linking development with security, asks for broadening the human security agenda further to include poverty, hunger, disease, natural disasters, and displacement. The concept has been further expanded by the Commission on Human Security as it reasons that "freedom from want, freedom from fear, and the freedom of future generations to inherit a healthy natural environment—these are the interrelated building blocks of human—and therefore national—security."[34] The wider definition of human security includes all sources of not only present but also future insecurity toward the individual, ranging from lack of development to increasing resource scarcity.

STUDY OF SECURITY IN THE MIDDLE EAST

Analytically, in this book, "security" will be understood in relation to existing and emerging security threats. In this globalized era, security threats in the Middle East are no longer limited to violent actions by armed groups and states. In this new interdependent and interconnected world, international issues have to some extent overtaken the importance of national issues. Globalization has created new opportunities as well as many risks and challenges. Globalization has generated more wealth and encouraged technological innovations, but at the same, it has failed to support and promote sustainable human development and thus it has generated anguish and deprivation.[35] So far, it has had a largely negative impact on the poor and underprivileged sections of the society and the region and has already resulted in growing civil unrest and in some cases contributed to armed conflicts in the developing world.[36] Moreover, new varieties of unconventional threats like climate change concerns, food and water scarcity, and energy crisis have been posing serious security challenges, shaping a more vulnerable and insecure region. These newly emerging threats are interrelated, and a threat to one country or region has often become a challenge to all in the region. Though our main focus in this study is to locate and analyze these important but often overlooked security threats, there is neither a direct preference for a state-centric security analysis nor a bias toward human security analysis. Neither is there an exclusive focus on the regional level or on the state level.

Though our focus will not be only region centric, we consider that the analysis of regional dynamics at play in the region will add quality and richness to the state-by-state analysis. Hence, we need to posit specific threats within the "security complex" in question, in which way it operates, and with what consequences; and, than, if the state's security and its security apparatus are not the beginning and the end of the security story, what dimensions, issues, and actors are then significant for the overall security situation? Although these theoretical developments of the security concept are generic, in their application they are highly context specific. There is a lot of ongoing theorizing around the broadened security concept. One dominant strand or relevance for the use of this security concept in the Middle East is the importance of eradicating "Islamic terror" for achieving peace and development in the region in order to enhance the security of the West, or, arguably, the entire global system.[37] The fear is that rebellion and terrorism grow most freely in failed states, hence the attempt at "securitizing development" by actors.[38]

In recent years, a lot of rethinking has been going on to locate the causes of violence in the global scenario. In this context, the relationship between development and security has become crucial. Although the nexus between security and development has seriously got into the policy agenda after the September 11, 2001 terror attack, the idea has been influencing international development policy for a long period of time. Even the Marshall Plan and Truman doctrine were a product of this idea. In the last one and a half decades, the issue of security and development has been one of the most prominent ones on the international agenda, primarily in the context of the work of the United Nations and other international and regional organizations. The international community is fond of "new solutions," and its focus is increasingly on how conflicts of various sorts can be prevented through greater focus on "development." The crucial position of the civil society in the context of security and development has been an issue on which international nongovernmental organizations have been devoting much effort as well.

As development and security are interactive conceptions, it may be asked that for whose security and for whose development is this nexus really focusing on. Short-term security considerations of the developed world increasingly undermine the long-term developmental challenges of developing regions. This approach also poses challenges for the international community's long-term engagements that are necessary for achieving sustainable peace. There are also severe coordination issues between different intergovernmental and aid agencies and their policies in connecting development and security. Though there are recent attempts toward policy standardization, in most cases, the so-called coordination is limited to rhetoric. Besides a lack of coordination among relevant agencies, the policy driven by the nexus approach also suffers from a huge disparity between policy and implementation, the absence of local stakeholder involvement, and a lack of resources.[39]

The Middle East, however, is perfectly situated to take advantage of the discourse on the security-development nexus. On the one hand, the region is highly securitized with multilayered and long-standing conflicts causing a prominent military presence where the security dilemma is the dominant process at play and where vast interests are protected by military means alone. Borders are obsessively guarded and sovereignty upheld to the extent that it negatively affects states to interact in the globalized system. On the other hand, it is obvious how political legitimacy deficits, unfulfilled development promises, and a strained and increasingly scarce natural resource base create to a large extent a series of insecurities. Thus, a deeper and sincere commitment to human security may be needed to unlock the security dilemma and establish a progressive spiral. This is, however, easier said than done.

THE MIDDLE EAST

The focus of the book is the Middle East and this regional composition is loosely confined to the Mashrek region and the Arab Peninsula. The Mashrek region can be defined as the geographical area placed east of Egypt and north of the Arabian Peninsula.[40] This concept originally came from the early dates of the Islamic conquest. The Mashrek region, Maghreb region, and the Arab Peninsula thereby constitute the Arab world. Traditionally, the region of Arabic-speaking countries to the east of Egypt and north of the Arabian Peninsula, within the Arab world, is known as Mashrek, and it literally means "east." It complements the term Maghreb, meaning "West." Egypt has a peculiar position: while it is unique in many ways, it has strong cultural, ethnic, and linguistic ties to both the Mashrek and the Maghreb. However, when it gets clubbed with one or the other, it is usually regarded as part of the Mashrek. Thus, this present study includes Egypt and focuses on six countries of the region, which also includes Jordan, Iraq, Lebanon, Syria, and the Palestine. Also, in an unorthodox way, we include Israel in the analysis

Table 1.1   Countries in the Middle East Region

Countries	Population (in Million)	GNI per Capita (in USD)	HDI Index	Life Expectancy at Birth	Freedom Rating
Egypt	82.06	3,140	0.682	71.16	5.5
Israel	8.060	33,930	0.888	81.8	1.5
Iraq	33.42	6,720	0.642	69.42	6
Jordan	6.46	4,950	0.745	73.85	5.5
Lebanon	4.46	9,870	0.765	80.01	4.5
Syria	22.85	1,850	0.658	74.55	7
Palestine	5.168	2,782	0.686	73.2	
Yemen	24.41	1,330	0.5	63.11	6
Bahrain	1.33	19,770	0.815	76.61	6.5
Kuwait	3.36	45,130	0.814	74.29	5
Oman	3.63	25,150	0.783	76.55	5.5
Qatar	2.16	86,790	0.851	78.37	5.5
Saudi Arabia	28.83	26,260	0.836	75.48	7
UAE	9.34	38,360	0.827	76.84	6

Sources of the Data: The World Bank (data.wprldbank.org), UNDP Human Development Reports (hdr. undp.org), and Freedom House (freedomhouse.org). UNDP Human Development Report ranks countries with HDI of less than 0.550 for low human development, 0.550–0.699 for medium human development, 0.700–0.799 for high human development, and 0.800 or greater for very high human development. Freedom House index ranks countries, level of freedom on the basis of available political and civil rights. Countries are ranked on a scale of 1–7: countries with a score from 1 to 2.5 are regarded as "free," 3 to 5 "partly free," and 5.5 to 7 "not free."

since it constitutes a major security player within the geographical area that historically has been known as the Mashrek. We will also include countries of the Arab Peninsula, including Yemen (the Gulf Cooperation Council (GCC) includes all Arab Peninsula states, except Yemen). Members of the GCC include Bahrain, Kuwait, Oman, Qatar, Saudi Arabia, and the United Arab Emirates. While the focus of the study is on the countries outlined above, in certain aspects also other countries will be included in the analysis where relevant for a particular issue (such as Sudan in relation to the food and water security analysis and Iran and Turkey while discussing energy and migration issues).

However, many more states, as well as other actors, are linked to other Middle East actors' securities. Thus, there is a need to analytically make a distinction of several subsecurity complexes within the Middle East that crisscross and link up with the rather artificial regional construction. Due to the fact that ethnic groups, as in the Middle East, extend over one, or in most cases several, territorial borders, interethnic as well as interstate relations shape the patterns of amity and enmity in the region.[41] The formation of the nature of the complexes is constantly changing, and the security issues also alter over time, which in turn can transform the sets of complexes in the Middle East. Robertson[42] explains the constantly changing complex formation in the following way:

Because these states (in the Middle East) are new, the pattern of their relation-ships is in an early stage of development. A prominent feature of the developing Middle East state system is a constant pattern of realignment, which has thus far prevented the rise of a hegemonic power. This feature underlines the supreme difficulty in establishing regional security, a feature within which the Arab statesmen move and breathe.

One could argue that various security issues among states link the states' national security concerns together. The Middle East could also be seen as a regional security complex full of other sets of security complexes, or sub-complexes, which all have their own security issues that connect the states together in inextricably entangled relations. For instance, the Palestinian issue is a security concern for many states in the region, even for countries in the Maghreb. Similarly, the Euphrates and Tigris rivers form the security issue for the four "riparian" states, Turkey, Syria, Iraq, and Iran, and thereby form another regional security complex.[43] Each of the states in the Middle East is linked to other security complexes in the larger region with other security issues that in turn create new analytical complexes.

The Middle Eastern countries have been directly linked to the external state actors since their foundation in the 1920s. After the collapse of the Ottoman Empire, the colonial powers, France and United Kingdom, had redrawn the map of the Middle East. Most of the countries in the region gradually gained their independence from the colonial influence in the 1940s and 1950s. The Arab League that was formed in 1945 had two main issues on its agenda: First, all Arab states were seen as artificial colonial creations that only tempo-rarily existed until a pan-Arab state was established. Second, Palestine should be under Arab control and the Jewish Zionist should be prevented from estab-lishing the Israeli State. After 1948, when Israel was established, the Arab League was very much united around its struggle against Israel. However, the pan-Arab unity did not last long, despite Egypt's and Syria's attempt to take the first merging step of forming the Arab Union in 1958. It turned out that national interests were stronger than the pan-Arab sentiments, and the union collapsed in 1962. Despite great popularity in the Arab world, the project of Egypt under its president Nasser, who aimed for Arab unity under its leadership, began to lose relevance after the disastrous defeat of the Arab countries in the 1967 war against Israel. Syria and Iraq which were ruled by the other major pan-Arab branch, the Baathist ideology, became bitter rivals and worked to undermine each other. Lebanon witnessed a long and violent civil war between 1975 and 1990, and the Israeli-Palestinian conflict is still far from being over. With time, various states have consolidated themselves, in clear dissonance with pan-Arabic visions, and often with the help of strong, repressive internal security apparatus.

INTERNATIONAL ACTORS AND REGIONAL
SECURITY IN THE MIDDLE EAST

In the last seven decades, the security scenario of the Middle East has been dominated by three major visible conflicts: the Cold War, the Arab-Israeli dispute, and the Iraq Wars, with the latent one being the Sunni-Shia sectarian divide. After the end of the Cold War, the contemporary security consciousness in the region can be attributed to the Israeli-Palestinian relations.[44] The regional identity received a jolt in the postcolonial period with the creation of Israel in 1948. The devastating defeat at the hands of Israel in the 1967 war brought down further the hope of the region to recover Arab glory and honor under the Egyptian leadership. Egypt, Syria, and Jordan suffered heavily militarily and economically and the Jordanian West Bank, the Egyptian Sinai Peninsula, and Gaza Strip, and the Syrian Golan Heights all came under Israeli control. In the 1973 war, Egypt and Syria made a surprise attack on Israel and had initial military success, but the war ended with the Israeli military having the upper hand. The involvement of the superpowers showed the risks involved in Arab-Israeli wars. The war escalated dramatically in which both the superpowers came close to a Third World War, warranting a comparison with the Cuba crisis.[45] At that time period, the Cold War was at its height and this conflict immediately became a proxy war between the Soviet Union and the United States. The Russians supported the Arab states and the United States supported Israel with arms and ammunition as well with military advice. The tide turned soon; Israeli forces got an upper hand and almost reached Damascus and came very close to Cairo.[46] Finally, after several ceasefire negotiations, the war came to an end. However, the outcome of the war brought some political success for the Arab states in spite of heavy military defeat.

In 1974, the Arab League recognized PLO as the sole representative of the Palestinian people. Thanks to American mediation, Egypt left its Arab allies in the cold and made a peace deal with Israel in 1978. This development brought a huge power asymmetry between Israel and its adversaries in the region. The war between Iran and Iraq started in 1980 and that diverted the region's attention from the Palestinian issue as Iran was gaining advantage. The Iranian revolution that brought Shia Islamic cleric Ayatollah Khomeini to power became a concern not only for external powers like the United States and the Europeans but also for the Sunni-dominated states in the Arab world who feared the export of Islamic fundamentalism to their societies. At the same time, many Arab states, not least Saudi Arabia and Egypt, feared a militarily strong Iraq led by Saddam Hussein. Hence, external parties' effort was mainly to ensure that neither Iran nor Iraq would win the war and thereby strengthen their regional position. Hence, most states in the region, including

Israel, were involved, indirectly, in the war. After nearly a million and a half losses of lives,[47] an end of the Iran-Iraq war that began with a ceasefire in 1988 and the beginning of intifada in 1987 in the Israeli-occupied territories brought back the attention of the region to the Palestinian issue.

After the end of the Cold War and the dissolution of the Soviet Union and in the aftermath of the Gulf War, the United States, using its diplomatic and military influence, brought all the relevant parties to the Palestinian conflict (Israel, Syria, Lebanon, and Jordanian-Palestinian representation) to the negotiating table in Madrid in 1991. The process resulted in several important decisions and led to the historic Declaration of Principle of September 13, 1993, in which the parties (Israel and the PLO) not only recognized each other but also committed themselves to solve the conflict through political means. However, the hope of achieving a comprehensive solution to the Arab-Israeli conflict gradually yielded to disillusionment. The United States' attempt to solve the final status issues in a summit meeting at the Camp David summit concluded on July 25, 2000 without achieving any substantial agreement, although the key issues were discussed formally at this level for the first time. The beginning of the Second Intifada in September 2000 finally brought a stalemate to the peace process. Some of the positive outcomes of the peace process were the mutual recognition between Israel and the PLO, the establishment of an autonomous Palestinian Authority (PA), and the Israel-Jordan Peace Treaty of October 26, 1994. The negotiation between Israel and Syria looked favorable in its initial stage but did not move further, and Israel withdrew from Lebanon unilaterally in 2000.

In March 2002, Saudi Arabia presented the "Arab Peace Initiative" at the Arab summit in Beirut, which proposed a multilateral approach to bring an end to this dispute. Under the initiative, Arab countries endorsed a two-state solution—Israel would respect the lines of June 1967, a Palestinian state would take over the West Bank and the Gaza Strip and also find a "just solution" to the refugee issue, and in return, Arab countries would formally recognize Israel. This led to establishing the "Quartet"—the United States, Russia, the European Union, and the United Nations, and in 2003, it suggested a "road map" for bringing about a settlement. The road map was not implemented, but it still remains a reference point for the slowly moving negotiations.

In 2007, US president George W. Bush hosted a conference at Annapolis, Maryland, to revive the peace process. Though the Israeli prime minister, the president of the Palestinian Authority, and the representatives from the "Quartet" including Arab countries took part in the conference, the hardline Palestinian group, Hamas, was not represented. However, it led to regular meetings between Israeli and Palestinian officials and both teams shared maps of a possible territorial solution. The negotiation process came to an end with Israel's military offensive in Gaza in December 2008. Direct talks resumed for a short period after another US-brokered meeting in Washington in September 2010, but the talks got into another deadlock again. Very little is left of the peace process in 2015, and there is increasing pressure from the international community, particularly from European states, on the parties to return to the negotiating table.[48] US Secretary of State, John Kerry, led intensive efforts in trying to revive the negotiations in 2013–2014, but these efforts were unsuccessful.

Europe had a very limited role in starting the peace process in the Middle East; however, in the post–Oslo Accord phase, it played a key role in bringing about economic development in the Palestinian areas. In spite of regular attempts by the European policy makers, the United States is reluctant to give up its primacy and let Europe play any significant role in the Israel-Palestine negotiations.[49] Some of the countries in the Middle East consider United States as a biased mediator, but they lack unity of purpose and the ability to oppose any political mediation by the United States. Except Syria, all other countries in the region have developed close working relations with Washington.

The September 11, 2001 terror attacks brought about a dramatic impact on regional security, particularly on the Middle East peace process and American involvement in the region. The Arab-Israeli conflict got overshadowed due to direct American military intervention in Iraq in 2003. Due to the lack of legitimacy in the eyes of the international law and the absence of support from a credible coalition, the Islamists in the region have used the invasion of Iraq to mobilize against "American hegemony." The security situation in the post–Saddam era Iraq is highly unstable to say the least. The presence of foreign fighters, particularly from Saudi Arabia and Syria,[50] created serious problems for the international forces to maintain security in the post–2003 period. In the absence of peace and stability, the US-led Western attempts for political and economic development in Iraq failed to achieve their objectives. Due to the increased presence of American troops in 2007 and the tactical mobilization of Sunni tribes against Sunni extremists, there was a drop in terrorist incidents in Iraq for a short period of time. However, as expected, this did not last long. By October 2011, American combat troops completely withdrew from Iraq and the security situation in Iraq fast turned extremely dangerous.

Many states in the region had traditionally considered Iraq as the only state capable of balancing Iranian dominance. But today these states face a problem as Iraq lacks the ability to play that role now and in the near future. Therefore, it is mainly Saudi Arabia and Iran that compete for regional dominance today. Not only strategic factors but also sectarian Sunni-Shia divisions in Iraq and its neighboring countries have become a serious concern. While

Iraqi intervention had strengthened strong anti-US sentiments in the Middle East, the insurgency, suicide bombing, and kidnappings in the lawless Iraq further added to Arab/Islam phobia in the West. After the early withdrawal of US troops under the present Obama administration, the Sunni minority and jihadi groups got the opportunity to challenge the weak central government in Baghdad. The popular uprising in Syria came soon after the exit of the American troops from Iraq. Since 2012, Iraq and Syria have turned to become another Lebanon, a perfect stage for the proxy war between Sunnis and Shias, supported by the two respective neighbors, Saudi Arabia and Iran.[51]

While the United States has been to some extent engaged in controlling the violence in Iraq, it has been simultaneously trying hard to force Iran to abandon its secret nuclear weapons program. The dispute over nuclear proliferation has escalated particularly since 2006. The American efforts to wage a coordinated effort by the international community against Iran's adventurism have been regularly challenged by the reluctance of China and Russia to go along with the United States. The United States also provides covert support to the Iranian resistance movement, particularly in the Arab majority oil-rich Khuzestan region. Iran also does what it can do best to create security challenges in the region for the United States in particular and for the international community in general. Iran actively supports and promotes the Shia majority in Iraq to declare a Shia state, which is seen as a direct threat to the important Western ally in the region, Saudi Arabia. Iran, in league with Syria, supports Hezbollah to wage a struggle against Israel. The strengthening of Hezbollah has brought not only security threats for Israel; it has also caused a serious internal crisis in Lebanon. Iran is also backing the Shia Houthi rebels in Yemen, while Saudi Arabia is backing president Hadi and has engaged in an extensive bombing campaign starting from March 2015. Iran also supports Hamas in the Palestinian self-rule areas, by providing it weapons and even military training.[52] However, the United States and its Western Allies have managed to get a deal with Iran in April 2015, and if it is ratified and implemented, it will bring Iran's entire supply chain of fissile material under broad inspections of the International Atomic Energy Agency (IAEA), in exchange for the threat to impose sanctions. The IAEA-led inspection will make it almost impossible for Iran to operate a secret nuclear weapons program. The success of this deal can lead to normalizing Iran's relations with the West and may curb Iran's aggressive policies toward Israel and lessen support for terror activities in the region.[53]

Besides the Palestinian conflict, the other long-standing dispute affecting the Middle East is the Kurdish issue. The Kurds, like the Palestinians, are a nation without a state, but their situation differs in many ways from that of the Palestinians.[54] Besides Iraq and Syria, the other two neighboring regional powers, Turkey and Iran, have substantially large Kurdish minorities. There are nearly 28 million Kurds in the region, of which 14.5 million are in Turkey, 6 million in Iran, 5 to 6 million in Iraq, and 2 million in Syria. However, they have refused to be assimilated into dominant ethnic groups of their respective states and have agitated for self-rule for nearly a century. In recent decades, Kurds have increasingly influenced regional security dynamics, waging a violent struggle for autonomy in Turkey and being important actors in the ongoing civil wars in Iraq and Syria.

Before the overthrow of the Saddam regime in Iraq, all the four states with significant Kurdish population had somehow followed a similar policy (use of force) toward containing the separatist struggles of their Kurdish minorities, but also sometimes providing help to rebels as they wage their struggle against the enemy state. However, the newfound semi-independence of Kurdish population in northern Iraq (own parliament and flag) brought serious worries for other three countries, as they perceived this development as a direct threat to their own domestic security. At the same time, for Turkey, the carrot of European Union (EU) membership has persuaded the country to deal with its Kurdish problem in an internationally acceptable manner. In 2002, Turkey abolished death penalty and allowed Kurds to broadcast and teach in their own language.[55] Besides the hope of the EU membership, Turkey also has a strong domestic constituency, which supports the expansion of human rights and improvements in the position of Kurds. In the Turkish elections, in June 2015, the pro-Kurdish party HDP (People's Democratic Party) received over 12 percent of the vote and made it with around 80 seats into the 550-strong Turkish Parliament.[56]

In the late 1970s, Abdullah Ocalan established the Kurdistan Workers Party (PKK). The group, which has Marxist-Leninist roots, engaged in an armed struggle against the Turkish government from 1984 demanding an independent state within Turkey. This resulted in the death of more than 40,000 people and huge population displacement. In the 1990s, the PKK scaled down its demand from independence to autonomy, but this was not accepted by Turkey, so the violent conflict continued. After Ocalan's arrest by Turkish authorities in 1999, there was a pause in the violence for some years, but it restarted in 2004. By 2009, PKK had around 3000 fighters based in the mountains of northern Iraq. Turkey had created a security zone inside Iraq for its military to prevent PKK infiltration and had secured an agreement with Iraq in 2008 which assured that Iraq's territory would not be used to launch attacks against neighboring countries. A trilateral commission consisting of officials from Turkey, the United States, and northern Iraq was established to deal with issues for a possible PKK amnesty,[57] but without much success.

From 2009 to 2011, high-level talks between PKK and the Turkish authorities took place secretly in Oslo, but ended without any significant progress, leading to the escalation of conflict in June 2011. On the last day of 2012, Turkey announced the revival of peace negotiations and in 2013, a ceasefire was agreed upon. In spite of initial progress, when the spillover of the Syrian civil war entrusted autonomy to Kurdish groups in Syria, it gave strategic strength to the PKK. This led to the resumption of clashes between Turkish forces and PKK fighters from September 2014. If Turkey, because of the lure of the EU membership, shows willingness to constitutionally recognize Kurdish identity and adopt a northern Iraq formula, it will be very difficult for Iran to ignore the Kurdish demand for long. Moreover, while European powers have played a subdued role in the Palestinian issue so far, they have a real opportunity, through Turkey, to take the Kurdish issue to the center stage and address it. In the fight against the Islamic State (ISIS), the Peshmerga (one who confronts death) forces of Iraqi Kurdistan have also grabbed the opportunity to attract international support, thus strengthening the Kurdish position.

Though regional, national, and sectarian conflicts have taken the center stage in the Middle East, the region faces many developmental challenges. As the Israeli-Palestinian conflict is still simmering and the conflicts in Iraq, Syria, and Yemen have become very violent, the economic and social conditions in the region are either stagnating or deteriorating. For the ruling elites, development policies are not a priority since they are very much occupied by the complex political dynamics of the region. The United States usually exerts more military and political influence in the region, while Europe has significant economic and cultural relations. In the Middle East, countries have limited trade relations between them, either because some borders are simply closed or when formally borders are open, security measures and politicization of economic relations reduce incentive to trade.[58]

THE RISE AND FALL OF THE ARAB SPRING
AND THE RISE OF THE ISIS

In the Middle East, the national security of individual countries is primarily equated with regime security. The ruling elites are extremely sensitive to any opposition to their authority. Some cosmetic political reforms, aiming to give space for the establishment of some democratic mechanisms, were initiated by the authoritarian regimes in the region in the late 1980s and early 1990s. Though there is a significant variation in political freedom among the countries, these "liberalization" processes have not yet resulted in genuine democratization in any one of them. Limited political and civil freedom are often initiated and often regulated by the states. In several cases, regimes have backtracked on even these limited reforms.[59] For over two decades, the international community has been consistently complaining about the lack of democracy and respect of human rights in the countries of the region. Till the advent of the Arab Spring in late 2010, the Western powers were moderately encouraging the states in the region to introduce political reforms. However, after September 11, regimes in the region, not least Egypt and Jordan, started arguing that the reform might pave the way for Islamic radicals to capture power.

After failing to establish new functional institutions in a post–Saddam Iraq and not being able to bring stability and peace to the country, the United States became reluctant to undertake military action for initiating regime change in the region. However, to some extent it increased financial and political support to civil society groups to strengthen the democratic support structure in the region. These democratization projects were being undertaken particularly in Egypt, Jordan, the Palestine, and Iraq. The official American and European position before the Arab Spring was that they did not want to impose regime change, but they repeatedly wished for such a change to take place. They provided support for election monitoring, training political parties, strengthening independent media, and promoting civil society groups. Americans and Europeans were also concerned about the instability that can follow from a regime change in pro–Western Arab states, such as Egypt, Jordan, and Saudi Arabia. However, as Laila Alhamad[60] argues, Western support for democracy failed to be effective as they were not able to understand the ground reality and lacked basic understanding of how political change could have taken place in the region. The regimes in this region more or less had been still able to protect themselves from various "waves of democratization." Almost all the countries in the region suffer from a serious democratic deficit and are far from starting a genuine democratization process.

Italian philosopher Norberto Bobbio defines democracy as a system that replaces the power of force by that of persuasion.[61] As he argues, "What is democracy, other than a set or rules, for the solution of conflict without bloodshed?"[62] When defining democracy, the usual inclination is to follow the archetypal definitions, which are minimalist in nature. Schumpeter[63] writes that democracy is merely a system in which rulers are selected by competitive elections, while Popper[64] defines it as a means by which people remove rulers without any resort to force. Democracy is certainly much more than rule of the people and by the people. Democracy needs to be defined as a system where the government is in power by the consent of the people and the government is accountable to the governed. Moreover, democracy also means that there are free elections, checks, and balances on executive power, a division of power, constitutional protection of minority rights, freedom of association, a free press, respect for human rights, and equal rights before law.

Since the end of the Cold War, the notion that democracy is the ideal form of government has almost become axiomatic, though the empirical evidence for such a normative conclusion is not yet definite.[65] Closely related is the belief that a community of democratic nations is the best way to maintain domestic and international peace. There is considerable evidence of democratic peace in international relations,[66] and democracy, or the promise of democratization, has been an integral component in several peace agreements since the end of the Cold War, which has ended civil conflict within nations. In the 1990s, several countries in Asia, Latin America, and Eastern Europe have become democratic. The so-called "third wave" of democratization,[67] which began in Southern Europe in the mid-1970s, moved on to Latin America and Asia in the 1980s, and then reached sub-Saharan Africa, Eastern Europe, and the Soviet Union.[68] However, it never showed up in the Middle East or North Africa. At least not till the end of 2010.

On December 17, 2010, the self-immolation of vegetable vendor Mohamed Bouazizi in the Tunisian town of Sidi Bouzid sparked the Arab Spring. Within a few months, a wave of dramatic political protests throughout North Africa and the Middle East swept away the authoritarian rulers of Tunisia, Egypt, and Libya. Popular protests and violent uprisings started spreading to the Mashrek region and also to the Gulf states. In Yemen, a transition government took over power from the country's long-serving authoritarian leader. In Syria, opposition to the ruling regime led to a civil war, which caused a serious humanitarian crisis with millions of internally displaced people and external refugees and increasing social-political tensions in neighboring countries, especially Jordan, Lebanon, and Turkey. The rulers of Morocco, Algeria, and Jordan have managed to stay in power by preempting serious political reforms with a combination of economic compensation and conceding some minor political rights. In the Gulf region, violent popular protests took place in Kuwait and Bahrain. To protect the regime in Bahrain, Saudi Arabia intervened militarily under the cover of the GCC. More than five years have passed since the Arab Spring began in late 2010. Almost in all the countries in the Middle East, which experienced popular uprisings, the political situation remains fluid and explosive. Despite some similarities in the cause and nature of popular opposition to authoritarian rule, the outcomes of these protests differed from country to country.

Within two months of the onset of the Arab Spring, one of the most stable autocrats in the Middle East, Egypt's Hosni Mubarak, was overthrown on February 11, 2011. The Egyptian popular opposition to the Mubarak regime broke out on January 25, 2011, on Police Day. Egypt commemorates January 25, 1952 as Police Day, the date of the Battle of Ismailia, in which Egyptian police officers in the city of Ismailia had battled against British colonial forces. Protest centered in Cairo's Tahrir Square and the protesters smartly used social media (Facebook and Twitter) to successfully coordinate their mobilization. Mubarak offered concessions but failed to appease the opposition and finally was forced to step down. This political transition was not a peaceful one as demonstrators and pro-Mubarak forces had fought many violent clashes resulting in significant bloodshed.

After the overthrow of Mubarak, the majority of the Egyptian electorate did not vote for secular candidates as the West had hoped for. Mohamed Morsi of Muslim Brotherhood won the country's presidential election with 51 percent of the vote. Even the Salafist Party, the political arm of the al-Qaeda, won almost a quarter of the total parliamentary vote, so a huge majority of Egyptians opted for Islamist parties. But Morsi's incompetent and confrontational policies did not take long to invite street protests against his regime, and taking advantage of this development, the Egyptian Army overthrew the elected government, outlawed the Muslim Brotherhood Party, and General Abdul-Fattah el-Sisi took over power in June 2013. The new regime is no way more liberal and democratic than Mubarak's or Morsi's.[69]

After the initial successes in executing the overthrow of the regimes in Tunisia and Egypt and creating a violent uprising in Libya, the Arab Spring started to spread to the east of Suez. Thanks to mounting opposition on the streets, President Ali Abdullah Saleh of Yemen was the fourth Arab leader to be forced out of power. In January 2011, public demonstrations against Saleh's 33-year rule began to take momentum in Yemen. Saleh promised not to seek reelection and his loyal forces launched a violent clampdown, but the protests not only sustained but also spread to other parts of the country. In April 23, 2011, his party, General People's Congress (GPC), signed a formal agreement under the auspices of the GCC to hand over power to his deputy, but Saleh refused to oblige. This led to serious clashes between forces loyal to him and the opposition, and in June 2011, Saleh was seriously injured in a rocket attack on his palace and he traveled to Saudi Arabia for medical treatment. He returned to the highly volatile Sana'a in September 2011 and in a signed deal in November 2011, he relinquished power to his deputy, Abdrabbuh Mansour Hadi. Hadi assumed power and led a unity government. After an election in February 2012, Hadi was sworn in for a two-year term as president.

Since assuming power, President Hadi has faced enormous challenges like extensive poverty and food scarcity[70] in the country and an al-Qaeda-led insurgency and rebellion by Zaidi Shiite, known as Houthis in the north. In late 2014, the emergence of groups affiliated to the ISIS further increased Hadi's challenges. While he had the backing of the Sunni-dominated southern part of the country, he failed to get full support of the country's security forces. To weaken the influence of the Houthis, Hadi revealed in February 2014 his plan to make Yemen a federation of six regions, which led to further aggravation of the crisis in the country. In February 2015, attack from Houthi rebels forced Hadi to flee from Sana'a to Aden, his southern stronghold. After

rebel forces started to attack Aden, a coalition led by Saudi Arabia compris-
ing four other Arab states, Jordan, Egypt, Sudan, and Morocco, intervened
on behalf of Hadi. Arab states accuse Iran of providing financial and military
support to Houthis. Still there is no sign of democracy or good governance in
Yemen, rather the country has witnessed huge political instability and civil
war in the post–Arab Spring period. As Adam Baron[71] describes, "Over the
course of the past six months, Yemen's once-celebrated post–Arab Awaken-
ing transition has come to a dramatic—if slow-burning—end."[72]

The winds of Arab Spring blew into GCC countries with varied repercussions and manifestations from one country to another. Some Gulf states, particularly Bahrain, and to some extent Oman, were heavily affected. In early
2011, inspired by the widespread Arab Spring movements in countries across
the Middle East, opposition groups in the small island nation of Bahrain rose
up in a series of protests against the ruling Al Khalifa family. After initial
days, the Shia opposition parties took over the leadership of the movement
but endorsed the same demands for a new constitution to transfer powers into
the hands of elected officials. The protesters turned the capital's Pearl Round-
about into Bahrain's Tahrir Square, as a symbol of the political challenge to
the authoritarian regime. With the assistance of the Desert Shield Force, the
military arm of GCC states, Bahrain ruthlessly clamped down the protest in
the dead of night in March 17, 2011. The day after the security crackdown,
bulldozers demolished the six sails holding a pearl statue in an attempt to
bury any trace of the symbolic political challenge. A large number of protesters were killed and hundreds of them were arrested. There were reports
that authorities in Bahrain had employed nonregular forces from Pakistan to
violently suppress public demonstrations.[73] More than four years have passed
now, and though the prodemocracy movement in Bahrain has grown quieter,
it has not died away. On the street, demonstrations appear sporadically, sometimes resulting in violent clashes.

In Oman, protests started to erupt in January 2011 and gradually spread to
different cities. Unlike Bahrain, Oman was successful in somewhat peacefully containing the reformist demand and popular protest within three
months. The regime's swift and flexible actions in promising a series of economic and political reforms were somewhat successful in containing popular
anger. Saudi Arabia also followed a similar successful strategy to prevent the
spread of the Arab Spring within its territory. The Saudi monarch decided to
employ an estimated $450 billion of the country's financial reserves to isolate
its society from the impact of the Arab Spring and to delay any significant
political reforms.[74] Despite the success of the regime in buying political
stability, the political situation in Saudi Arabia continues to remain on the
brink. In Kuwait, which already has a parliament with power to veto government decisions and vote ministers out of office, people protested demanding

a constitutional monarchy and rights to form political parties. In the beginning, the regime wanted to buy out the challenge in dispensing substantial financial grants and food subsidies. However, it did not satisfy the protesters, so the regime was forced to hold general elections in February 2012, which was declared illegal by the Constitutional Court in June 2012 and then the second general election in one calendar year took place in December 2012, which was boycotted by the opposition groups. Though the opposition supporters protested against the election, the public opposition to the regime in the country has subsided to a large extent.

Though the regime in Jordan did not face major unrest like many other Arab rulers, in Syria it was a different story. In the initial months of the Arab Spring, Syrians appeared to support their young president, Bashar al-Assad, who had projected an image as a populist modernizer. When street demonstrations finally reached Syria in March 2011, in the southern town of Deraa, the protesters did not demand the overthrow of Assad but only wanted greater freedom and an end to corruption. However, the faith in Assad as a reformer soon evaporated when security forces opened fire on demonstrators and the regime offered only superficial political reforms. The regime branded the protestors as criminal armed gangs and sectarian thugs. In the early days, however, the protestors were mostly peaceful and inclusive, while violence inflicted on them was carried by the regime-supported Shabiha militia from Assad's own Alawi sect.

The Syrian opposition in the early stages modeled itself after its counterparts in Tunisia, Libya, Egypt, and Bahrain in an attempt to peacefully capture public places, portraying "a civic, non-sectarian and non-Islamist face at home and abroad, and in some cases hoping to attract a NATO intervention like Libya's."[75] The violent response from the security forces and militias did not deter the opposition, rather a large number of people across the country started filling up the streets to demonstrate against the regime. Soon, peaceful demonstrations took the shape of an uprising as the opposition groups began to take up arms to defend themselves and to drive away regime forces from their areas. The popular protest came to Syria late, but fast transformed into a brutal and increasingly sectarian armed conflict. The regime's determination to employ all means at its disposal in order to clutch on to power pushed what began as a peaceful protest into an unrelenting spiral of militarization.[76] By the end of April 2011, the situation deteriorated significantly as security forces started using tanks and heavy armor to quell any protests, resulting in a large number of civilian deaths. The UN Security Council condemned the attacks on civilians on August 3, 2011. The response of the international community to the unrest and brutality was limited to some sanctions against the regime, but not in the form of military intervention. While, at the regional level, the Assad regime cleverly used its strategic partnership with Iran and

Hezbollah to obtain arms and military training, at the international level, its long-standing good relations with Russia and China provided much-needed support within the UN Security Council, besides military and financial support.[77]

In spite of the international community's perplexity regarding its scope of engagement in the conflict, pressure continued to build on Assad as rebel groups occupied large areas in the north and east of the country and launched attacks on Damascus and Aleppo. Many countries started recognizing opposition National Coalition as the legitimate representative of Syria. However, because of the refusal of the Western powers and Saudi Arabia to provide heavy weapons to rebels, the momentum of the conflict started tilting in favor of the Assad regime in the first half of 2013. The concerns regarding rebel groups' links with al-Qaeda-affiliated jihadists contributed to the hesitation of the Western countries. The alleged chemical weapons attack on a Damascus suburb in August 2013 put serious pressure on the United States to militarily intervene, but the US administration used diplomatic means to reach a "Russian-brokered" agreement to remove Syria's chemical weapons.[78]

By 2014, both the warring parties reached a stalemate. Assad refused to relinquish his position, while the National Coalition insisted on this demand for any negotiated settlement. The conflict led to a huge humanitarian disaster, resulting in the death of more than 100,000 people and displacing millions from their homes. According to a UN estimate, as of March 2015, four years of conflict in Syria had resulted in the deaths of more than 220,000 Syrians and had forced more than 11 million people out of their homes, including 7.6 million people internally and more than 3.9 million people to neighboring countries (UN News Center, March 31, 2015). Russia's direct military intervention in support of the Assad regime in the autumn of 2015 has further complicated the dynamics of this conflict. The conflict began in March 2011 as a relatively peaceful popular uprising for limited political demands. The refusal of the regime to listen to protesters and the use of force to restore order turned the public protest to a violent civil war involving regional and international backers. The IS took advantage of this crisis and fast became a party to the conflict and now controls a self-declared caliphate in a large part of territory in Syria and Iraq.

The IS started as a group called Jamaat al-Tahwid wa-i-Jihad (JTWJ) established by Abu Musab al-Zarqawi in 1999. In the beginning, this group was devoted to effect a regime change in Jordan. In the post–2003 period, Zarqawi moved his group to Iraq and started an insurgency against American forces. The JTWJ soon came into prominence after its attack on the UN compound in Baghdad in August 2003 and a series of attacks on Shia holy shrines and religious festivals. In 2004, the JTWJ formally became an al-Qaeda affiliate when Zarqawi agreed to work under Osama bin Laden and the group changed its name to al-Qaeda in Iraq or AQI. After this, it started to build its own network of fighters during the Iraq insurgency and developed a power structure to enforce the sharia law. In 2006, Zarqawi brought together a number of smaller Iraqi jihadi factions under the AQI leadership under the umbrella of the Majlis Shura al-Mujahedin (MSM).

After the death of Zarqawi following an American airstrike in 2006,[79] the AQI was led by Abu Ayyub al-Masri and then by Abu Omar al-Baghdadi. It then changed its name to Islamic State in Iraq in order to focus on capturing Iraqi territory to establish a sharia-based state there. The group was initially successful in gaining control of the Sunni-dominated Anbar province, but it was ousted by the tribal militias with the help of an American troop surge in 2007. In 2010, Abu Bakr al-Baghdadi assumed the leadership of the IS after the deaths of al-Masri and Abu Omar al-Baghdadi by a tank shell. He became successful in regaining some of the popular support after being able to exploit the growing sense of alienation and persecution among the Sunni population and started to set up a stronger organizational structure. The Shia-dominated Iraqi regime might have been able to suppress the IS, but the uprising by Sunnis in Syria started to change the sectarian balance of power in the region.[80]

Baghdadi decided to take part in the Syrian Civil War in April 2013 in spite of opposition from Jabhat al-Nusra (JN), the al-Qaeda-affiliated group in Syria, and renamed the organization as the Islamic State in Iraq and Syria (ISIS) (or the Islamic State in Iraq and Lavant—ISIL).[81] After its formation, ISIS, throughout late 2013 and early 2014, devoted its attention toward gaining control of Syrian territory. Maintaining its stronghold in Raqqa, where it was able to get total control after overthrowing other rebel groups, the ISIS started expanding its territory over other areas by getting new allies and defeating their enemy forces. After gaining significant territorial victory in Syria, the ISIS moved to regain large parts of Anbar province and in early June, it captured Iraq's second largest city, Mosul. On June 29, 2014, the very first day of Ramadan, the ISIS proclaimed itself a caliphate and Abu Bakr al-Baghdadi as Caliph Ibrahim, demanding the loyalty and obedience of all Muslims throughout the world. While al-Qaeda-affiliated jihadi groups usually use the methodology of social integration for expanding their influence, the ISIS has adopted a clear strategy to control territory through military force. In 2015, the ISIS has practically obliterated the border between Syria and Iraq and established in its place a caliphate that rules an area larger than the United Kingdom. With the present political instability in both Iraq and Syria, the ISIS is poised to have a long-term presence.

The ISIS, unlike the al-Qaeda, prioritizes occupying territory and has created a top-down structure for civil and military to rule it. A large number of foreign Muslims, mostly from Europe, Australia, Indonesia, and the United States, are joining the ISIS. A smaller number of "lone wolf" enthusiasts of the ISIS have also attacked Western targets.[82] Although the ISIS is part of a larger global jihadist movement in its ideology and worldview, its social origins are rooted in a specific post–Saddam Iraqi situation and Arab Spring-induced Syrian civil war. After the overthrow of the Saddam regime, Sunnis in Iraq had been protesting unsuccessfully the marginalization and discrimination under the new Shia-dominated regime. Similarly in Syria, the long-standing Sunni resentment under the minority Alawite sect regime became pronounced after the violent crackdown of the Arab Spring. With the rapid decline of state institutions and the spread of civil wars in Iraq and Syria, the ISIS provided an opening for these grievances to organize and wage a powerful opposition. However, in Syria, as Heydemann[83] argues, "If democracy as an outcome of the uprising was always uncertain, democratic prospects have been severely crippled by the devastation of civil war and the deepening fragmentation of Syrian society."

The failure of the Arab Spring to bring about democracy and the rule of law in the region created an environment that was conducive for radicalism to thrive. The Arab Spring has turned out to be, as a Twitter handle calls it, "Jihadi Spring," spreading al-Qaeda in Libya, Muslim Brotherhood in Egypt, and the ISIS in Syria. What really went wrong with the Arab Spring? Why did the democratic transitions not turn out to be quick and successful like in Eastern Europe? A weak state structure, segmentation of societies along sectarian, ethnic, and regional lines, and Islam providing an alternate political ideology can all possibly explain why the Arab Spring did not turn out to be as it was expected.[84]

Democratic transition is an area where unexpected and sudden events have repeatedly challenged conventional wisdom. Some countries regularly move in and out of democratic rule. Most of the established theories on how democratic societies emerge are regularly challenged by new developments. Whether referring to the "Lipset's Law,"[85] the role of "pacts,"[86] or more Marxist-influenced explanations on the role of the working class,[87] there is still a lack of solid and reliable theories. The democratic transition process appears as emerging from utterly complex combinations of underlying factors, putting the viability of predictability and "engineering" into serious doubt. So, it is not easy to locate any one critical reason for the origin of the Arab Spring and its failure to establish a democratic Middle East.

However, Arab Spring was probably the very first successful attempt in the Middle East to remove authoritarian dictators through popular uprisings. Previously, the countries in the region had witnessed regime transition mostly through military coups. The regional media and access to modern technology probably contributed somewhat to the diffusion of the popular uprising at the regional level.[88] However, Western analysts and scholars usually view this popular uprising as a result of the diffusion of democratic norms, supported by modern media and a digitally connected aspiring youth population. They fail to recognize that the Arab Spring was predominantly due to the domestic structural changes in the region. The political factors behind the origin of the Arab Spring are straightforward: Countries in the region have overall failed to develop pluralistic and open political systems. Part of the contribution of the West to the political factors came indirectly through popular opinion mobilizing against the US occupation of Iraq, its continuing and unwavering support for Israel, and Western backing of authoritarian oppressive regimes in the region. The popular uprisings in the Middle East, in spite of their loose links with one another and their broadly related opposition to corrupt authoritarian administrations, do not fit into a single template. However, economic underpinnings like slow economic growth, growing inequality, high unemployment, and rapidly growing young and aspiring populations[89] contributed significantly to the mobilization of protesters. Economic grievances, and to some extent, grievances over corruption at the lower level, dominated the agendas of participants in protests in the initial period. The core support base for the uprisings varied significantly from country to country and depended primarily on how policies of different regimes in the years prior to these protests had contributed to societal and economic grievances.

The open protests against authoritarian regimes indicated a critical rupture to the long-standing social contract that had existed between the ruler and the ruled was based on the fact that the regime was providing valuable socioeconomic benefits to its citizens in return for their subservience. In the post–Cold War period, many regimes were forced to follow liberal economic policies and gradually lost the ability to buy political loyalty by providing socioeconomic benefits. To offset the declining popular support base, authoritarian regimes strengthen their internal security forces to repress the majority of the population and to create a state of fear. The Arab Spring was most probably provoked by the desire of human security goal of achieving freedom from want and freedom from fear.[90] A variety of critical socioeconomic issues, including abject poverty, higher unemployment rate, widening wealth gap, and corruption by the ruling elites, contributed to the popular uprisings.[91] Nearly 23 percent of Arabs youth had no employment, while the overall regional unemployment rate was over 10 percent.[92] The countries in the Middle East were far behind their potential to attain wealth. Some countries had experienced impressive macroeconomic growth since early 2000, but due to a lack of social and distributional justice and inequitable distributional arrangements, they suffered from growing economic inequalities.[93]

Thanks to oil revenue, most of the countries in the Middle East went through rapid economic transformation from an agriculture-based economy in the 1970s to a service and trade-based economy. This led to loss in the farming sector and to a situation where a few beneficiaries who were close to ruling regimes accumulated valuable land, water, and other ecological resources. This transition has made the rural Arabs poor and marginalized and the Middle East as one of the most food-insecure regions of the world.[94] Recurring droughts, increased farming costs, and decades of neglect by the regimes made the situation further worse. However, the reasons for the uprisings were certainly not limited to the food prices and jobs. Not only was the region afflicted by growing poverty, inequality, and food insecurity, but also political oppression defined the relationship between rulers and the ruled.

In 2009, immediately before the arrival of the Arab Spring, the fifth Arab Human Development Report (pp. V–VI) was published, which was entitled "Challenges to Human Security in the Arab Countries." This report had made an attempt to examine the relationship between human development and human security. The report argued that "human security and state security are two sides of the same coin" and clearly suggested that "the trend in the region has been to focus more on the security of the state than on the security of the people." The report[95] also concluded that "while the state of human security is not uniform throughout the Arab countries, none can claim to be free from fear or free from want and many are affected by spillovers from insecurity in neighboring countries."

FUTURE SECURITY THREATS: EMERGING SCENARIOS

While the Middle East is in a flux, what then are the emerging threats and what potential risks can we identify for the future? Furthermore, how do these threats and risks impact the security situation in the region and outside? Before and after Arab Spring, many studies, as well as security analyses, have predicted that the Middle Eastern states, due to their weak status, are on the way to collapse. Though Iraq, Syria, and Yemen are experiencing civil wars and the ISIS is gaining strength and territory, most of the states in the Middle East have survived despite their initial conflictual establishments and consolidation phases, and challenges from pan-Arabism, interstate wars, internal conflicts, international interventions, violent protests, and serious development challenges. The states have survived mostly with the help of oppressive regimes built up of internal and external security needs and military forces. This massive bias of placing most resources on the security sectors has had a negative impact on the remaining fewer social and socioeconomic resources that have been unequally distributed and shared among the populations. In combination with high demographic transformation with high fertility rates, and an increasingly younger age structure, the welfare needs increase dramatically in the Middle East.

The combination of having regimes that are determined to stay in power and at the same time are unable to meet the development and economic needs of the people carries the risk of creating internal instability. This creates an insecure environment for the individual citizen as well as for the regimes themselves. The protests in Jordan against the IMF-backed high prices in 1998, which led to riots in Egypt in 2008, and the recent Arab Spring in most parts of the region are a few examples of how societal reaction follows when the states fail to provide the basic survival needs. Many of the states, particularly Egypt, have become so weak that they have accepted that a great portion of the basic socioeconomic and social welfare distribution is taken care of by the local grassroots organization, that is, by the Islamic sector of society. Hence, despite the fact that the Islamic fundamentalist sectors are also seen as a security threat vis-à-vis the state, some sort of division of labor has occurred, where parts of the Islamic civil society sector provides this basic welfare for people in most need. This is also why a kind of social mobilization is taking place at the grassroots. But a mobilization that voices criticism against the regime also becomes a challenge for the regime, which at the same time cannot risk criticizing the Islamists, as it will make the state weaker, thereby risking further protests against the regime. Most of the countries in the region have strong grassroot Islamic movements that provide for health, education, and social welfare to the poorest people in society.[96]

One of the most difficult problems in the Middle Eastern states is that they have failed to transform themselves as strong states institutionally in which its populations and civil society are taken care of. The states are not homogenous nation-states but rather multiethno/religious or multinational states. The Middle East is characterized by a variety of state-building projects, with each state containing several different ethnic or ethno/religious groups. Due to direct or indirect Great Power influence in creating "new" states within the region,[97] these groups extend over one or, in most cases, several territorial borders. Turkey (Turkish majority dominating the Kurdish minority), Syria (with a dominant religious Alawi-minority), and Iraq (a Sunni Arab minority that during the Saddam era dominated the Shia-Arabs and Sunni-Kurds) are some examples of states where different ethnoreligious groups strive to strengthen and expand their own interests in relation to the dominant ruling elites.[98] In turn, this creates a situation where the security concerns of various states are inextricably linked to each other. The Middle Eastern state elites have rather seen themselves as representatives for their own groups and not for the "nation" as a whole. Most states have a "weak" degree of institutionalization and thereby gain legitimacy only from parts of its population.

Hence, a weak state, with the absence of democratic institutions and a low degree of popular support, entails the risk of becoming repressive. The ruling elites usually divide various ethnic groups in the security system of the state where those belonging to the same ethnic group of dominant elites are perceived as more reliable citizens, while others are conceived of as less reliable in a hierarchic order.[99] The region's security faces serious challenges from disputed state-building projects, radical jihadi groups, authoritarian nondemocratic repressive regimes, and an ethnically segmented population, which all adds to the "traditional" security problems. The region also has very limited institutional and cultural ability to solve its own security problems. Most of the existing academic works on this region focus on these traditional and hard security challenges. However, as it has become very apparent with the Arab Spring, increasingly the region and its growing population face a highly complex and fragile security system, where the above-mentioned security issues critically interact with a number of somewhat overlooked but extremely critical issues that are vital for peace and stability.

Although the Middle East is presently experiencing high population growth, it has rich deposits of attractive natural resources of high value like oil and gas, but it seriously suffers from a strained renewable resource base that is vital for survival, like water and arable land. The region suffers from huge environmental challenges of water scarcity, desertification, and land degradation. Due to increasing population and urbanization, the region needs a lot of food supplies. A number of scientific projections of climate change have been made in recent years, though agreement on the timing and extent of this change has not been reached. However, these projections are consistent in one aspect— agricultural productivity in the region would generally suffer and the losses in this sector would be huge.[100] In spite of limited data on which these scenarios are based, there are a number of reasons to focus more attention on this aspect. Already, today the climatic variability (with large fluctuations in precipitation between years) creates challenges for the countries in the region.[101] Less agricultural output will lead to more demands for creating new agricultural areas in the region and/or to look for agricultural investment (land and water investments or "grabs") in other parts of the world to meet the growing food demand. The already heavy reliance on "virtual water"[102] will increase.

Energy insecurity is not generally associated with the Middle East, but the countries in the Eastern Mediterranean part have been traditionally vulnerable to it as their fossil fuel endowments have been low. However, the finding of major natural gas deposits in that part of the region heralds a new dimension to the existing energy-power structure within the region, creating new challenges as well as opportunities for interstate relations and improved cooperation.

The countries in the region have a migratory history between them dating back to the collapse of the Ottoman Empire, but migration on a large scale began in the 1970s to the oil-rich Gulf states. In this interdependent globalized world, a series of demographic, economic, sociocultural, and psychological issues influence the nature, pattern, and direction of voluntary human migration, while forced migrations are the result of civil war, political and ethnic persecution, famine, climate change, and environmental disasters.[103] The migration pattern in the Middle East is a combination of both voluntary and forced migration of large number of population. In the last four decades, large-scale temporary labor migration has taken place in the region. However, most of the countries in the region, particularly in the Mashrek part, are primarily remittance-receiving countries. Remittances represent an important source of income for some of the countries, particularly for Egypt, Lebanon, and Jordan. The region not only has economic migrants, it is also a source or host of a large number of forced migrants, refugees, and internally displaced persons. Besides long-standing issues involving Palestinian and Kurdish refugees, the region today grapples with increasing displacement of population due to the ongoing violent conflicts in Iraq, Syria, and Yemen.

Given the above, this book will make an attempt to analyze emerging security challenges in a comprehensive and systematic manner, applying a broad security concept as well as a theoretical frame. It will, moreover, as a key aspect, draw the tenants from the regional security issues into both the global security analysis and human security perspective that this approach obviously calls for. It will, furthermore, outline some possible scenarios as to where the security issues are evolving in this region in the context of globalization and climate change and subsequently open a discussion on policy responses.

Chapter 2, "Achieving Food Security: A Critical Challenge," will analyze the enormity of the task of ensuring food security for the region's growing and fluctuating population. Several challenges, including increased food demand in richer economies, population growth, forced migration, and land and water diversion for housing and urbanization, pose serious risks for the region's food security. Hunger has not yet become a major problem in the Middle East. However, with its scarcity of arable land and rainfall, the region is not self-sufficient in food production. The region has, since the 1970s and onward, been highly reliant on import of food. It is, therefore, argued that there is an urgent need to boost the region's agricultural production in sustainable ways that do not negatively impact the economy or the environment. While previous food shortages were mitigated by increasing food imports, this option is less reliable now due to increasing food scarcity and also climate change–related uncertainties. Thus, the region needs to adopt a broader range of options such as applying technological innovation in the food system, making sustainable use of land and water for agricultural production, as well as reducing waste through improved storage and transport infrastructure, that is, effecting improvements in the food supply chain.

Chapter 3, "Water Scarcity: Threat to Peace and Stability," examines the impact of the increasingly scarce arable land in the Middle East. Increasing demand for water for domestic, municipal, and industrial use makes the commodity more scarce for agriculture. Fresh water availability is also rare in many parts of the region. Moreover, the weather of the region is also highly unpredictable, with a large part of it suffering from both droughts and floods. The region is the location of two-thirds of world's capacity to desalinate water, largely made possible because of the availability of cheap energy. However, the desalinated water is still not cheap enough to be used for agricultural purposes. Moreover, the process is not only economically expensive and energy intensive, but also ecologically disastrous. There is no doubt that the region suffers from huge water stress. Thanks to climate change, the region is predicted to get much hotter, precipitation will decline more, and the sea level will rise and affect its coastal areas. In the pursuit of meeting the increasing water demand, besides the struggle to acquire more waters from the shared river systems like the Nile, Jordan, and Euphrates-Tigris, political and legal positioning by countries in the region over transboundary ground aquifers is another major sticking point. There is an ongoing race in the region to gain control of shared water resources. However, cooperation and joint management rather than control is needed to make the best use of scarce water supply.

Chapter 4, "Energy Security and its Changing Dynamics," argues that while most of the world is preoccupied with the impact of instability in the Middle East on oil prices and the world economy, a different kind of energy crisis in the region is developing due to the ongoing reshuffle in natural gas supplies. The energy status quo in the region has started to change dramatically. The old oil and natural gas developers like Iraq and GCC countries may be losing their historic advantages in fuel development, while a new group of potential energy developers are taking advantage of recent technological advances that have unlocked previously inaccessible reserves. The global oil price has become highly volatile and its use has become seriously controversial. The traditional oil-producing countries are expanding their gas exploration and also some of them are even switching to the renewable energy sector. These potentially dramatic changes will have major repercussions for the entire region. In general, the politics of Middle Eastern gas will probably be just as dramatically affected by the upheaval as that of oil, but it will follow a separate trajectory. Its effect will, at least initially, be more local in nature, and will vary from one country to another. Energy development, particularly of natural gas, is a long process and needs interstate cooperation and large and long-term investment. The broader political and economic effects of this development will not likely be felt immediately. Nevertheless, it will be wise for the countries in the region and the international community to plan how best to adapt to the new energy landscape of the Middle East.

Chapter 5, "Managing Large Population Migration," analyzes the impact of the region's large-scale forced and voluntary population migration. In the last four decades, large-scale temporary labor migration has taken place in the region. Many migrants from the region and from outside have come to the oil-rich Gulf countries in search of work. They have been the major contributors to the economic development of the host countries and highly valuable remittances for the home countries. The region not only has remittance-sending economic migrants, it is also source or host of a large number of forced migrants, refugees, and internally displaced persons. Large-scale transborder migration has several dimensions for inducing conflict between host and home states in the region. In some cases, refugees, after settling in the host countries, indulge in antiregime activities against their home governments. Antiregime activities against their home government by Iraqis after settling in Syria or in Iran have become a major source of tension in the region, creating further negative implications for regional security. Kurdish militants' frequent use of the host state's territory against homeland regimes is a very common security problematic in the region as well. It is also a fact that large displacements because of the Israel and Palestinian conflict and the Iraq War have posed a structural threat to many refugee-receiving countries in the region. Competition with the local population over resources has become a serious law and order concern. In some cases, particularly in Jordan and Lebanon, the Palestinian refugees have become serious threats to their host regimes. Countries in the region are increasingly getting worried about the threats posed by large-scale migration from civil wars in Iraq, Syria, and Yemen. Migrant groups not only act as spoilers of peace and stability, but also have the capacity to positively affect conflict resolution processes.

The concluding chapter of this book, entitled "In Search of Sustainable Regional Security," discusses the linkages among the four emerging security threats in the context of existing fault lines within the regional security structure. While identifying immediate security risks for region, the chapter highlights the importance of efficient management of the natural resources in providing stable and sustainable peace. Countries in the region, in their effort to achieve political stability, have usually neglected sustainable economic development and favored short-term, situational development. The negative outcome of this approach has been not only unsustainable destruction of natural resources, but also, in some instances, the creation of further conflicts and insecurity in society.

NOTES

1. This chapter has borrowed liberally from Ashok Swain, Joakim Öjendal and Michael Schulz, *Security in the Middle East-Increasingly Multidimensional and Challenging,* A Study Commissioned by the Strategic Perspective Project within the Swedish Armed Forces Headquarters, Stockholm, August 2009.

2. Markus E. Bouillon, *The Middle East: Fragility and Crisis* (New York: IPA, 2007).

3. Louise Fawcett, *International Relations of the Middle East* (Oxford: Oxford University Press, 2009); Beverly Milton-Edwards, *Contemporary Politics in The Middle East* (Cambridge: Polity Press, 2006).

4. Barry Buzan, Ole Waever, and Jaap de Wilde, *Security: A New framework for Analysis* (Boulder and London: Lynne Rienner Publishers, 1998).

5. Dan Caldwell and Robert E. Williams Jr., *Seeking Security in an Insecure World* (Lanham, MD: Rowman & Littlefield Publishers, Inc., 2006).

6. Mike Bourne, *Understanding Security,* (New York, Palgrave Macmillan, 2014).

7. Kenneth N. Waltz, *Theory of International Politics* (Reading, MA: Addison-Wesley, 1979).

8. Ellie Kedourie, *Politics in the Middle East* (Oxford: Oxford University Press, 1992); Roger Owen, *State, Power, and Politics in the Making of the Modern Middle East* (London: Routledge, 2003).

9. Barry Buzan, *People, State and Fear* (Brighton: Harvester Wheatsheaf. 1983); Richard Ullman, "Redefining Security," *International Security* 8 (1983): 129–53.

10. Ashok Swain, *Understanding Emerging Security Challenges* (London: Routledge, 2012).

11. Carl Johan Åsberg and Peter Wallensteen, "New Threats and New Security: The post-Cold War debate," in *Preventing Violent Conflicts. Past Record and Future Challenges,* ed. Peter Wallensteen (Uppsala: Department of Peace and Conflict Research, Uppsala University, 1998), 168.

12. Michael Sheehan, *International Security: An Analytical Survey* (Boulder: Lynne Rienner, 2005).

13. Helga Haftendorn, "The Security Puzzle. Theory-Building and Discipline Building in International Security," *International Studies Quarterly,* 35 (March 1991), 3.

14. David Held and Anthony McGrew, eds., *The Global Transformations Reader: An Introduction to the Globalization Debate* (London: Polity Press, 2003).

15. Bull Hedley, *The Anarchical Society. A Study of Order in World Politics* (London: Macmillan, 1977).

16. Buzan, *People, State and Fear.*

17. Barry Buzan, Ole Waever, and Jaap de Wilde, *Security: A New framework for Analysis* (Boulder and London: Lynne Rienner Publishers, 1998); Barry Buzan, *People, State and Fear*; Joakim Öjendal, "The Elusive Pacific Region," in Hettne et al, eds., *National Perspectives on the New Regionalism in the South* (MacMillan, London, 2000); Michael Schulz, Fredrik Söderbaum and Joakim Öjendal, eds., *Regionalization in a Globalizing World* (London, Zed Press, 2001).

18. Barry Buzan, *People, State and Fear.*

19. Bull Hedley, *The Anarchical Society. A Study of Order in World Politics.*

20. Buzan, Waever and de Wilde, *Security: A New framework for Analysis,* 11.

21. Barry Buzan and Gowher Rizvi, *South Asian Insecurity and the Great powers,* (Basingstoke: MacMillan, 1986).

22. Karl W. Deutsch, Sidney A. Burell, Robert A. Kann and Maurice Lee Jr., *Political Community and the North Atlantic area; international organization in the light of historical experience* (Princeton: Princeton University Press, 1957).

23. Rick Fawn, 'Regions' and their study: wherefrom, what for and whereto? *Review of International Studies*, 35 (2009): 5–34.

Andrew Hurrell, "Explaining Regionalism in World Politics," *Review of International Studies*, 21 (October 1995): 331–58; Fredrik Söderbaum and Timothy M. Shaw, *Theories of New Regionalism* (Basingstoke: Palgrave Macmillan: 2003).

24. United Nations Development Programme, *New Dimensions of Human Security* (New York, United Nations, 1994).

25. Pauline Kerr, "Human Security," in Alan Collins, ed., *Contemporary Security Studies*, 3rd Edition (Oxford: Oxford University Press, 2013), 105.

26. Mary Kaldor, *Human Security* (London, Polity Press, 2007), 122.

27. Björn Hettne, Andras Inotai and Osvaldo Sunkel, eds., *The New Regionalism and the Future of Security and Development* (London: MacMillan, 2000).

28. Lloyd Axworthy, "Canada and Human security: the Need for Leadership," *International Journal*, 52 (1997): 184.

29. UNDP, *New Dimensions of Human Security*.

30. Des Gaspers, "Securing humanity: Situating 'human security' as Concept and Discourse," *Journal of Human Development*, 6 (2005): 221–45.

31. Richard Jolly and Ray Deepayan Basu, "Human Security–National Perspectives and Global Agendas: Insights from National Human Development Reports," *Journal of International Development*, 19 (2007): 457–72.

32. Des Gaspers, "Securing humanity: Situating 'human security.'"

33. David Chandler, "Review Essay: Human Security: The Dog That Didn't Bark," *Security Dialogue*, 39 (2008): 428.

34. The UN Commission on Human Security, 2003, 4. The Commission on Human Security was established in January 2001 under the initiative of the UN Secretary-General Kofi Annan and was co-chaired by Mrs. Sadako Ogata and Professor Amartya Sen. The commission finalized its report in February 2003.

35. Ashok Swain, "Agenda 21," in *Encyclopedia of Globalization,* Roland Robertson and Jan Aart Scholte, (New York: Routledge, 2006).

36. Ashok Swain, Ramses Amer and Joakim Öjendal, eds., *Globalization and Challenges to Building Peace* (London: Anthem Press, 2007).

37. Mark Duffield, *Development, Security and Unending War: Governing the World of Peoples* (Cambridge: Polity Press, 2007); Daniel Lambach, "Security, development and the Australian Security Discourse about Failed States," *Australian Journal of Political Science*, 41 (2006): 407–18.

38. This is pertinently pointed out in the US' "National Security Strategy," stating that "America is now threatened less by conquering states than (it is) by failing ones" (2002: 1).

39. Ramses Amer, Ashok Swain and Joakim Öjendal, eds., *The Security-Development Nexus: Peace, Conflict and Development* (London: Anthem Press, 2012).

40. "Mashrek" means "east" in Arabic and "Mahgreb" (north African states excluding Egypt) means "west."

41. Michael Schulz, "The Palestinian-Israeli Security Complex: Inconciliatory Positions or Regional Cooperation?," in *Case Studies of Regional Conflicts and Conflict Resolution,* ed. Leif Ohlsson (Gothenburg: Padrigu Papers, 1989), 119.

42. Barry Buzan and Gowher Rizvi, *South Asian Insecurity and the Great powers,* (Basingstoke: MacMillan, 1986), 160–61.

43. Ashok Swain, *Managing Water Conflict: Asia, Africa and the Middle East* (London: Routledge, 2004); Ashok Swain, "A New Challenge: Water Scarcity in the Arab World," *Arab Studies Quarterly,* 1 (1998): 1–11.

44. Shiblev Telhami, *The Stakes: America in the Middle East* (Boulder, Col.: Westview, 2004).

45. Jerome Slater, "The Superpowers and an Arab-Israeli Political Settlement: The Cold War Years," *Political Science Quarterly,* 4 (1990–1991): 557–77.

46. Sidney D. Bailey, *Four Arab-Israeli Wars and the Peace Process* (London: Palgrave MacMillan, 1990).

47. More than 1 million Iranians lost their lives and around 250,000–500,000 Iraqis also died. Rajaee Farhang, *The Iran-Iraq War: The Politics of Aggression* (Gainesville: University of Florida Press, 1993).

48. Peter Beaumont, "UN Resolution to Impose 18-Months Deadline on Palestinian State Talks," *The Guardian,* May 21, 2015.

49. Rodrigo Tavares and Michael Schulz, "United States' Relations with International Organizations," in *Handbook of US-Middle East Relations,* ed. Robert E. Looney (London: Routledge, 2009).

50. Magnus Ranstorp, *Perspectives on Terrorism: What Will It Look Like 2018 and Beyond?,* (Stockholm: National Defense College, 2008).

51. Nearly 10 percent of 1.3 billion Muslims worldwide are Shias and most of them live in the Middle East. Shias form the majority of the population in Iran, Iraq, and Bahrain and are the largest religious group in Lebanon. They also constitute significant minorities in the Arabian Gulf states, especially in Saudi Arabia, Yemen, and Syria.

52. However, before the ongoing crisis in Syria, some others suggest that Hamas was receiving more support from Syria than from Iran. *The Economist,* January 17, 2009.

53. Jessica T. Mathews, "The New Deal," *The New York Review of Books,* May 7, 2015.

54. Ted Robert Gurr, *Minorities at Risk: A Global View of Ethnopolitical Conflicts* (Washington DC: United States Institute of Peace Press, 1993).

55. Kerim Yildiz, *The Kurds in Turkey: EU Accession and Human Rights* (London: Pluto Press, 2005).

56. Constanze Letsch and Ian Traynor, "Turkey Election: Ruling Party Loses Majority as pro-Kurdish HDP Gains Seats," *The Guardian,* June 7, 2015.

57. Pelin Turgut, "In Turkey, Signs of Change for the Kurds," *Time,* April 13, 2009.

58. Alfred Tovias, Sema Kalaycioglu, Inon Dafni, Ester Ruben and Lior Herman, "What Would Normalization of Economic Relations between Mashrek Countries, Turkey and Israel Imply?," *The World Economy,* 4 (2006): 665–84.

59. Kaye, Dalia Dassa Kaye, Frederic Wehrey, Audra K. Grant and Dale Stahl, *More Freedom, Less Terror? Liberalization and Political Violence in the Arab World* (Santa Monica: Rand Corporation, 2008).

60. Laila Alhamad, "Formal and Informal Venues of Engagement," in *Political Participation in the Middle East*, eds. Ellen Lust-Okar and Saloua Zerhouni (Boulder, Col.: Lynne Rienner, 2008): 33–47.

61. Danilo Zolo, *Democracy and Complexity: A Realist Approach* (Cambridge: Polity Press, 1992), 99.

62. Quoted in Ian Shapiro and Hacker Cordon Casiano, eds., *Democracy's Value*, (Cambridge: Cambridge University Press, 1999).

63. Joseph A. Schumpeter, *Capitalism, Socialism and Democracy* (New York: Harper & Brothers, 1942).

64. Karl Popper, *The Open Society and its Enemies* (London: Routledge and Kegan Paul, 1962).

65. The classic exposition of this thesis is Fukuyama's normative idea that democracy and free markets will continue to expand as the dominant organizing principles for much of the world, though there is not much empirical evidence for such a conclusion; Francis Fukuyama, *The End of History and the Last Man* (Simon and Schuster, 1992). International organizations as well as individual developed nation-states have been for many years actively engaged in encouraging and supporting democracy and civil society.

66. Michael E. Brown, Sean M. Lynn-Jones and Steven E. Miller, eds., *Debating the Democratic Peace: An International Security Reader* (Cambridge: MIT Press, 2002); Spencer Weart, *Never at War: Why Don't Democracies Fight One Another?* (New Haven: Yale University Press, 1998); Peter Wallensteen, *Understanding Conflict Resolution: War, Peace and the Global System*, (London: Sage Publications, 2002); Bruce Russet, *Grasping the Democratic Peace* (Princeton: Princeton University Press, 1993); Morgan, T. Clifton and Sally Howard Campbell. "Domestic Structure, Decisional Constraints, And War: So Why Kant Democracies Fight?," *Journal of Conflict Resolution*, 35 (1991): 187–211. There are some works that are critical to this democratic peace concept and these are: Dean Babst and William Eckhardt, 1992, "How Peaceful Are Democracies Compared With Other Countries," *Peace Research*, 24 (1992): 51–57; Stuart A. Bermer, "Dangerous Dyads: Conditions Affecting the Likelihood of Interstate War, 1816–1965," *Journal of Conflict Resolution*, 36 (1992); Steve Chan, "Mirror, Mirror On The Wall . . . Are Democratic States More Pacific?," *Journal of Conflict Resolution*, 28 (1984): 617–48; Alex Mintz and Nehemia Geva, "Why Don't Democracies Fight Each Other? An Experimental Study," *Journal of Conflict Resolution*, 37 (1993): 484–503.

67. Samuel Huntington, *The Third Wave: Democratization in the Late Twentieth Century* (Norman: University of Oklahoma Press, 1991).

68. David Potter, David Goldblatt, Margaret Kiloh and Paul Lewis, eds., *Democratization* (Cambridge: Cambridge University Press, 1997).

69. Michael J. Totten, "Year Four: The Arab Spring Proved Everyone Wrong," *World Affairs*, July/August 2014.

70. Ashley J. Clements, *Yemen: Fragile lives in hungry times* (Oxford: Oxfam, 2011).

71. Adam Baron, *Civil War In Yemen: Imminent And Avoidable*, European Council on Foreign Relations Policy Memo, March 2015.

72. Adam Baron, *Civil War In Yemen: Imminent And Avoidable*.

73. Bruce Reidal, "The New Bahrain-Pakistan Alliance," *The National Interest*, August 2, 2011.

74. Abdulkhaleq Abdullah, *Repercussions of the Arab Spring on GCC States*, Arab Center for Research & Policy Studies Research Paper, Doha, May 2012.

75. Marc Lynch, Deen Freelon and Sean Aday, "Syria in the Arab Spring: The integration of Syria's conflict with the Arab uprisings, 2011–2013," *Research & Politics*, 1 (2014): 1–7.

76. Marc Lynch, "How Syria Ruined the Arab Spring," *Foreign Policy*, May 3, 2013.

77. Steven Heydemann, "Syria and the Future of Authoritarianism," *Journal of Democracy*, 24 (2013): 59–73.

78. Ian Bremmer, "What Does America Stand For?," *Time*, 185 (June 2015): 16–21.

79. Fawaz A. Gerges, "ISIS and the Third Wave of Jihadism," *Current History*, (December 2014): 339–43.

80. Patrick Cockburn, *The Rise of Islamic State: ISIS and the New Sunni Revolution* (London: Verso, 2015).

81. We acknowledge that there are different views on which terminology is to be used when describing the ISIS or ISIL. In this book we have chosen to use the various names (also including IS and Da'esh) interchangeably.

82. Graeme Wood, "What ISIS Really Wants," *The Atlantic*, March 2015.

83. Steve Heydemann, "Syria and the Future of Authoritarianism," *Journal of Democracy*, 24 (2013): 59.

84. F. Gregory Gause III, "The Year the Arab Spring Went Bad," *Foreign Policy*, December 31, 2012.

85. Seymour Y. Lipset, "Some Social Requisites of Democracy," *American Political Science Review*, 53 (1954): 69–105.

86. Guillermo O'Donnell and Philippe C. Schmitter, *Transitions from Authoritarian Rule: Tentative Conclusions about Uncertain Democracies* (Baltimore: Johns Hopkins University Press, 1986).

87. Göran Therborn, *The Rule of Capital and the Rise of Democracy, New Left Review*, 103 (1977): 17–41.

88. Henry E. Hale, "Regime change cascades: What we have learned from the 1848 revolutions to the 2011 Arab uprisings," *Annual Review of Political Science* 16 (May 2013): 331–53; Muzammil M. Hussain and Philip N. Howard, "What best explains successful protest cascades? ICT and the fuzzy causes of the Arab Spring," *International Studies Review*, 15 (2013): 48–66; David Patel, Valerie Bunce, Sharon Wolchick, *Diffusion and demonstration* in *The Arab Uprisings Explained: New Contentious Politics in the Middle East*, ed., Marc Lynch (New York: Columbia University Press, 2014), 57–74; Kurt Weyland, "The Arab Spring: Why the surprising similarities with the revolutionary wave of 1848?," *Perspectives on Politics*, 10 (2012): 917–34.

89. AfDB, *Jobs, Justice and the Arab Spring: Inclusive Growth in North Africa*, Paper prepared for the North Africa Operations Department (ORNA), African Development Bank, 2012, at www.afdb.org (accessed May 12, 2015).

90. Mohammed Nuruzzaman, "Human Security and the Arab Spring," *Strategic Analysis*, 37 (2013): 52–64.

91. Larbi Sadiki, "The 'bin Laden' of Marginalization," Al Jazeera English, January 14, 2011, at www.aljazeera.com, (accessed May 10, 2015); Danny Schechter,

"The Hidden Roots of Egypt's Despair," Al Jazeera English, January 31, 2011, at www.aljazeera.com, (accessed May 11, 2015).

92. Anthony Cordesman, *Rethinking the Arab "Spring": Stability and Security in Egypt, Libya, Tunisia, and the Rest of the MENA Region* (Washington DC: Centre for Strategic and International Studies, 2011).

93. Ali Kadri, "A Depressive Pre-Arab Uprisings Economic Performance," *The New Middle East: Protest and Revolution in the Arab World, ed.* Fawaz A. Gerges (New York: Cambridge University Press, 2014), 80–106.

94. Rami Zurayk and Anne Gough, "Bread and Olive Oil: The Agrarian Roots of the Arab Uprisings," in *The New Middle East: Protest and Revolution in the Arab World, ed.,* Fawaz A. Gerges (New York: Cambridge University Press, 2014), 107–31.

95. Arab Human Development Report, *Challenges to Human Security in the Arab Countries (New York: UNDP 2009),* 190.

96. Björn Olav Utvik, *Islamist Economics in Egypt: The Pious Road to Development* (Boulder: Lynne Rienner Publishers, 2006).

97. After the defeat of the Ottoman Empire, the Great Powers did divide the Middle East into new "nation-states." The old Ottoman districts of Mosul, Bagdad, and Basra became the new state of Iraq. Parts of the maimed former Greater Syria became Jordan, Palestine, Lebanon, and Iraq and the remaining parts became the state of Syria. The rest of the Ottoman Empire became what today is Turkey, a part of the old Empire that was liberated by Kemal Ataturk.

98. Still, the power relations among the various ethnoreligious groups within each of the above-mentioned states are far more complicated than what is described here. First, there are more ethnoreligious groups involved in each state. Second, it creates an even more complex relational web between the states in the Middle East.

99. Khaled Salih, *State, Nation Building and the Military: The Case of Iraq from 1920 to 1942,* (Göteberg: Arbetsrapport: statvetenskapliga institutionen, 1992).

Cynthia Enloe, *Ethnic Soldiers. State Security in Divided Societies* (Athens: The University of Georgia Press, 1980).

100. Gerald C. Nelson, Mark W. Rosegrant, Jawoo Koo, Richard Robertson, Timothy Sulser, Tingju Zhu, Claudia Ringler, Siwa Msangi, Amanda Palazzo, Miroslav Batka, Marilia Magalhaes, Rowena Valmonte-Santos, Mandy Ewing, and David Lee, *Climate Change: Impact on Agriculture and Costs of Adaptation,* International Food Policy Research Institute Washington, D.C., October 2009.

101. Wilco Terink, Walter W. Immerzeel and Peter Droogers, "Climate Change Projections of Precipitation and Reference Evapotranspiration for the Middle East and Northern Africa," *International Journal of Climatology,* 33 (2013): 3055–72.

102. Virtual water is the water used to produce various agricultural products, primarily food grains, fruits, and vegetables. J. A. Allan, "Virtual Water-the Water, Food, and Trade Nexus: Useful Concept or Misleading Metaphor?," *Water International,* 28 (2003): 4–11.

103. Ashok Swain, "Environmental Migration and Conflict Dynamics: Focus on Developing Regions," *Third World Quarterly,* 17 (1996): 959–73.

Chapter 2

Achieving Food Security

A Critical Challenge

During the global food crisis in the early 1970s, the concept of "food security" came into prominence. The World Food Conference of 1974 focused on increasing production in food-deficit countries and also encouraging a coordinated system of national and international food reserves.[1] The debates were mostly about ways to achieve national and global food security.[2] However, with the severe food crisis in Africa in the years 1984–1985, the discussion underwent a significant shift toward achieving food security more at the household and individual level as it became clear that adequate food availability at the national level did not ensure the accessibility of individuals and households to food.[3]

In the post–Cold War period, the concept of food security expanded itself to embrace many themes and subthemes, highlighting the relationship between food security and nutrition to wider concerns of livelihood security and long-term sustainability. In addition, socially or culturally determined food choices became a consideration. The core concept of food security has evolved over time and has gradually become more complex. Overall, the concept of food security has transformed from a basic one to a multidimensional phenomenon, in which concerns relating to household food and nutritional security have shifted to household livelihood security. Also, emphasis is being given to the dynamic relationships between the political economy, poverty, complex individual strategies, and malnutrition. The most widely accepted definition at this point of time is the one given by the Rome Declaration on World Food Security and the World Food Summit Plan of Action in 1996: "Food security exists when all people, at all times, have physical and economic access to sufficient, safe and nutritious food to meet their dietary needs and food preferences for an active and healthy life."[4]

In this context, the task of achieving food security in the Middle East is an enormous one. Even at the global level, food security is an increasing concern, not least because of the water and land needed to sustain an increasing need for food but also because of a more water-intensive food demand, which is largely the impact of when an increasing part of the global population is becoming middle class and changing its food consumption into more water-intensive food products.[5] Not only the lack of water but also energy (e.g. to transfer the water to where it is needed for irrigation) and arable land (including degrading soil quality, which is an increasing challenge in the region) are but some of the main challenges of increasing food production. Both the per capita availability of water and arable land in the region are the lowest in the world. The long-term structural factors driving food insecurity at the global level remain even more prominent in the Middle East, which is characterized by high population growth, small and shrinking level of arable land, and dwindling availability of per capita water resources.[6] Add to this the high population growth, violent conflicts with large-scale forced migration, increasing food demand, poor food supply chains, and the lack of well-developed trade regimes for food in the region, and the picture becomes even bleaker. Moreover, the efficient management of water in most of the countries of the region leaves much to be desired.

Even in the oil-rich but water-scarce Gulf countries, the efficiency of water use is poor both on the supply and demand side. High level of leakage and low level of reuse of treated wastewater are major challenges. At the domestic level, only around 50 percent of the water is treated and the reuse out of this is less than 40 percent. In the agricultural sector in the Gulf countries, the water use efficiency is around 50 percent.[7] Furthermore, the policies adopted in the water sector are not suited to improve efficiency in the Gulf. For example, the use of groundwater is free in these countries, which only leads to overuse as well as depletion of aquifers.[8]

Not surprisingly, countries in the region see food security through the lens of national security considerations. Even more so, political stability in the region is connected to the price of bread and thus the wheat price. The Arab region imports over 50 percent of the calories it consumes and it is the region that imports most cereals in relative terms, in the world, thus making it extra sensitive to large fluctuations in cereal prices. The region imports the largest quantity of the global wheat, that is, around 30 percent that is being traded.[9] While the Arab Spring was not directly about bread, soaring prices of wheat in the aftermath of the food price hikes in 2007–2008 have arguably contributed to the erosion in regime legitimacy and increase in political instability.[10]

In the wake of the global food price crisis, the Arab world witnessed an additional four million undernourished people, and in countries like Yemen, seed stocks were utilized one year earlier than planned, thus jeopardizing future food security.[11] There is no dispute to the fact that the region is quite heterogeneous. The rich countries in the Gulf region as well as Israel can be deemed to be largely food secure, primarily because they have substantial oil revenues or a highly diversified economy. Still, the Gulf countries face an increasing dependence on world markets to satisfy their food demands, something that can be considered somewhat risky, as the reliance on the global food trade system has become less reliable. Thus, as Woertz[12] notes, the Gulf countries have become increasingly wary of risks of food supply disruptions as a result of embargoes and export bans. Therefore, these countries have opted for land acquisitions abroad as a means to boost their food security and reduce their dependence on world markets.[13]

With its scarcity of arable land and water, the region is not self-sufficient in food production. The region has, since the 1970s and onward, been highly reliant on import of food.[14] Several policies have been undertaken to achieve a greater degree of food self-sufficiency,[15] but the fact is that the region is still heavily dependent on food imports from outside of the region, in particular, relating to cereals, which is the main staple food commodity. This exposes the region to a higher vulnerability as a result of volatility of food prices and also the lack of efficiency in food supply chains.[16] As Elhadj[17] describes, the idea of food self-sufficiency in arid and semiarid countries such as Syria and Saudi Arabia is "more of a romantic dream than of a reasoned strategy." Projections for the region point to the need for increasing its reliance on food imports by 64 percent during the period 2010–2030.[18]

According to the UN Food price index, food prices hit an all-time high in 2011. Notably, world grain prices had then doubled from what it was in 2007.[19] It has since gone down (primarily during 2013) but is illustrative of the challenges that food prices pose to this region. To mitigate some of the challenges, the Jordanian as well as the Egyptian government has introduced higher procurement prices for wheat as a means to encourage increased domestic production.[20] At the regional level, the United Nations Economic and Social Commission for Western Asia (UNESCWA) has started a program on the linkages between food and water security. The security implications of this policy are something that the states in the region are well aware of and are trying to manage by adopting various measures. For, the richer countries in the region that can afford higher food prices for some period of time (as long as the oil price does not at the same time drop significantly) are better positioned than some of the poorer or middle income countries in the region. As outlined below, the 2007–2008 food price crises sparked an intensification of efforts to "outsource" part of the region's food security by means of land acquisitions in primarily Africa by some of the countries of the region.[21]

There is an urgent need to boost the region's agricultural production in sustainable ways that do not negatively impact the economy or environment.

This is a sustainability question as well as one of security. While previous food shortages were mitigated by increasing food imports, this option is now less reliable due to increasing food scarcity and a less reliable food market. Moreover, the global climate change can bring further uncertainties, which will mean that rainfall will become less reliable and that some parts of the region are likely to receive even less rainfall than today. Thus, the region needs to adopt a broader range of options such as applying technological innovation in the food system, making sustainable use of land and water for agricultural production, as well as reducing waste through improved storage and transport infrastructure, that is, effecting improvements to the food supply chain.

While hunger has not previously been a major challenge in the region, the increasing pressure on some countries in the region primarily due to raging civil wars in Syria and Iraq and the resulting regional refugee crisis, but also to some extent the conflicts in Yemen and the situation in Gaza, makes the task of providing enough food an increasing challenge. Due to the civil war, it has not been possible to use arable land in large parts of Syria as well as in neighboring Iraq for agricultural purposes. The ongoing crisis in Syria has contributed, among other things, to food scarcity. According to FAO, cereal production is down by 50 percent and the infrastructure for agriculture (roads, dams, canals, etc.) has been significantly damaged. The yield levels in the country are also significantly down. In May 2014, FAO and the World Food Program (WFP) estimated that around 6.5 million Syrians were food insecure, a figure that has since increased.[22] The Syrian crisis also has important spillover effects on food security that can, and arguably does, affect the stability of neighboring countries. Lebanon, Jordan, Iraq, and Turkey all receive a substantial number of Syrian refugees. The official registered figure from the United Nation Refugee Agency (UNHCR) was close to four million refugees in April 2015. This figure does not include refugees that are not registered in the neighboring countries as well as the internally displaced within Syria (estimated at 7.6 million in April 2015). In Lebanon, for example, the significant number of refugees, close to a third of the country's total population, is putting pressure on the food security systems. In particular, as the majority of the refugees are located in the southern and mostly poorer parts of the country, it necessitates increased government expenditure on food subsidies.[23] Since 2013 and increasingly during 2014 and 2015, the flow of refugees crossing into neighboring countries has, in spite of continued heavy fighting inside Syria, significantly decreased. According to the Norwegian Refugee Council (NRC) and the International Rescue Committee (IRC), all states neighboring Syria have started to regulate entry into countries, citing security, social, and economic concerns.[24]

According to the *The State of Food Insecurity in the World 2014*, the world is slowly progressing toward less hunger, but in the Middle East, the trend during the last few years has been the opposite. The Arab region has seen a trend that shows both an increase in the number of undernourished and the prevalence of undernourishment. During 1990–1992, FAO estimated that 6.3 percent of the population was undernourished, but in 2012–2014, this figure rose to 8.7 percent, amounting to around 33 million people.[25] Instability and conflict arguably contributed to the increase in undernourishment in the region, and it can also be assumed that the undernourishment and lack of food security has contributed to social and political instability in places such as Syria, Yemen, and Gaza. Going beyond mere food availability, the nutritional value of the available diet needs to be highlighted as well. If food is important, the quality of food, or micronutrients, is equally important. Without good nutrients, malnutrition will, for example, lead to decreased immunity and the stunting of children and will be an additional burden on the food systems, not least in the region, since a very high level of the calorie intake is made up of wheat-based bread which lacks many of the key micronutrients.[26] As a matter of fact, the region is the only one in the world where chronic malnutrition is rising.[27] In addition to undernourishment, there is another trend occurring at the same time and that is the increase in the number of overweight and obese in the region. The regional average of overweight and obese is close to 25 percent, while the global average is less than 12 percent.[28]

Before the start of the civil war, Syria was facing a very challenging food security situation due to recurring droughts during 2006–2011. It has been noted that the combination of factors relating to drought, climatic variability, and poor governance indirectly contributed to creating a fertile ground for the protests against the Syrian regime in 2011.[29] As Gleick argues,

> Severe multiyear drought beginning in the mid-2000s, combined with inefficient and often primitive irrigation systems and water abstractions by other parties in the eastern Mediterranean, including especially Syria, contributed to the displacement of large populations from rural to urban centers, food insecurity for more than a millions people, and increased unemployment—with subsequent effects on political stability.[30]

Syria's huge internally displaced population and Syrians who have taken refuge outside the country (primarily in Jordan, Lebanon, and Turkey) account for nearly 10 million and are in need of sustained food and agricultural assistance. In Yemen, the long-standing political crisis has also severely affected the food security situation, with around 10.6 million people in need of food supplies during 2014. These figures are prior to the start of the regional military intervention in March 2015 led by Saudi Arabia. The Houthi rebels ousted the Yemeni government and this led to the evacuation of most of the UN staff and the withdrawal of much of the international humanitarian support programs. In Gaza, even before the Operation Protective Edge launched by Israel during the autumn of 2014, an incomprehensible 72 percent of families were estimated to be food insecure. Also in Iraq, the trend is spectacularly negative, with an estimated 23 percent deemed to be undernourished in 2014, as compared to only 8 percent in 1990–1992.[31]

A somewhat new challenge in the region that has become more evident after the advances of ISIS is how water installations can be (and are) used as a weapon with a direct or indirect effect on food security. ISIS has on some occasions shut water to villages, which has included agricultural water and on other occasions flooded agricultural plains in Iraq, thus destroying parts of the agricultural yield.[32] When nontraditional actors such as ISIS gain ground in the region, as they did at a significant pace during 2014, it opens up new security challenges with repercussions on food security. As such, control over primarily dams becomes a potential weapon in the arms of these actors that they seemingly do not shy away from using.

INCREASING FOOD DEMAND IN THE REGION

It is often in the water-scarce regions (who are often also scarce of arable land) that population growth rates are the highest. About 90 percent of the population growth during the next 40 years is expected to take place in Asia and Africa where water availability per capita often is much lower than in other regions.[33] A significant part of this population growth will occur in the Middle East. Indeed, the food demand in the region is slated to increase rather significantly during the coming decades. The structural factors that are particularly critical for food security—population growth, urbanization, and income growth—are all increasing at a relatively high rate.[34] This will all serve to increase the demand for food in the region but also put additional pressure on the societies of the region.

From 2010 to 2050, the number of people in the Middle East is expected to have risen from around 340 million to around 590 million. It should, however, be noted that family planning is starting to have an impact in the region. Moreover, with increasing income in the region, more people are entering the middle-class group, and birth rates are generally going down.[35] Still, in the Middle East, the population growth rate is among the highest in the world. In Israel, the growth rate is also rather high at 1.9 percent. Apart from the population growth in the region, there is also an income growth, a trend similar across the globe. This does have implications for food security as the middle class tends to adopt a more water-intensive diet.[36] This puts an increasing burden on the already scarce water resources of the region.

While an increasing population will mean more mouths to feed, it will also mean that the cost for the food subsidies in the region—which is significant (in Egypt, for example, around 2 percent of GDP in 2005)—will go up. Although food subsidy schemes in general have proven to be rather costly, ineffective, and hard to target to those in most need, they continue to exist. According to the World Food Program, close to 220 million people in the region access food subsidies and around 6 percent of GDP of the region is spent for this purpose.[37] The regimes in the region have reached the conclusion that the subsidies can be reduced and eventually taken away only over a long period of time.[38] In addition—if food subsidies are taken away—other schemes of subsidizing food will need to be found. However, because of the decreasing ability of some of the countries to uphold the subsidies due to budgetary limitations, the sustainability of the subsidies is increasingly in danger.[39]

Another challenge posed by faster population growth is the need to improve policies for job creation in the countries of the region. Currently, the unemployment figures in the region are very high, especially among youth. According to the International Monetary Fund (IMF), the youth unemployment in the region is around 25 percent.[40] The high degree of unemployment and the increasing political unrest in countries such as Egypt since the Arab Spring are also leading to the migration (discussed in more depth in chapter 5) of low-skilled workers to markets (in the Gulf region primarily) where jobs are available. As population increases and urbanization continues unabated, there is also loss of fertile and arable land, leading to subsequent loss in food security.[41]

If the region is to meet the challenges related to food and water in a better way, there is a need to diversify economies away from agriculture. Countries reliant on virtual water for their food supply need to diversify their economies so as to be able to continue to develop.[42] A diversified economy is dependent on progress in a range of sectors, for instance, in the quality of education, the institutional arrangements in a country, openness to innovation, private sector development as well as social mobility. Needless to say, such changes cannot materialize overnight but will take a long time to achieve since they are often to a large extent culturally embedded in a society.[43] For societies to be able to diversify economies, a certain level of social adaptive capacity is needed within a country. In many of the countries in the region, such adaptive capacity is mostly lacking. A large portion of the labor force is, directly or indirectly, engaged in the agricultural sector and it mostly lacks competencies to work outside of this sector. Thus, while diversifying economies of the region is a means to achieve a more sustainable solution in terms of water and food, the conditions necessary for such diversification to be successful will still take time to be created and probably will not happen without some degree of societal conflict.

The water scarcity in the region—discussed in greater depth in chapter 3—puts limits on what is possible in terms of production of food. The Middle East has about 1 percent of the globally available freshwater resources but over 5 percent of the global population. Not only the lack of water but also the lack of arable land is a challenge for the region. The global increase in arable land was around 2.3 percent during the years 1995–2005, while in the Arab region (excluding Sudan where it was significantly higher) it was around 1.7 percent.[44] Often there is a disconnect between land and water management practices in water-scarce regions, leading to a situation where the full potential is not realized.[45] To exemplify, it is noted that the green water[46] potential of the region is not being captured to the extent possible.[47]

Another area that has not received enough attention in the region relates to the food supply chain. A lot of water, food, and energy is actually wasted from the "field to the fork," to use the terminology pioneered by Lundqvist et al.,[48] thus increasing food insecurity at the global as well as at the regional level. At the global level, increasing attention has been paid to the fact that resources are being lost or "wasted" along the food supply chain.[49] Farmers globally as well as regionally have to produce much more agricultural output than what would be needed to feed the global population. Still around 800 million people face hunger in the world. It is clear that the global, regional, national, and local food supply systems do not function properly. Addressing the waste and losses in the system has multiple benefits in that it can help save precious food, water, as well as energy. In developing countries, much of the waste happens close to the field as a result of poorly developed harvesting practices, poor storage and packaging, lack of proper infrastructure, and transport systems as well as poorly functioning trading routes. Significant losses also occur in the sale, retail, and the households where the food is consumed. In many cases, up to a staggering 50 percent of what is produced on the field may be lost before it is consumed by a person. Clearly, there is scope for improvements in many points along this chain. This is not to say that it is easy to effect such improvements, but significant gains can be made through targeted approaches.[50] There are not many studies available that focus on food waste and losses in the region, but the FAO[51] has come up with one study that focuses on the Near East and North Africa and Central Asia. It notes that waste in the region is estimated at 32 percent at the consumption stage and that qualitative losses are very high. The qualitative losses are due to, among other things, poor market infrastructure, lack of adequate cooling storage, poor means of transportation, but also contamination and deficient protection standards, thus turning the issue of loss into one of *food safety*. The most striking example in the region is the case of fruits and vegetables, where close to 60 percent is being lost from the "field to the fork." Apart from increasing food insecurity, the food waste and losses also cause waste of water, energy, and land. In terms of land, an area of over 360 million hectares is used for the production of food, which will, in the end, not be consumed, and this area is much higher than in any other region.[52] Another aspect of the food security situation relates to overeating and obesity. Obesity in the Middle East, which exists alongside with hunger, is increasing the risk for diseases such as diabetes and cancer. The obesity rate in Egypt is a stunning 45 percent and it is being increasingly noted by governments and organizations that there is an urgent need to address the matter.[53]

A related challenge to the supply chain efficiency (or lack thereof) is the one associated with changing diets. With the growth in population, there is also growth in the middle class, and this section of the population has changed its dietary patterns over the years and has adopted a more water-intensive diet (focusing more on meat that needs a lot of water and less on a vegetarian diet that requires less water). Thus, while the development of a growing middle class is, of course, positive, it is also bringing about food security (and water security) challenges.

Connected to the challenges discussed above is the challenge of adequate governance systems that can facilitate proper participation, ensure low levels of corruption, and put in place management systems that are efficient. Tropp and Jägerskog[54] identified the water governance challenges in the region as having clear deficiencies. Likewise, the UNDP Arab Human Development Report from 2005 identifies governance as the main challenge for the region. In that sense, the region is facing the double challenge of both a deficiency in proper and inclusive governance systems and water and arable land scarcity. The governance challenges were identified well before the Arab Spring, but unfortunately many of the same challenges remain even after the Arab Spring.

As noted above, the fact that the region has been able to import virtual water is an important reason why tensions have not been higher over water. The high dependency on water from outside of the region shows that the external water footprint of many Middle Eastern countries is very high. The external water footprint is a measure to what extent a country is dependent on import of virtual water. This does not only include water for food, although the water used to produce food is by far the largest component.

IMPORT AND EXPORT OF WATER FROM THE REGION

The Middle East's food security relates very much to the global market, often more than is officially acknowledged. Thus, to understand how water, food, and security are related, it is important not only to analyze the food trade flows but also to understand the underlying narratives and discourses that permeate the region in relation to food and water.

There are different narratives being espoused in relation to food security and not least food self-sufficiency in the Middle East. As has been discussed above, it is clear that the region is heavily dependent on the import of virtual water to satisfy its increasing food demand. Food security is thus dependent on the global food market and food self-sufficiency has not been there for a long time. In 2008, the overall ratio in the Arab region of food self-sufficiency was around 60 percent and with increasing population and potential decreased rainfall this figure is scheduled to go down to around 35 percent by 2050 according to some estimates.[55] Larson[56] shows through economic analysis that the cost of increasing the level of food self-sufficiency in the region is very high and would almost double the demand for blue water, which is, of course, very unrealistic given the availability. However, the discourse has been (in most countries) one that has emphasized the national (or perhaps regional) production of food drawing the resources needed from within the region, even if the dream to fully do so for most countries disappeared in the 1970s or 1980s.[57]

It has, however, been important in the respective national discourses to emphasize the food self-sufficiency argument as a means both to project responsibility and to highlight the importance of both the agricultural and water sector(s).[58] The deficiency has been covered through imports, although this has largely been done in a discreet manner. As noted by Elhadj, "Importing foodstuff runs in the face of the well-propagated slogan of food independence, so the government-controlled media ignores discussing food imports."[59] In the case of Syria, as Barnes[60] argues, the water scarcity was, in fact, *constructed* and was a result of the Syrian government's efforts to promote irrigation (beyond what was renewable in terms of water availability, thus leading to depletion of resources), and the aim was to achieve food *self-sufficiency*. Since the 1960s, the ruling Baath Party has had agriculture as its main focus, including centrally managed irrigations systems. There was heavy subsidization of crops such as wheat and barley and the country achieved self-sufficiency in such crops. Francesca De Châtel notes that

> the relentless drive to increase agricultural output and expand irrigated agriculture blinded policymakers to the limits of the country's resources. Unrealistic agricultural targets, corruption, a failure to implement and enforce legislation, and the absence of a long-term strategy have thus devastated a region that was considered a breadbasket for the region.[61]

In the case of Saudi Arabia, the efforts to move toward food self-sufficiency have been grandiose to say the least. From the early 1980s, the kingdom spent a large part of its national budget on pumping primarily nonrenewable water resources for irrigation in the desert in an effort to achieve food self-sufficiency. It is estimated that between 1984 and 2000, Saudi investment in agricultural development was around 85 billion USD, which was around 18 percent of the value of the oil exports during the same period.[62] During this period, Saudi became a wheat exporter, thus in essence exporting away its finite and largely nonrenewable water reserves. In early 2008, however, the government announced that its food independency was to be phased out and that by 2016 it would import wheat to meet the needs of the country.[63] The strategy to pump largely nonrenewable groundwater sources to feed agricultural ambitions was clearly not sustainable in the long run. The fact that the renewable water resources of Saudi Arabia were not enough to sustain the food independence strategy, coupled with one of the highest population growth rates in the world, made this evident. Elhadj[64] outlines three key factors for the Saudi strategy to, in spite of being an arid country with limited water resources, start massive desert agricultural development. First, the idea of food self-sufficiency (or independence) had a clear nationalistic appeal and clearly communicated control over the country's political and economic future to the people. The national discourse emphasized that such a strategy would protect the country from a potential wheat boycott by food-producing countries. Second, the policy may have been inspired also by an effort to appease and settle the Bedouins of the Kingdom. However, the size of the land that was distributed to the Bedouins in the 1970s was too small. Third, it was seen as a way to enrich the elites. It is noted that by 1993 Saudi Arabia was the world's sixth largest wheat exporter and produced much more than what was needed for wheat self-sufficiency in the country itself. And since agricultural development had been supported by massive subsidies, the investors were able to gain substantially.

In many senses, the policies promoted by the states in the region have also been counterproductive to adopting a sound water and food policy, since water has rarely been given its correct value and therefore it has not been possible to see its true economic footprint.[65] As noted above, the prevalence of policies promoting food self-sufficiency, but even more a discourse promoting the same, has been and are, to some extent, still strong in the region. This is related to challenges that have been identified by Lundqvist, Grönwall, and Jägerskog,[66] as well as by Elhadj.[67] One particular challenge noted in the region is related to the notion of national security and the need to protect a country from the risk of food boycott and also from fluctuations in global food prices. This has led to policies in agriculture and water, in particular, that are often wasteful and largely nonsustainable in the long run. In addition, for some countries there is a need to generate foreign exchange to be able to pay for the import of food from international markets. For the oil-rich countries in the region, this is not a problem, but for some of the developing countries in the region, this poses a serious challenge. Last, the rural employment that often has most of its livelihood connected to agriculture (either directly or indirectly) is dependent on a large in-country agricultural sector.

As will be further elaborated in chapter 3, there is a clear link between the food and water discourses in the region. In the 1990s and early 2000s, it was widely believed that water was a source of violent conflict and even war.[68] This belief was based on the fact and realization that there was not enough water in the region to produce the food needed for the region, and therefore, the conclusion by researchers was that this will lead to war.[69] This was also further "backed up" by statements from leading politicians that they would be willing to go to war over water.[70] However, what was not included in the analysis was the importance of the virtual water being traded into the region.[71] Egypt had basically run out of water (from a food self-sufficiency perspective) in the 1970s but had since imported increasing amounts of grain from the global food market to make up for the deficit. It is evident how food in increasing amounts has been imported by the Middle East. Thus, the global food market acted as an ameliorating factor for countries facing shortage of water (and therefore of food). This has not meant that the Middle East has not been exporting agricultural produce and food, but that the net has been an inflow—and in particular of key food stuffs such as wheat. It is also worth noting that the statements emanating from politicians in the region were initially taken at face value, while further analysis has drawn the conclusion that the statements were made more to reinforce a sense of reassurance to the public that water was a key resource that the politicians took seriously and that the water security of the country was of key importance. As such, the statements should be analyzed and understood within the context in which they were uttered.[72]

Trade in foodstuffs has increased dramatically over the last century. According to WTO, the global food trade has increased by a factor of 4 only in the last 25 years. This has led to countries and regions becoming more interdependent on each other and also to the continued well-functioning of the global food trading system.[73] Indeed, as Hausman and Patrick[74] have clearly noted, there will always be a need for trade in food. This is so since the world's water and arable lands resources are not evenly distributed and neither is the global population. Some regions will be exporters of food (or grain), while others will be importers. The Middle East is and will continue to be a food importer. However, trade cannot be considered a panacea and is by no means an easily implementable solution. While increasing import of food would free up water resources to be used elsewhere in more economically productive sectors, it also brings important social considerations to the fore. In many poorer but also middle income countries, a large portion of the workforce is employed directly or indirectly in the agricultural sector. Thus, redirecting agricultural water (currently on average around 75 percent of the freshwater resources being used in the Middle East) to industry and domestic use will also mean that many people will lose their livelihoods in the agricultural sector. For some countries in the region with a high degree of economic diversification, this may not be a major problem, but for many of the countries with a less developed economy, it will be much more costly.[75] Embarking on such a strategy could also have a potentially very negative effect on the security and stability of the regimes in the region.

Given the magnitude of the trade of foodstuff, food has increasingly been viewed from a security and strategic perspective. Not least the United States has viewed the stability of the Middle East to be dependent on a continuous reliable food import. To grasp the importance for the region, it is important to understand the magnitude of the input to the food being produced and traded into the Middle East. When Egypt imports a kilo of wheat, it also imports—in its virtual sense—the production factors behind the kilo of wheat, with water being the most significant component. For one kilo of wheat, approximately 1000 liters of water is needed. And when Lebanon imports a kilo of rice, about 2500–4000 liters of water has been added to its water budget.[76]

Trade is an important factor for promoting economic development. Increased participation in global trade and regional integration is also something that will increase economic development in the region. Still at an aggregate level, the regional trade regime in the Middle East is not well developed. It remains one of the least integrated regions in terms of trade. The trade in the Arab region was less than 8 percent in 2012, far beyond Europe at over 60 percent, the Americas at 49 percent but also south and central America at 17 percent, and sub-Saharan Africa at 13 percent. While the intraregional trade is very low, the Arab region has still seen a substantive growth in its exports to other countries outside the region. From 1995 to 2013, the Arab region managed to increase its part of total global exports from 3 to 7 percent. While most of this is fuel (oil and gas), there is also a doubling of export growth of other commodities during the same time period.[77]

The food trade within the region is low in spite of a good possibility to trade between countries that are well endowed with water and arable land (at least in relative terms) and those that have less of those resources. There is no doubt that the potential for trade within the region is far larger than what is currently taking place. The reasons for the lack of trade are many. It is a fact that in general terms trade in the region is not as well developed. Already in the 1970, the Arab Organization for Agricultural Development (AOAD) was established in Sudan, intending to improve Arab agriculture but also increasing cooperation within the region. Its location was also, at least partly, related to the fact that Sudan was seen as a "breadbasket" for the region.[78] This has, however, never fully materialized and agricultural efficiency in Sudan is still very low, both by way of global and regional comparisons.[79] The interstate agricultural cooperation that was aimed at has largely not been developed, thereby resulting in missing some of the benefits of a regional approach and the possibility of achieving comparative advantages within the region. The potential to increase intraregional food trade is relatively large, not least in light of the current underutilized potential. Going beyond trade, it is also possible to increase capacity building and knowledge exchange and sharing in the region to increase food security.

In other regional fora, such as UNESCWA, there are discussions on increased intraregional collaboration over food production and trade. However, it is noted that the states' desire for political control over food supplies is taking various directions, including a renewed interest in "food sovereignty"—in particular, in the wake of the food price hikes of 2007–2008.[80] There is also an identification of areas where improvements in food production can be made, areas such as aquaculture. UNESCWA notes that the Egyptian freshwater aquaculture alone has the potential of satisfying the supply of the whole regional market.[81] According to Al-Zadjali,[82] there is a great potential to increase the development of fish resources in the Arab world. Governance mechanisms are weak, the availability of qualified labor is low, functioning markets are largely absent, and production is relatively primitive, to mention a few challenges. Targeted investments could assist the fish sector of moving beyond one that is characterized by import (in its totality) rather than export. The potential for development is strong in this sector.[83] Since fish is, in relative terms, a cheap source of protein, a healthy commodity, and does not consume the same amount of water as do animal protein in production, it would be a good strategy to invest more in fish production.

LAND INVESTMENTS AS A STRATEGY TO ADDRESS FOOD SECURITY

The increased focus on land investments in particular in the wake of the food price crisis of 2007–2008 at the global level has caught on the Middle East, and in particular, the Gulf countries. The investments in foreign land are not new but have gained more momentum since 2007–2008 and a range of different actors are operating in this space with differing objectives and priorities. Private actors seeking profit alongside state-owned companies as well as Sovereign Wealth Funds are making investments. Investments are taking place primarily in Africa, parts of Asia, and Latin America.[84] The increased focus on investments from the Middle East need not only to be understood from the perspective of the increased prices in the global food market but also from the fact that certain countries (among them Russia, a key wheat exporter) enacted export bans on grains. The investments in foreign land can be seen as a way to gain more control and thus reduce one's own vulnerability in relation to key resources in a global situation that is becoming increasingly insecure. Indeed, it can be seen as a risk-mitigating strategy.[85]

Woertz[86] discusses the land investments (or "grabs") from the Gulf perspective. The narrative, and indeed policies pursued in many of the Gulf countries aiming at food self-sufficiency, has contributed to this phenomenon. The policy pursued during the last forty to fifty years in the Gulf region has meant that water resources (both renewable and nonrenewable) in many cases have been exhausted, leading to groundwater levels dropping beyond sustainable levels and contributing to salt water intrusion and degrading water quality and leading to a need to phase out water-intensive crops. In addition, in order to avoid vulnerability to the global market price shocks, and realization of the nonsustainability of achieving food self-sufficiency at home, efforts to look beyond one's own borders have become increasingly popular. While the strategies behind investing in land have been different, with some looking for food security and others for profitable investments, the trend to invest in land has been on the increase. The investment in overseas land by Gulf states is inconclusive and unclear[87] much as are the global figures.[88] The Gulf investments have been happening in different places around the globe, including Ukraine, Sudan, Cambodia, and Australia. It is also important to note that it is not primarily the hike in prices that has led to a scare in the Gulf region but rather the export restrictions put in place by some of the major exporters of wheat and other central agricultural produce.[89] In this sense, the strategy of investing on agricultural land works as a risk-mitigating one. It provides a means to be able to control the virtual water (primarily food) flows of the country, and it can also be argued that it is a diversification strategy.[90]

In a historical perspective, the current investments by the Middle East (and in particular Gulf countries but also countries like Jordan) are less focused on Sudan now than during the 1970s. (During that period, there was a more concerted Arab effort, but this failed largely because of reasons related to a lack of proper governance and capacity.) Today, investments are taking place in countries that also, to some extent, are suffering from increasing water scarcity. Thus, the investments in countries such as Sudan, Pakistan, and Ethiopia have already become controversial. They may become even more controversial as population growth puts additional pressure on demand in countries where large-scale investments are taking place.[91] In addition, in some cases, the water that is being used to irrigate some of the investments is transboundary in its nature and this aspect draws investing countries into the hydropolitics of regions such as the Nile basin.[92]

It is often state actors who are at the fore of the Middle East land investments. The Gulf governments have been instrumental as drivers of this
policy. It is, however, often Sovereign Wealth Funds (SWFs) or the private
sector that are concerned with the implementation of the investment projects.
Though many announcements were made around 2008, implementation of
many projects has yet to begin. The reasons for this tardy progress can be
partly attributed to the financial crisis and also to the fact that some of the
investments have become politically controversial.[93]

CLIMATE CHANGE, WATER AVAILABILITY, AND FOOD PRODUCTION

Projections for climate change in the Middle East vary and sometimes reach
somewhat differing conclusions. However, what seems to be a consensus in
the research community is that the region is likely to receive less rainfall than
before. Indeed, IPCC has reported that "annual rainfall is likely to decrease
in much of Mediterranean Africa and Northern Sahara, with the likelihood of
a decrease in rainfall increasing as the Mediterranean coast is approached."[94]
The area around the Jordan Basin might be most affected in terms of precipitation changes in the Middle East. In addition, the region is also expected to
be subject to an increase in average temperatures. Averages for the Middle
East suggest between a 10 percent and 30 percent decrease in rainfall during
the twenty-first century. Projections show that by 2050, renewable rainfall in
the region may fall below 500 cubic meters per capita.[95] This is a very significant figure for a region already plagued with scarce (very variable) water
resources.[96] Furthermore, the 2014 IPCC Fifth Assessment Report has concluded that arid and semiarid regions are vulnerable to climate change. The
Middle East is certainly vulnerable and by the end of the twenty-first century,
it is estimated that the region will face a temperature increase of 0.9 to 4.1
degrees Celsius. This range may not be very accurate, but the indications are
clear—there will be an increase in temperature. This increase accompanied
by a significant decrease in rainfall and increase in evaporation will affect the
available water resources, and thereby the potential for food production in the
region significantly.[97] This means less water will be available for irrigation
but also much less soil moisture (green water). The dominant agricultural
system in the region is rain-fed and therefore any changes (or variations) in
the pattern of rainfall will severely affect agricultural output. It has also been
noted that the incidence of droughts and floods has been on the increase in
the region already.[98] It seems beyond doubt that, even if efficiency gains are
taken into account, the agricultural output in the region will decrease in the
long term, thus making the region even more dependent on virtual water from

outside. In terms of agricultural productivity, it has been estimated that until 2080, production is slated to decline in the Arab region by around 25 percent as a result of climate change. While cereal yields in the region are currently only about half of the global average per square meter, investments in technology could significantly improve the situation.[99] Significant variations also exist in the region in which, for example, Egypt has low levels of agricultural efficiency, while, for example, Israel has a high level of efficiency.

An additional challenge related to the climate variability and change in the region is water related. Since much of the water in the region is transboundary in nature, increased variability (which seems inevitable given the above predictions) will, therefore, have international and regional repercussions. In many cases, the decreased flow adds more pressure to the already conflictual relations on transboundary water (see chapter 3). In many cases, transboundary waters in the region lack agreements between the states sharing them, and where agreements exist, they are often based on multiyear averages of flows and defined in volumetric allocations and not in flow percentages, which means that, as less water can be expected during some years, increasing tensions over the sharing of water are likely.[100] Furthermore, in the basins of the region, the agreements are (where they exist) largely bilateral instead of multilateral, covering all of the riparian states in the basin.

Climate change, as Kishan[101] argues, can be seen to affect food security in primarily four different ways—in terms of availability, access, utilization, and stability. With regard to *availability*, climate change brings increased risks to availability of arable land as well as livelihoods primarily as it affects water availability and contributes to desertification and floods and droughts. In relation to *access*, it is possible that climate change could result in increased food prices, market volatility, and thereby increasing poverty (primarily rural but also urban). With regard to *utilization*, climate change often aggravates societal tensions and conflict since competition for resources increase and new conflicts may surface. Finally, *stability* may also be negatively affected, since climate change can increase the stress on often already hard-pressed social welfare and social safety nets. However, it is not only the actual or real aspects of climate change in a region that are important but (perhaps) equally important are the perceptions of how climate change will affect. When there is ambiguity on how climate change will materialize, it can often be used to support one's own narrative and political interests through a subversive process.[102]

There is an ongoing discussion establishing relations between water, drought, and the start of the Syria crisis in 2011.[103] In this context, the probable contributions of the climate variability and change are also important to note. It has been observed that there have been longer periods of droughts in this region (and in the case of Syria) and this is being seen by some as effects of climate change. Research, however, has not clearly confirmed this link.[104] However, before the onset of the civil war, there was large migration within Syria from the rural areas to the cities. The drought that took place in Syria led to severe crop failures in many areas, thus putting many farmers out of work. In 2009, over 200000 Syrians left the rural areas due to their inability to sustain their livelihoods.[105] However, it has also been argued that the drought and "climate change" as key drivers of the crop failures or even the protests in Syria may have been inflated both by the media and by the regime. De Châtel claims that rather than being the drought *per se* that led to the loss of livelihoods and subsequent uprising, it was the failure of the Syrian government to respond to the ensuing crisis triggered by the drought during consecutive years that was the key reason.[106] The occurrence of drought is not a new phenomenon in Syria but rather a recurring event. Syria's neighbors were also affected by the drought, but it was only Syria that experienced a humanitarian crisis as a result. Syria had for long, against better knowledge, ignored to put sensible agricultural and water policies in place and when that coalesced with the long drought, the result was crop failure as well as loss of livelihoods.[107] While much analysis has focused on the recent decade when analyzing the drought and climate change as drivers for the uprising against the Syrian regime, it makes more sense to analyze the recent events in the broader context of the last fifty to sixty years of mismanagement of water and agricultural resources in Syria. The weak policies that allowed overuse of aquifers as well as surface water resources for agricultural production (often to gain political favors with the rural poor) slowly built up a crisis that finally led to a situation where a drought (that occurred during 2006–2010) resulted in loss of livelihoods on a large scale. De Châtel is even more clear in her analysis, when she points out that the ". . .possible role of climate change in this chain of events is not only irrelevant; it is also an unhelpful distraction. In the context of the future of water management in Syria, it distracts from much more tangible and real problems; in the context of the uprising, it strengthens the narrative of the Assad regime that seizes every opportunity to blame external factors for its own failings and inability to reform."[108]

While attempting to go beyond the headlines of the discussions about climate change as source of the conflict and uprising in Syria, a deeply multifaceted picture emerges, one in which the combination of various factors and their relations serve as explanations as to why the conflict emerged. The poor governance systems and the inability to respond to the drought hitting the region rather than the drought itself seem to be more plausible reasons. The neighboring countries, particularly Jordan, which also experienced a serious drought (and which also has more water scarcity), fared much better, arguably because better systems were in place to tackle the drought. As Sowers, Woertz, and Waterbury[109] conclude, "Rather than demonstrating that drought caused the conflict, the Syrian tragedy highlights the capacity of political systems and economic policies to exacerbate vulnerability to environmental events." Indeed, the Syrian misguided policies actually negatively contributed to create an increased vulnerability to drought.

CONCLUDING THOUGHTS

The security aspects of food have not always been all that well understood. However, it is not a secret that the availability of affordable food, and in particular bread, is something that has been an important feature of stability in the Middle East. Subsidies on food (and in particular bread) have been seen as a means to gain political acceptance in the region. It has been observed that higher food price was also a contributing factor to the situation that allowed for the Arab Spring to emerge.[110] The stability of mostly undemocratic regimes in the region is linked to and dependent upon an undisturbed import of wheat into the region. Political actors, for example, the United States, have understood this and made efforts to support their key allies in this endeavor. Thus, the challenge of achieving food security is reliance on outside factors, in particular, in times of protracted crisis and conflict such as the one being experienced presently in the region. It is likely that from a food security perspective, the work to increase stability and good governance will be even more important in the future. Improving governance is a challenge that is not new to the region and it should be noted that efforts aimed at policy reforms to address this challenge will be contentious since they will result in winners and losers—or perception of it.[111]

A key strategic aspect of the global trading system for food is that it requires a certain degree of trust from those relying on it. In the current global climate of increased regional instability, not least in the Middle East, the dependence on the trading system is being increasingly questioned. Unless states in the region feel that they have enough trust in the system, the tendency to reach for policies will be more geared toward increased food self-sufficiency or investments (land acquisitions or "grabs") that can substitute for a well-functioning trading system.[112] An added and related challenge for the region is that there is a general lack of diversified economic framework, which works as a challenge for improved food security. This restricts people from moving from the agricultural sector to another sector of the economy. Coupled with this is the challenge that the economies of the region, in general terms, will have to produce other products that can allow them to substitute and trade for the food produced in the region presently.

There is an urgent need to boost the region's agricultural production in sustainable ways that do not negatively impact the economy or environment.

While previous food shortages were mitigated by increasing food imports, this option is less reliable now due to increasing food scarcity, a less reliable food market, and also climate change–related uncertainties, which will mean that rainfall will become less reliable and that some parts of the region are likely to receive even less rainfall. Thus, the region needs to adopt a broader range of options such as applying technological innovation in the food system, making sustainable use of land and water for agricultural production, as well as reducing waste through improved storage and transport infrastructure.

Achieving food security, "a fundamental need, basic to all human needs and organization of social life,"[113] is of critical importance for a highly fragile region like the Middle East. Food security is the key organizing principle for achieving development, as it contributes to several aspects of livelihood and human security, ranging from health, sustainable growth, environment to trade. In addition, food security—or insecurity—continues to play a powerful part in the ongoing violent conflicts and is setting the stage for potential new conflicts in the region. Thus, comprehensive steps need to be taken to address food insecurity to avert potentially devastating consequences and to seek peace and stability for the region.

NOTES

1. Adebayo Adedeji, *Interaction between Structuralism, Structural Adjustment and Food Security Policies in Development Policy Management,* European Centre for Development Policy Management (ECDPM) Occasional Paper (Maastricht: Von Braun, 1989), 13.

2. Simon Maxwell and Marisol Smith, "Household food security: a conceptual review," in *Household Food Security: concepts, indicators, measurements,* eds., Simon Maxwell and Timothy Frankenberger (Rome: IFAD and UNICEF, 1992), 6.

3. Timothy R. Frankenberger and M. Katherine McCaston, *From Food Security to Livelihood Security: The Evolution of Concepts* (Atlanta, Georgia: CARE USA, 1998), 1.

4. FAO, "Rome Declaration on World Food Security," *World Food Summit,* 13–17 November 1996, Rome, Italy.

5. Anders Jägerskog, Ashok Swain, and Joakim Öjendal, "Water Security—Origins and Foundations," Volume I, in *Water Security,* (4 vols.), eds., Anders Jägerskog, Ashok Swain, and Joakim Öjendal (SAGE Publications, London: October 2014).

6. Håkan Tropp and Anders Jägerskog, "Meeting the Water Scarcity Challenges in the Middle East and North Africa," *Arab Journal of Water* 1 (2008).

7. It should be noted that an ineffective irrigation system will not necessarily lead to a loss of water as some of it will end up as soil moisture, create run-off, or flow into groundwater systems.

8. Waleed Al-Zubari "Sustainable water resources management in the Gulf Cooperation Council countries," in WWAP (United Nations World Water Assessment Program, *Facing the Challenges. Case Studies and Indicators* (Paris, UNESCO, 2015).

9. World Bank and FAO, *The Grain Chain: Food Security and managing wheat imports in Arab Countries* (Washington, DC: The World Bank, 2012).

10. Kishan Khoday, "Sustainable Development & Green Economy in the Arab Region," *Arab Development Challenges Background Paper 2011*, UNDP Regional Centre in Cairo (UNDP Cairo, 2011).

11. World Bank, FAO and IFAD, *Improving Food Security in Arab Countries* (Washington, DC: 2009).

12. Eckart Woertz, "The Governance of Gulf Agro-investments," *Globalizations* 10, 1 (2013): 87–104.

13. Eckart Woertz, *Oil for Food: The Global Food Crisis and the Middle East* (Oxford: Oxford University Press, 2013), 32.

14. Tony Allan, "Watersheds and Problemsheds: Explaining the Absence of Armed Conflict Over Water in the Middle East," *Middle East Review of International Affairs* 2 (March 1998): 49–51.

15. Food self-sufficiency is defined as having the means (primarily water and land) to produce the food needed for the population in any given country.

16. Abdul-Karim Sadik, "The State of Food Security and Agricultural Resources," in *Arab Environment: Food Security, Annual report of the Arab Forum for Environment and Development*, eds., Abdul-Karim Sadik, Mahmoud El-Solh and Najib Saab (Beirut: AFED, 2014).

Anders Jägerskog and Kyungmee Kim, "Land acquisition as a means to mitigate water scarcity and reduce conflict?" Accepted in *Hydrological Sciences Journal* (2015).

17. Ellie Elhadj, "Saudi Arabia's Agricultural Project: From Dust to Dust," *Middle East Review of International Affairs* 12 (2008): 6.

18. World Bank et al., *Improving Food Security in Arab Countries.*

19. Khoday, "Sustainable Development & Green Economy in the Arab Region."

20. Clemens Breisinger, Perrihan Al-Riffai, Oliver Ecker and Danielle Resnick, "Regional Developments: Middle East and North Africa," in International Food Policy Research Institute—IFPRI, *Global Food Policy Report 2014* (Washington, DC: IFPRI, 2015).

21. Woertz, *Oil for Food: The Global Food Crisis and the Middle East;* Jägerskog and Kim, "Land acquisition as a means to mitigate water scarcity and reduce conflict?"; Martin Keulertz, *Drivers and impacts of farmland investment in Sudan: water and the range of choice in Jordan and Qatar* (London: King's College, Department of Geography, 2013).

22. Sadik, El-Solh and Saab, *Arab Environment: Food Security.*

23. Sadik, El-Solh and Saab, *Arab Environment: Food Security.*

24. Norwegian Refugee Council (NRC) and International Rescue Committee, *No Escape: Civilians in Syria struggle to find safety Across Borders,* November 2014, at www.nrc.no (accessed May 12, 2015).

25. FAO, IFAD and WFP, *The State of Food Insecurity in the World 2014. Strengthening the enabling environment for food security and nutrition* (Rome: FAO, 2014).

26. International Food Policy Research Institute, *Global Food Policy Report 2014* (Washington DC: IFPRI, 2015).

27. Carlo Scaramella, Regional Director at World Food Programme (WFP) Presentation entitled "Sustainable Development for the most Food-Insecure and Vulnerable: the Role of Social Protection and Safety Nets in Building Resilience," at the Arab High Level Forum on Sustainable Development, Manama, Bahrain, 5 May, 2015.

28. World Health Organization Database, at http://www.who.int/nutgrowthdb/database/en/, (accessed May 15, 2015).

29. Peter Gleick, "Water, Drought, Climate Change and Conflict in Syria," in *Weather, Climate and Society*, 6, 3 (2014): 331–340. doi: http://dx.doi.org/10.1175/WCAS-D-13-00059.1

30. Gleick, "Water, Drought, Climate Change and Conflict in Syria," 338.

31. FAO et al., *The State of Food Insecurity in the World 2014. Strengthening the enabling environment for food security and nutrition.*

32. Strategic Foresight Group, *Water and Violence: Crisis of Survival in the Middle East* (Strategic Foresight Group, Mumbai, India, 2014).

33. C. Hausmann and S. Patrick, "Contingency planning: Trade's role in sustainable world food security," *Aquatic Procedia 1* (2013): 20–29.

34. World Bank et al, *Improving Food Security in Arab Countries.*

35. World Bank et al, *Improving Food Security in Arab Countries.*

36. Jan Lundqvist, Charlotte de Fraiture and David Molden, "Saving Water: From Field to Fork – Curbing Losses and Wastage in the Food Chain," SIWI Policy Brief (Stockholm: SIWI, 2008).

37. Scaramella, "Sustainable Development for the most Food-Insecure and Vulnerable: the Role of Social Protection and Safety Nets in Building Resilience."

38. UN ESCWA, *Food Security and Conflict in the ESCWA region*, UN ESCWA, United Nations, New York, 2010, at http://www.escwa.un.org/information/publications/edit/upload/ECRI-10-1.pdf, (accessed May 14, 2015).

39. Scaramella, "Sustainable Development for the most Food-Insecure and Vulnerable: the Role of Social Protection and Safety Nets in Building Resilience."

40 Masood Ahmed, Dominique Guillaume, Davide Furceri (2012) "Youth Unemployment in the MENA Region: Determinants and Challenges," in World Economic Forum's *Addressing the 100 Million Youth Challenge—Perspectives on Youth Employment in the Arab World in 2012,* June 2012, at https://www.imf.org/external/np/vc/2012/061312.html (accessed May 12, 2015).

41. World Bank et al, *Improving Food Security in Arab Countries.*

42. J.A. Allan, *Virtual water: tackling the threat to our planet's most precious resource* (London: I. B. Tauris, 2011).

43. Jan Lundqvist, Jenny Grönwall and Anders Jägerskog, "Water, food security and human dignity – a nutrition perspective," Ministry of Enterprise and Innovation, Swedish FAO Committee, Stockholm, July 2015.

44. World Bank et al., *Improving Food Security in Arab Countries*.

45. Malin Falkenmark, Anders Jägerskog, and Karl Schneider, "Overcoming the Land-Water Disconnect in Water Scarce Regions – Time for IWRM to go contemporary," *Water International 30*, 3 (2014).

46. Green water is the water in the topsoil layer.

47. Martin Keulertz, Purdue University. Personal communication. Amman, Jordan, November 25, 2014.

48. Lundqvist et al, "Saving Water: From Field to Fork – Curbing Losses and Wastage in the Food Chain."

49. It is important to note that the FAO and Arab Organization for Agricultural Development (AOAD) data measure production and net trade in relation to population numbers only. Thus, they do not include waste along the food supply chain, often do not cover subsistence farming, and do not generally provide a great level of detail on micronutrient deficiencies. Nevertheless, the figures provided at this level of aggregation are arguably the best data for analysis. Woertz, *Oil for Food: The Global Food Crisis and the Middle East*.

50. Lundqvist et al, "Saving Water: From Field to Fork – Curbing Losses and Wastage in the Food Chain."

51. FAO, *Global Food Losses and Waste – Extent, Causes and Prevention*, FAO, Rome, 2011.

52. FAO, *Global Food Losses and Waste – Extent, Causes and Prevention*.

53. Hafez Ghanem, "Food Price Volatility and Implications for Arab Food Security," in *Arab Environment: Food Security. Annual report of the Arab Forum for Environment and Development*, eds., Abdul-Karim Sadik, Mahmoud El-Solh and Najib Saab (Beirut: Lebanon), 2014.

54. Håkan Tropp and Anders Jägerskog, "Meeting the Water Scarcity Challenges in the Middle East and North Africa," *Arab Journal of Water*, 1, 2 (2008).

55. Elie Elhadj, "Dry Aquifers in Arab Countries and the Looming Food Crisis," *Middle East Review of International Affairs*, 12, 4 (December 2008).

56. David F. Larson, "Introducing water to an analysis of alternative good security policies in the Middle East and North Africa," *Aquatic Procedia 1* (2013): 30–43.

57. John Anthony Allan, *The Middle East Water Question: Hydropolitics and the Global Economy* (London, I.B. Tauris, 2001).

58. Anders Jägerskog, "Why states cooperate over shared water: The water negotiations in the Jordan River Basin," (PhD Dissertation, Linköping University, 2003); Elie Elhadj, "Dry Aquifers in Arab Countries and the Looming Food Crisis."

59. Elhadj, "Dry Aquifers in Arab Countries and the Looming Food Crisis," 6.

60. Jessica Barnes, "Managing the Waters of Bath Country: The politics of Water Scarcity in Syria," *Geopolitics*, 14, 3 (2009).

61. Francesca De Châtel, "The Role of Drought and Climate Change in the Syrian Uprising: Untangling the Triggers of Revolution," *Middle Eastern Studies*, 50, 4, (2014): 529.

62. Elie Elhadj, "Saudi Arabia's Agricultural Project: From Dust to Dust," *Middle East Review of International Affairs*, 12, 2 (June 2008).

63. "Saudi Scraps Wheat Growing to Save Water," Reuters, January 8, 2008.

64. Elhadj, "Saudi Arabia's Agricultural Project: From Dust to Dust."

65. Larsson, "Introducing water to an analysis of alternative good security policies in the Middle East and North Africa."

66. Lundqvist, Grönwall and Jägerskog, "Water, food security and human dignity—a nutrition perspective."

67. Elhadj, "Saudi Arabia's Agricultural Project: From Dust to Dust."

68. Jägerskog, Swain and Öjendal, "Water Security – Origins and Foundations," Volume I.

69. Joyce R. Starr, Water Wars, *Foreign Policy* 82 (1991): 17–36; John Bullock and Adel Darwish, *Water Wars: Coming Conflicts in the Middle East* (London: St. Dedmundsbury Press, 1993).

70. Jägerskog, *"Why states cooperate over shared water: The water negotiations in the Jordan River Basin"*; Ashok Swain, *Managing Water Conflict: Asia, Africa and the Middle East* (London: Routledge, 2004).

71. Allan, *The Middle East Water Question*.

72. Jägerskog, *"Why states cooperate over shared water: The water negotiations in the Jordan River Basin."*

73. Lundqvist, Grönwall and Jägerskog, "Water, food security and human dignity—a nutrition perspective."

74. Hausmann and Patrick, "Contingency planning: Trade's role in sustainable world food security."

75. Allan, *Virtual water: tackling the threat to our planet's most precious resource*; Lundqvist, Grönwall and Jägerskog, "Water, food security and human dignity—a nutrition perspective."

76. Lundqvist, Grönwall and Jägerskog, "Water, food security and human dignity—a nutrition perspective"; Marta Antonelli and Stefania Tamea, "Food-water security and virtual water trade in the Middle East and North Africa," *International Journal of Water Resources Development* 31, 3 (2015): 326–42.

77. UNCTAD database, at www.unctad.org (accessed May 20, 2015).

78. Eckart Woertz, *Oil for Food: The Global Food Crisis and the Middle East*.

79. Keulertz, *Drivers and impacts of farmland investment in Sudan: water and the range of choice in Jordan and Qatar*.

80. UN ESCWA, "Food Secure Arab World: A Road Map for Policy and Research," Report, February 6–7, 2012, Beirut.

81. UN ESCWA, "Food Secure Arab World: A Road Map for Policy and Research."

82. Tariq Al-Zadjali, "Developing Fish Resources in the Arab World," in *Arab Environment: Food Security. Annual report of the Arab Forum for Environment and Development*, eds., Abdul-Karim Sadik, Mahmoud El-Solh and Najib Saab (Beirut: Lebanon, 2014).

83. Al-Zadjali, "Developing Fish Resources in the Arab World."

84. Anders Jägerskog, Ana Cascao, Mats Hårsmar and Kyungmee Kim, "Land Acquisitions: How Will They Impact Transboundary Waters?" Report Nr. 30, SIWI, Stockholm, 2012.

85. Lundqvist, Grönwall, Jägerskog, "Water, food security and human dignity—a nutrition perspective."

86. Woertz, *Oil for Food: The Global Food Crisis and the Middle East.*

87. Jägerskog and Kim, "Land acquisition as a means to mitigate water scarcity and reduce conflict?."

88. Woertz, *Oil for Food: The Global Food Crisis and the Middle East.*

Keulertz, *Drivers and impacts of farmland investment in Sudan: water and the range of choice in Jordan and Qatar.*

89. Woertz, *Oil for Food: The Global Food Crisis and the Middle East.*

90. Suvi Sojamo *et al.*, "Virtual water hegemony: the role of agribusiness in global water governance," *Water International*, 37, 2 (2013): 169–82.

91. Woertz, *Oil for Food: The Global Food Crisis and the Middle East.*

92. Jägerskog et al, "Land Acquisitions: How Will They Impact Transboundary Waters?."

93. Woertz, *Oil for Food: The Global Food Crisis and the Middle East.*

94 IPCC, "Climate change 2007: Synthesis Report," Chapter 11, 866, at www.ipcc.ch, (accessed May 12, 2015).

95 World Bank et al, *Improving Food Security in Arab Countries.*

96. Jeannie Sowers, Avner Vengosh and Erika Weinthal "Climate change, water resources and the politics of adaptation in the Middle East and North Africa," *Climate Change*, 104 (2011): 599–627.

97. Abou-Hadid F. Ayman, "Impact of Climate Change on Food Security," in *Arab Environment: Food Security. Annual report of the Arab Forum for Environment and Development,* eds., Abdul-Karim Sadik, Mahmoud El-Solh and Najib Saab (Beirut: Lebanon), 2014.

98 AFED, "Arab Environment: Climate Change – Impact of Climate Change on Arab Countries," in *Report of the Arab Forum for Environment and Development 2009,* eds., Mostafa K. Tolba and Najib W. Saab.

99. World Bank et al, *Improving Food Security in Arab Countries.*

100. Anton Earle, Ana Cascao, Anders Jägerskog, Ashok Swain, Joakim Öjendal and Stina Hansson, *Transboundary Water Management and the Climate Change Debate* (London: Routledge, 2015); Malin Falkenmark and Anders Jägerskog, "Sustainability of Transnational Water Agreements in the Face of Socio-Economic and Environmental Change," in *Transboundary Water Management: Principles and Practice,* eds., Anton Earle, Anders Jägerskog and Joakim Öjendal (London: Earthscan, 2012).

101. Kishan, "Sustainable Development & Green Economy in the Arab Region."

102. Earle et al, *Transboundary Water Management and the Climate Change Debate.*

103. Gleick, "Water, Drought, Climate Change and Conflict in Syria."

104. Ralf Klingbeil and Fidele Byiringiro, "Food Security, Water Security, Improved Food Value Chains for a more Sustainable Socio-economic Development," Unpublished paper, UNESCWA, 2013.

105. Center for Climate and Security, at www.climateandsecurity.org (accessed January 15, 2015).

106. De Châtel, "The Role of Drought and Climate Change in the Syrian Uprising: Untangling the Triggers of Revolution."

107. De Châtel, "The Role of Drought and Climate Change in the Syrian Uprising: Untangling the Triggers of Revolution"; Jeannie Sowers, John Waterbury and

Eckart Woertz, *Did Drought trigger the Syria Crisis?*, September 12, 2013, at http://
footnote1.com/did-drought-trigger-the-crisis-in-syria/.

108. De Châtel, "The Role of Drought and Climate Change in the Syrian Uprising:
Untangling the Triggers of Revolution," 32.

109. Sowers, Woertz and Waterbury, *Did Drought trigger the Syria Crisis?*, 3.

110. Khoday, "Sustainable Development & Green Economy in the Arab Region."

111. Breisinger et al, "Regional Developments: Middle East and North Africa."

112. Lundqvist, Grönwall and Jägerskog, "Water, food security and human dignity
– a nutrition perspective."

113. Raymond F. Hopkins, "Food security, policy options and the evolution of
state responsibility," in *Food, the state and interactional political economy: Dilemmas
of developing countries,* eds., F. L. Tullis and W. L. Hollist, (Lincoln and London:
University of Nebraska Press, 1986).

Chapter 3

Water Scarcity

Threat to Peace and Stability

The demand for water for human and industrial use has increased, so also the competition for water used for irrigated agriculture. Many regions in the world are already facing serious problems in meeting the rapidly increasing demands for water. In order to meet their demands, they are overexploiting the available water resources. This overexploitation of water resources further results in acute shortage. In this scarcity situation, water has increasingly become a source of social tension as users are worried about the present or future availability of water resources. They work purposefully and consciously to maximize the availability of water resources. Therefore, water scarcity has the potential to bring further competition and create conflict that can destroy the ongoing arrangements of water sharing. Thus, achieving water security has become a major challenge at the global level. However, it was not until the 1980s and 1990s that the environment, and predominantly water, increasingly became a concern for policy makers from a security perspective.

Water scarcity in the Middle East is particularly a cause for serious concern.[1] The countries in this region have to make do with a more or less static resource, while more pressure is being put on the resource as the populations in these countries increase; pollution is on the rise and new habits of people "demand" more water. This Malthusian[2] reasoning is that conflict is assumed to be the outcome of the increasing competition for resources. With a primary focus on the Middle East, it was concluded more than two decades back that competition over water would lead to "water wars."[3] The increased focus on water (among other "new" security concerns) coincided with the end of the Cold War and arguably made it possible to address "new" or "alternative" security issues.[4] This situation led to a "securitization" of new issues in which water moved up higher in the order of political importance.[5] While the focus early on in the debate was on water as a reason for conflict and thereby had a supply-side focus, it moved over time into a realization that managing demand and putting proper governance systems in place was also (and perhaps more) important.[6]

Water security includes a range of different aspects.[7] Without adequate supply of water, societies cannot function. Global food production is dependent on water[8]; energy production is dependent (directly and/or indirectly) on a secure access to water; health provision is dependent on safe and reliable water supply; and general societal development is dependent on a safe access to water. These critical roles of water have been highlighted internationally in the UNDP Human Development Report of 2006[9] and in the Rio+20 conference 2012.[10] The United Nations has reiterated water security as a key issue and has devised strategies to address it.[11] Water also features prominently in the follow-up to the Millennium Development Goals (MDGs), in the newly created Sustainable Development Goals (SDGs) where water and sanitation have been given a separate and important place (Goal number 6). It is estimated that around 1.8 billion people in the world lack access to clean water and 2.5 million lack access to adequate sanitation. Out of the 2.5 billion people lacking access to adequate sanitation, around 1 billion are children. As a result of inadequate access to sanitation and clean water, a staggering 1.5 million people die every year of preventable and curable water-related diseases such as diarrhea.[12] These aspects of water and sanitation directly relate to human security.

While water scarcity is a major challenge, many argue that an even more important challenge is the governance of water.[13] In order to meet the needs of a growing global population, responding to development aspirations, as well as providing food security with adequate governance systems, is imperative.[14] In the areas of water and food, governance and management challenges (and also opportunities) are larger and complex in relation to the food supply chain, though there are massive losses in this chain, and in some regions and countries, up to 50 percent is lost from the "field to the fork."[15]

From a classic security perspective, the fact that water crosses boundaries and is "shared" between countries is what makes it more interesting. However, as noted above, this is not the only aspect of water security. More than 40 percent of the available freshwater is found in shared rivers, lakes, or groundwater systems between two or more countries. When water is plentiful and relations between the countries that are sharing the resource are good, cooperation over a shared water resource is usually not challenging. Unfortunately, such a situation is the exception rather than the rule. In many areas, not least in the Middle East, shared water resources are subject to contestation and controversy. Several river basins in different parts of the world, particularly in Asia, Africa, and the Middle East, experience a fair degree of interriparian disputes and the most well known of them are the Nile River, the Mekong, Amu and Syr Darya, the Jordan River, the Congo River, the Indus, and the Ganges. The Oregon State University has developed the Transboundary Freshwater Dispute Database (TFDD), and it has identified 276 international river basins across the globe. Add to this over 300 shared groundwater systems and the magnitude of the challenge becomes even more evident. As population soars with a growing demand for food production and increasing industrial and municipal use, it comes as no surprise that water has increasingly been treated as a national security issue at the highest political level.[16] Some argue that while early on in the debate it was hypothesized that water would be a reason for conflict and even war, most of the interactions over shared river basins were of a cooperative nature.[17] Some others have highlighted the ameliorating role that "virtual water"—water that has been used to produce food grains, for example—has had for regions where water scarcity has been most acute.[18] This has enabled a country like Egypt—which basically ran out of water in its effort to produce the food it needed in the 1970s—to compensate through increased import of virtual water (see also chapter 2 for a more elaborate discussion about virtual water trade and in particular its importance for the Middle East).

However, in about two-thirds of the river basins, cohesive and negotiated agreements and frameworks are lacking, thus making them even more vulnerable to conflict. Furthermore, when agreements do exist, the institutions that are set to manage them are often lacking a proper mandate and/or are underfinanced, thus making their task challenging and increasing the risk of conflict.[19] While a few decades back water was seen as a reason for war, the debate moved from a focus on cooperation over transboundary waters to one that discusses equitable cooperation and the fact that conflict and cooperation are often components present at the same time at various scales between countries sharing a river, lake, or groundwater system. In addition, the power asymmetries between states in a basin and how this affects prospects for equitable cooperation have dominated the debate.[20]

In addition, new challenges have emerged to the water security framework. One of the most critical ones is climate change and climate variability. The available water resources in the world are far from equally divided, and some regions and countries are better endowed with water than others. With increasing global warming, meaning increased variability in flow and more droughts as well as floods, some already arid and semiarid regions are predicted to receive even less rainfall than before.[21] Even in cases where agreements between states do exist, they are most often not flexible in allocation but rather have a volumetric focus and are based on multiyear averages.[22] These factors make them vulnerable to deal with an increasing climate variability, which will mean increasing fluctuations in the flow of shared water systems. Another challenge is the increase that has been seen in foreign land investments (see also chapter 2), where outside actors often invest in a basin and become hydropolitical actors in that basin.[23] Other security challenges are the use of water as a weapon in an armed conflict, which has gained in significance and increasing attention particularly with the Syrian crisis, where the ISIS has taken control of water infrastructure and dams and has started using them to punish its adversaries.

Considering the complexities and challenges, transboundary water relations may best be described as a form of continuous negotiations as the parameters are changing, more or less quickly, over time.[24] The actors wanting to engage in the basin and support riparian cooperation need to do so with a long-term financing perspective understanding that promoting and eventually achieving sustainable cooperation takes time and energy.[25] Here, it is important to analyze water scarcity problems of the Middle East and discuss it in light of the governance mechanisms put in place in the region, both nationally and regionally. For this, it is necessary to explore existing conflicts around transboundary waters and also various, often embryonic and cooperative, mechanisms that exist for joint management. The aim is to link water conflicts to broader political conflicts and situate the water challenges within a wider regional security discussion, particularly with the focus on food, energy, and migration challenges in the region.

WATER SCARCITY AND WATER GOVERNANCE IN THE MIDDLE EAST

On per capita terms, the Middle East is the region in the world that has the least water available. Roughly, 1 percent of the available water resources are to be found in the region, while it harbors over 5 percent of the global population. Much of the water is furthermore not always easily accessible but found in groundwater systems. Most of the region has water resources that are either heavily exploited or overexploited as per the water stress indicator. This means that water resources are either used to their limits (in terms of what is annually renewable in rivers, lakes, and groundwater systems) or often cross the limits, thus making use unsustainable. This leads to depleting groundwater tables, sinking water levels in surface water systems, decreased flow in rivers, and subsequently salinization of freshwater sources and increasing pollution problems. The region is dependent on a few key water resources, some of them being surface water and some groundwater. A challenge but also an opportunity is evident in the use of *green water* resources.[26] No doubt that rainwater is not being put to efficient use in the region. A more efficient use of the green water in the region could ease some of the pressure on the other water systems. Thus, while the overall water situation is quite bleak in the region, there are still opportunities that exist.

Even before the end of the Cold War, US intelligence services had warned that there were at least ten places in the world where armed conflict could break out over water shortages—the majority of them were in the Middle East.[27] The region has not experienced these "water wars," but the situation is still conflictual. Many of the countries in the Middle East rely heavily on imported surface water, which comes through their shared river systems.[28] In a situation of increasing water demand and with climate change–related uncertainties, these rivers have the real potential to become even more conflictual among the riparian states if not managed appropriately.

The Nile River is the primary source of water for Egypt, which receives over 95 percent of its freshwater from the river.[29] Changes in the current management regime are, therefore, seen in Cairo as a potential threat to the water security of the country. In terms of formal agreement for cooperation on

Table 3.1 Water Availability in the Middle East[1]

Country	Total Internal Renewable Water Resources (km³/Year)	Ground Water: Produced Internally (km³/Year)	Surface Water: Produced Internally (km³/Year)	Water Resources: Total Renewable Per Capita (m³/ Capita Year)
Iraq	35.20	3.20	34.00	2 652[F]
Iran	128	49.30	97.30	1 957
Lebanon	4.80	3.20	4.10	1 110
Syria	7.13	4.84	4.29	865
Egypt	1.80	1.30	0.50	773
Oman	1.40	1.30	1.05	550[F]
Israel	0.75	0.50	0.25	261[F]
Jordan	0.682	0.45	0.485	164[F]
Bahrain	0.004	0.00	0.004	157
Saudi Arabia	2.40	2.20	2.20	99.3[F]
Yemen	2.10	1.50	2.00	96.6[F]
Palestine	0.812	0.74	0.072	94.7*
Qatar	0.056	0.056	0.00	70.6
United Arab Emirates	0.15	0.12	0.15	35.3
Kuwait	0.00	0.00	0.00	7.20

F, FAO estimate.

*Data from Palestinian Water Authority 2007. Includes approximately 53.4 cmc purchased externally from an Israeli company. If the externally purchased water is excluded, the total renewable water resources per capita and year for Palestine would be approximately 79.6m³.[2]

[1]FAO AQUASTAT, Online database, 2007, at http://www.fao.org/nr/water/aquastat/data/query/index.html (accessed June 1, 2009). Availability of neighboring countries to the Middle East region is included as it is relevant from a transboundary perspective (e.g., Turkey and Iran in the case of Euphrates and Tigris).

[2]Palestinian Water Authority. Water database. Palestinian National Authority, Palestinian Central Bureau of Statistics, 2007, at http://www.pcbs.gov.ps/Portals/_pcbs/Water/c6f0eba6-3f6a-41b3-baad-c6b13a24ddc8.html (accessed June 1, 2009).

the Nile River, there exists a colonial 1929 agreement and 1959 agreements between Egypt and Sudan basically dividing the bulk of the water between them. Before major developments on the river took place in the other riparian states also sharing the Nile in East Africa, this did not constitute a major challenge, but as they started to develop and gain independence, this became a growing challenge. Development aspirations centered around water have led to increasing discussions on the division and use of the Nile waters among the riparian states of the Nile River.[30]

The Nile River is about 6800 km long and the area of the Nile basin covers almost 10 percent of the area of Africa. In total, eleven riparian states share the Nile waters with a combined population of around 400 million people. Population growth is also very high in the river system. If the current population growth rates continue, the estimates for the main riparian countries of the Nile, Egypt, Ethiopia, and Sudan alone are that they will be around 340 million people by 2050. The Nile River basin is characterized by a complex hydrological as well as hydropolitical system. A range of tributaries feed the Nile River and cross both different climatic zones and political boundaries, and the river is prone to large variations within and between years in flow. It is also prone to drought and flood events. Poverty levels are very high in the basin. The Nile River has two main tributaries. The White Nile emanates from the Nile Equatorial Lakes region and the source of the Blue Nile is from the highlands in Ethiopia. The level of rainfall in the basin varies considerably. The difference between the rainfall in the Nile Equatorial Lakes region and the rainfall in Egypt and North Sudan is massive. While the water dependency ratio in Rwanda and Burundi is close to nil, it is 77 percent in Sudan and around 97 percent in Egypt. Most of the water (86 percent) in the Nile system emanates from the Ethiopian highlands.[31] From a development perspective, it is also important to note that the basin is still to a large degree dependent on agriculture for livelihood. In the basin as a whole around 75 percent of the water is used in the agricultural sector, and in Ethiopia and Egypt, the figure is around 85 percent, while in Sudan it is over 90 percent.[32] This makes those countries very dependent on rainfall (and thereby climate) variability in the basin. The rapid population growth in the basin (not least in Egypt) puts additional pressure on the water resources in the region, both from a food security and energy security perspective. The basin has also seen significant economic and political change during the last five years, including the birth of a new state (the Republic of South Sudan), the Arab Spring in Egypt with social and political changes, large-scale investments in land in parts of the basin (with unclear effects on the water in the basin), the discovery of oil and mineral resources in Uganda, and the construction of many dams on the river, with the Grand Ethiopian Renaissance Dam (GERD) being by far the most significant development to take place.[33]

The development of the Nile Basin Initiative (NBI), which was a program aiming at achieving joint development of the Nile Basin region, started in early 2000 led to increased international focus not only on the river but also on the region as such. Parallel to the development program, negotiations on a new agreement, the "Cooperative Framework Agreement (CFA)," progressed. After around ten years of negotiations, six states signed the CFA in 2010, but this has led to diplomatic challenges now as the two downstream riparian states (Egypt and Sudan) have refused to sign the agreement as they view it as not catering enough to their interests and not protecting what they view as their historical rights over the Nile waters. The CFA is not yet a legally binding agreement as it has not yet been ratified by a minimum of six countries, but it affects the political as well as the NBI development track (Earle et al, 2015). Furthermore, Ethiopia has since decided to embark on a construction of the Grand Ethiopian Renaissance Dam (GERD) on the Nile River, which further aggravates the situation in the Eastern Nile.[34] Over 80 percent of the Nile waters emanate from Ethiopia and any efforts to obstruct this flow are seen by Egypt as a threat to its national security. The dam will, when finalized, be one of the largest in Africa and will mainly work to generate hydropower. Thus, water use is largely nonconsumptive (although the large lake that will be generated after filling the dam will increase evaporation) and will still provide both Egypt and Sudan with water. It seems one of the key challenges is how to deal with the situation when the dam is being filled and also the pace of this activity, since filling will significantly reduce the flow of the Nile to the downstream countries, particularly Egypt. A longer period will make the impact on the flow less significant. Another challenge relates to the safety of the dam as a potential collapse of the dam structure would be detrimental to both the downstream countries, Sudan and Egypt. A tripartite committee between Egypt, Ethiopia, and Sudan has been established to study the impact of the GERD, and the process is ongoing at present. The impact on the regional security in the region as a result of the developments in the basin (primarily the Eastern Nile region and in particular the GERD) should not be underestimated. With continued population growth, a heavy reliance on the agricultural sector for livelihoods in the basin, increasing pressure from climate change (and variability), and ongoing political challenges in the region (the conflict in South Sudan and the ongoing political instability in Egypt in the post–Arab Spring period) will continue to (and increasingly so) affect the regional security discussions.

The Jordan River basin has been marred in conflicts and tense negotiations over its division and use. The conflict over the waters of the Jordan River is part of the Arab-Israeli conflict having five riparian states (Israel, Jordan, Lebanon, Palestine, and Syria) that in some cases do not have formal relations and in others a less than good cooperation.[35]

Between Israel and Jordan, it is the Jordan River and its drainage basin that is the bone of contention. Between Israel and the Palestine, the dispute is over the Jordan River drainage basin and the aquifers (groundwater systems) in which the water flows. The water flows mainly west from the heights of the West Bank toward the Mediterranean into Israel. The sources of the upper Jordan River are three major springs. One of these, the Hasbani, has its source in Lebanon, while the Dan has its source in Israel, and the Banias in the Israeli-occupied Golan Heights. The Hasbani, the Dan, and the Banias join at a length of six kilometers inside Israel and flow into the Hula Valley where they are joined by some smaller tributaries. The upper Jordan River then flows south into Lake Tiberias/Kinneret before it continues southward toward the Dead Sea. Lake Tiberias/Kinneret covers 166 square kilometers and when its level is 213 meters below sea level, it stores 538 million cubic meters (mcm) of water.[36] Around ten kilometers south of Lake Tiberias/Kinneret, the Jordan River is joined by another main tributary, the Yarmouk, which has its source in Syria and flows through Jordan. It is the main water source for Jordan. Actually, Jordan does not use any water from the Jordan River directly but draws its water from its tributaries before they discharge into the river.

During the last decades, Jordan has not received its share of water in the Yarmouk since Syria has withdrawn more than it has been entitled to upstream. For Israel and Jordan, the Jordan River Basin (which includes its tributaries) is of immense importance as both states withdraw large percentages of their water from it. For the other riparian states in the basin—Syria and Lebanon—the basin is not as important as it is for Israel, Jordan, and the Palestine since Lebanon gets a greater share of its water from the Litani and Awali Rivers, while Syria receives most of its water from the Euphrates and the Orontes. Moreover, the quantity of water in the Jordan River is constantly dwindling along the course of the river because more water is withdrawn from it than is renewed every year. This is especially significant in years of drought. The reduction in the flow threatens the quality of the water as saline water infiltrates and salinizes the water, making it impossible to use. Agricultural drainage water, draining into the river from both sides of the river, is accelerating the deterioration of the water quality. Hence, the water problem in the basin is not only one of quantity but also one of quality.

In addition to the dispute over surface water between Israel and Jordan, there is the dispute over the groundwater of the mountain aquifer between Israel and Palestine. The mountain aquifer, which is divided in the western aquifer, flows from the highest parts of the West Bank westward, the northeastern aquifer flows northeast into Israeli territory, and the eastern aquifer flows east toward the Jordan River. The eastern aquifer is not considered to be a transboundary water resource as its flow is almost entirely within the

West Bank. The western and northeastern sections of the mountain aquifers had reached their productive limits by the mid-1970s. In these areas, the groundwater table has started falling alarmingly for several decades now. The overextraction of water has also led to a deterioration of the quality of the water in the aquifer. The Palestinians blame Israeli settlers for overpumping, and the control of groundwater sources has been one of the major constraints to peace in this region.

These aquifers are recharged through the precipitation that falls over the West Bank. The recharge is subject to major variations as precipitation over the area varies considerably from year to year. These variations obviously complicate relations among the riparian states, and this is particularly evident in the years of drought. The variations in water availability are in a sense possible to account for. If the parties could agree to negotiate allocations on the basis of "reliable" water and include provisions for the allocation of the "nonreliable" extra water, the problem of allocation in times of drought would be more easily dealt with. The data on river flows are multiyear averages and thus not a very rational base for yearly allocations,[37] particularly as the Jordan River Basin is subject to high seasonal and multiannual variances in precipitation and attendant stream flow.[38]

In the conflict between Israel and Palestine, a further source of dispute is the Israeli coastal aquifer, which runs along the Mediterranean coast and connects from Israel into the Gaza aquifer, which underlies the Gaza Strip. There is a general agreement that the Gaza aquifer is an extension of the coastal aquifer in Israel, although there are different views on the extent to which they are connected. Some argue that the flow in the aquifer is predominantly east to west, which seems to suggest that Israeli activities north of the Gaza Strip will not seriously affect the part of the aquifer that lies beneath the Gaza Strip. Similarly, the activities in the Gaza Strip will not affect the Israeli coastal aquifer.[39] However, Palestinians complain that the settlements in the area have hindered the recharge of the groundwater. The unsustainable water extraction from the aquifer by the Jewish settlers (before they were all evacuated) has reduced the water table in many places to below sea level. The resulting infiltration of salt water from the Mediterranean Sea has made the Gaza aquifer water somewhat unsuitable for agricultural use. Gaza is already experiencing serious food and water crisis and increasing salinization of the aquifer will only aggravate the situation.[40]

There is no agreement covering the whole basin, but there are bilateral agreements. Jordan and Syria have an agreement on the Yarmouk River, although Syria has been using more than what the agreement stipulates.[41] Israel and the Palestinian Authority signed in 1993 the Declaration of Principles (DOP), commonly referred to as the Oslo agreement, as well as the "Oslo II" in 1995. Both of these "agreements" represent more of road maps for negotiation, and the intention was to finalize these negotiations within a five-year period, something that has yet to materialize. They furthermore relate primarily to the groundwater aquifers shared by the Israelis and the Palestinians. Water is identified as one of five key aspects of agreement in the final status negotiations. Thus, the current framework, which provides for the so-called Joint Water Committee (JWC) between the parties, and states that the Palestinians do have "water rights" (without defining what these are), does not cover all relevant aspects and is skewed in favor of Israel.[42] Between Israel and Jordan, water is dealt with in some detail in their peace agreement which is effective from 1994.[43] Relations between Israel and Jordan on water have seen some improvement over the last more than twenty-year period. There are also provisions for a Joint Water Committee (JWC) between the two countries and they meet regularly and discuss common issues. In 2015, they signed another agreement for joint desalination and trading of water. The Israeli-Jordanian relations need also to be viewed in the light of the larger cooperation between them where there is a strong mutual dependence in areas such as energy, security, and intelligence.[44]

Regarding the *Euphrates-Tigris Rivers*, there exists no all-inclusive framework for cooperation. The relations around the waters of the Euphrates and Tigris have been guided primarily by unilateral riparian action and occasional cooperation. The river sharing engagement is primarily between Turkey, Iraq, and Syria, but Iran is also part of the discussion.

The annual discharge of the Euphrates is 32 billion m^3, while the Tigris has an annual flow of 52 billion m^3. The Euphrates-Tigris River system is, however, characterized by a very high annual as well as interannual variation in flow. During the last decades, the flow has also been largely affected by the undertaking of large-scale irrigation as well as hydropower (energy) projects in all the riparian countries, driven (at least in part) by a rapid population growth and a craving for more agricultural development for increasing food production.[45] The Euphrates basin covers an area in the order of 444,000 square kilometers out of which around 33 percent is in Turkey, 19 percent in Syria, and 46 percent in Iraq. The Tigris basin covers an area of close to 388,000 square kilometers out of which 15 percent lies in Turkey, 0.5 percent in Syria, 75 percent in Iraq, and 9.5 percent in Iran.[46] Iraq derives the majority of its water from the Euphrates-Tigris system. For Syria, this system is strategically very important, although it is part of other basins such as the Orontes and the Jordan because of its importance from an agricultural development as well as hydropower perspective. For Turkey, it contributes around a third of the country's surface water resources and the basin includes a fifth of its agricultural area. The water dependency ratio is very high in the region as well. Syria has around 72 percent of water that stems from outside the country and for Iraq it is 61 percent.[47] The high fluctuations in flow within and between years provide a case for close coordination and cooperation between the riparian states of the basin. The hydrointerdependence is high among the basin countries.[48] Still, the development of cooperative mechanisms has been far from ideal. Added features that will further complicate future cooperation are the water conditions along the Euphrates, which are projected to be around eight times more stressed in 2025 compared to 2010.[49] According to projected climate changes, there will be increased temperature in resulting evaporation and more frequent extreme weather events. While the basin is experiencing rapid population growth now, all the stakeholders will have to make do with a likely decreased overall water availability and significantly lower on a per capita basis.

Kibaroglu and Scheumann[50] describe the evolution of transboundary relations in the basin as having had four more or less distinct periods. The first period (early 1920s to late 1950s) coincided with a phase of nation building where water was (in relative terms) abundant and the focus was more internal (domestic needs and socioeconomic development) rather than on their respective neighbors. The second phase (from the late 1950s to 1980s) was characterized by an increasing competition between the riparian states in the Euphrates-Tigris systems as a result of growing development aspirations where the hydropolitical relations were shaped by national projects, in principle not coordinated with their neighbors. During this period, Turkey started its Greater Anatolia Project (GAP), which was a major development scheme intended to utilize large parts of the Euphrates-Tigris waters. The third period (from the 1980s to the late 1990s) is seen as the most complex where linkages between transboundary water management and broader security considerations became increasingly evident. During this period, the Turkish-Syrian relations on water were affected by the Kurdish question where Syrian support to the PKK (Kurdistan Worker's Party) became a thorny issue. During the fourth period (from the early 2000 to around 2011), cooperative attempts increased between the countries in the basin. Not least did the signing of the so-called Astana Security Agreement from 1998 between Syria and Turkey also lead to more cooperative efforts on the water side.[51]

Between Iraq and Turkey there exists a committee (Joint Technical Committee) that has met irregularly over the years to discuss the sharing of the waters. The discussions have from time to time seen bellicose statements over the sharing of the waters. In spite of many meetings, the outcome has not moved the cooperation forward that much. Still, various other initiatives have been tried, including the establishment of a "track-two" process involving an academic network (The Euphrates-Tigris Initiative for Cooperation—ETIC), which has brought together academics from the different riparian countries to discuss potential ways to increase cooperation. Simultaneously, the governments in the basin have moved ahead with the signing of protocols showing an intention to cooperate more closely.[52] However, after the civil war erupted in Syria, the progress that was imminent during the first decade of 2000s quickly took a slide backward. Regional relations, which have become significantly more fragile since 2011, have also largely brought a halt to the progress on water cooperation in the basin. The problem has been further complicated by the ISIS advances in both Syria and Iraq, with subsequent taking over of dams and water installations, thus showing how transboundary water relations are intimately linked to broader regional security politics. The control of ISIS of water installations means that potentially cooperation between all riparian states may not be possible indefinitely and the threat of stopped (or decreased) flow as well as destruction of dams could foretell a catastrophe.[53]

The power relations between the parties have been largely determining the outcome of the cooperation, largely in favor of Turkey at the expense of the less strong (and downstream) riparian states. Another complicating factor is the regional divisions of Iraq, which has led to the situation where the Kurdish Regional Government (KRG) in Northern Iraq controls much of the water coming from Turkey before reaching the rest of Iraq. In addition, the current situation in Syria and parts of Iraq, with ISIS having in control of parts of the water, has put any plan for improving the cooperation to appear more like aspirations for the distant future than something that is remotely likely in the near future.

Presently, in all the major transboundary river basins in the Middle East, a race is going on to gain as much control of water resources as possible. However, cooperation rather than control is needed among the riparian states to get the best possible use of scarce river water resources. In spite of many attempts, still no basin-based agreements regarding the use of the international rivers have been possible in the region for the mutual benefits of all the riparian states. Thus, any unilateral riparian development plan over shared river water is being perceived by another as a threat to its national interest. In this context, there is a real need of basin-wide cooperative arrangements, involving at least the major riparian countries. Without the active cooperation of the riparian states, the water potential of the international rivers in this region cannot be fully developed. The most efficient use of these river waters with the help of a joint river management mechanism is very much needed to address the growing water scarcity in the region.[54]

In addition to the major river systems, there are also groundwater resources available in all countries—some of them are transboundary in nature. One example is the *Disi aquifer* shared between Jordan and Saudi Arabia. While exploitation started sometime back in 2000, there has not been a formal agreement between the countries until the spring of 2015. While there previously existed some form of tacit understanding between the two kingdoms, a formal agreement was signed on April 30, 2015, on the management and utilization of the shared systems.[55] It can be hypothesized that the agreement between Jordan and Saudi Arabia was actually agreed upon at this point in time, after many years of deliberations, as a result of the need for improved cooperation in the region and the need for strengthening certain alliances in the region against common threats such as ISIS.

As discussed before, much of the available waters in the region are of a transboundary nature. The available water also varies within the region, with some countries being almost totally dependent for their total water use on water emanating from outside of their territory. Moreover, some countries import water (in its virtual form) from abroad, making them highly dependent on water from elsewhere. From a security perspective, this carries huge importance. As availability is low and dependence on outside sources is high, it elevates the water issue for most countries in the region to one of high national security concerns.

There are various ways to address the water challenges in the region. As discussed earlier, there were a lot of apprehensions a few decades back on water being the reason for armed conflicts and wars in the region.[56] The persistent narrative on food self-sufficiency (craving for more water than what was, and certainly is, available) in the region led to the conclusion that fighting over water resources will increase. While political conflict has increased, the conflicts over water have been ameliorated by the fact that massive amounts of "virtual water," that is, water used to produce the much-needed food, have been imported to the region, thus easing part of the pressure on the water resources in the region.

In addition to the current challenges in the region, increased demand from various sectors of the economies, high population growth, and climate change are exerting further pressure on the available water.[57] Most projections indicate that the Middle East will have longer and more frequent droughts, higher temperatures, and generally reduced water availability.[58] These will pose an additional challenge on the already hard-pressed region. Also, from a transboundary perspective, these add further complication as the fluctuation in flows will be larger, and on the rivers where agreements do exist, they will not be flexible but rather will be based on multiyear averages.[59] However, in the Euphrates-Tigris system, annual and interannual fluctuations in flow are significant and need to be managed in a coherent manner, but presently no institutional structure is in place to manage these challenges effectively.[60]

As the challenges in the region are predicted to become more severe in relation to climate variability, the existing river water agreements are largely based on multiyear averages and they are far from being equipped to adapt to address increasing fluctuations.[61] The already existing large flow fluctuations between years are affecting all the major river systems in the region. This is likely to lead to increasing challenges for governments in the years to come.

Generally, transboundary water actors are responding to the climate change in three distinct ways: *adapting* to predicted impacts; *resisting*, as in avoiding or ignoring the issue; or *subverting*, as in exploiting the debate to fulfill their own agenda.[62] Arguably, actors understand (or *choose* to understand) the issue against the background of their own interests and intentions. What scientists say about climate change and what action needs to be taken about it will be viewed in a different light depending on whether a riparian state is upstream or downstream or whether a state represents a powerful entity or a less powerful one. Often one can see proof of responses to the climate change debate becoming securitized in the region. The increasing flow variations in transboundary basins are clearly an example where increasing politicization and securitization is evident in the discourse.

While there is a growing competition among the riparian states over the scarce and dwindling water resources, the challenges within each of these countries are also getting severe. Competition within countries between the agricultural, industrial, and domestic sector is fast becoming severe as well. Generally, regimes in the Middle East have (and in many cases do still) subsidized the agricultural sector. However, a major governance challenge in the water sector in the region is the lack of a proper pricing system for water (and the service to provide the water).[63] The agricultural sector still receives a large amount of subsidies. The importance of the food self-sufficiency narrative (discussed in chapter 2) underlines this and explains why it may be seen as the politically desired option to subsidize the agricultural sector. Besides, unsustainable and huge agricultural subsidies, corruption, low levels of public participation, and inadequate management systems are other challenges affecting not only the water sector but also related sectors such as agriculture and food.[64] In the region, much of ongoing national water reform policy documents contain elements of increased stakeholder participation, but on the ground "voice and accountability" are very low. Poor accountability mechanisms, in combination with insufficient water legislation, and weak implementation and monitoring of the existing legislation create unfavorable conditions for the establishment of sound water management and obstruct the development of good governance in the region.

SUPPLY VERSUS DEMAND SIDE SOLUTIONS

The water challenges can be overcome by various strategies. One is to focus on increasing the supply and another is to focus on managing the demand better. Often, however, a combination of the two approaches is used. This is also the case in the Middle East, although there is generally a stronger focus on supply-side solutions.

In most parts of the region, subsidy of agricultural water is a cornerstone of the agricultural policy. In fact, the region has the highest level of agricultural subsidies for water in the world measured as part of GDP.[65] Perhaps the clearest example of the excessive subsidies is Saudi Arabia's decision to grow wheat in the desert using primarily fossil water.[66] In Saudi Arabia, the price of one cubic meter of water for the farmer is 0.08 cent, while the real price before subsidies is 1.09 USD. In Yemen, the heavy subsidies on diesel have also had negative effects on the water situation in the country as it has allowed cheap pumping of scarce water to irrigate the water-intensive qat crop.[67] The issue of subsidies illustrates the importance of the food self-sufficiency narrative in the region. The fact that water is subsidized has led to unsustainable agricultural practices as well as wastage of this scarce and valuable resource. The subsidies for irrigation also lessen the need to find innovative and more water-efficient techniques for irrigation practices, and the policy of providing subsidies does not provide the economic incentives to move to less water-intensive crops. The Saudi experiment with growing wheat in the desert, which brought them at one point to become the world's sixth largest wheat exporter, was reversed in 2008 when they adopted a policy of phasing out the growing of wheat and increase reliance on wheat import.[68] Given the scarcity in the region, one would assume that the water productivity in the region would be higher than in other parts of the world, but in reality, the water productivity is only half of that of the rest of the world.[69]

An example of a massive supply-side solution is the Red Sea-Dead Sea Water Conveyance project. The project was originally intended to help save the Dead Sea, whose level has been sinking with around one meter annually for the last three decades, and build a symbol of peace for the region. The reason for the decline in the water level in the Dead Sea is that much of the water from the Jordan River has been diverted before it enters the Dead Sea. Syria diverts much of the water in the Yarmouk River (a tributary to the Jordan River) before it enters Jordan (more than what is entitled to in relation to its agreements with Jordan), and later, Jordan diverts water from the Yarmouk and captures some of the water coming from the wadis (the periodic rivers that form during the rainy season at higher elevation) before it enters the Dead Sea. Israel is also heavily diverting water along the Jordan River, primarily through almost completely damming the Jordan River south of the Tiberias Lake and pumping water from the lake into its National Water Carrier. Today, the Jordan River is a trickle compared to what it used to be and it is estimated that only around 5–20 percent of the natural flow of the Jordan River ends up in the Dead Sea. The Red Sea-Dead Sea program, managed by the World Bank, focused on studying the feasibility of the project and has had three prime pillars: (i) saving the Dead Sea from environmental degradation, (ii) desalinating water and generating energy at affordable prices, and (iii) building a symbol of peace and cooperation in the Middle East. The bulk of the studies were geared toward studying the feasibility from a range of angles, but an "alternative study" was also done, which had the task of looking at alternate options, including more demand-oriented projects/ approaches.[70] The project has a clear supply-side focus. Environmental organizations, such as Friends of the Earth Middle East (now called EcoPeace Middle East), have constantly been arguing that there are alternate ways to stop the decline of the Dead Sea, which include more demand-oriented measures such as focusing on water use efficiency and improved irrigation techniques in the Jordan Valley.

In many of the oil-rich Gulf countries like Saudi Arabia, UAE, Qatar, Kuwait, Oman, and Bahrain, the use of desalination (drawing on the access to cheap energy) is another supply-oriented solution to their water scarcity, coupled with a high reliance on imported food and agricultural products. In spite of having very little natural freshwater, these countries are using more water per capita than most countries in the world.[71] A heavy reliance by the Gulf states as well as Israel on desalination has contributed significantly in increasing their water budget but at the same time has decreased the pressure on their own natural water resources. Besides challenges of energy consumption, the desalination process also produces a huge quantity of by-products of brine (very salty water from the desalination plants). In the case of Israel, the water budget has increased by almost 50 percent when compared to a situation without desalinated water. This should potentially make Israel much more forthcoming toward Palestine in future negotiations over water (as part of the final status negotiation). However, it is not likely to happen without a solution to the larger political impasse. Furthermore, desalination needs a lot of energy and in some of the countries of the region like Jordan this is proving to be an increasingly hard challenge partly because of lack of their own energy sources or because of conflicts and political unrests that may disrupt energy supply (natural gas export from Egypt is being targeted by terror groups in Sinai desert). Though desalination is forming a part of the solution of the region's water supply, it cannot be a sustainable solution. As desalination is energy intensive, there is a limit as to how much of it can be used as a provider of water for the agricultural sector. The cost of a cubic meter of desalinated water is (at best) around 0.5 USD and even this is not a price that is economically viable for irrigation.

To be able to meet water scarcity challenges, the countries in the region need to increase efficiency in the agricultural sector. The subsidies for water in the region are the highest in the world, while water productivity is the lowest.[72] This is the result of poor policies, with wrong incentives, which has resulted in poor governance and management of the water resources of the region. Trade in food has provided a means for the Middle East to make up for its "water deficit" through the import of virtual water. At the global level, this food trade will continue to be needed (and increasingly so) since most of the population growth will take place in countries that are water scarce and has a water availability that is very limited in comparison with other regions.[73] For a region like the Middle East, the situation is more precarious and it is imperative to improve the incentive structure for agricultural production on the home front. Increasing efficiency of water use is a must, as well as increasing the reuse of treated wastewater.

A combination of governance reforms (including subsidies, management cultures, etc.) with a focus on demand management, together with increased supply-side approaches (primarily desalination, but also increased reuse of treated waste water), will continue to be much needed in the region. This combination has to be combined with continued reliance on trade and import of "virtual water." However, because of the prevailing narrative of food self-sufficiency and the (natural) unwillingness of the countries in the region to be overly reliant on a global food market, with its associated risks of price fluctuations and potential export restrictions, there is an increasing interest for investments in land for production outside of the region. The land investments—which also become water investments—are seen as a risk-mitigating strategy and are intended to increase the agricultural production of the countries in the region.[74]

HIGH DEGREE OF SHARED WATER RESOURCES

Not only is the Middle East plagued by water scarcity, but also the limited water resources are often shared between two or more countries. Not only are the surface water resources (rivers and lakes) shared, but also much of the groundwater is. The groundwater of the region has largely been overlooked in research and analysis, partly because data is harder to get but also because it is not seen in the same way as a river or a lake. However, groundwater extraction and depletion in the Euphrates-Tigris basin is severe, the situation in the West Bank is worrisome, and the Gaza aquifer is severely overused.[75] Already today the Gaza aquifer suffers from a shrinking groundwater level, increasing salinization and increasing pollution.[76] The dependency ratio (the level on which a country is dependent on another country for freshwater) in the region ranges from 50 to nearly 100 percent in the region.[77] A country like Egypt is almost completely dependent on water coming from outside of its borders (primarily from Ethiopia). Almost all of the water in Egypt comes from the Nile and almost all of the Nile waters emanate from outside of its borders. For the downstream countries in the Euphrates-Tigris system, the dependency on Turkey is significant, and lately both Iraq and ISIS have been accusing Turkey of withholding too much water upstream.[78]

What has been evident during the last three to four decades is a securitization of the water issue in the region where water has moved into the national security scene. Even if it has been argued that "water wars" are not evident[79] and the riparian countries have signed a number of river agreements,[80] water is still viewed through a "security lens." The securitization of water is likely to stay, given an increasing water scarcity driven by population growth and large migration (in receiving countries such as Jordan and Lebanon), high level of dependence on transboundary water, and a volatile political situation in the region. The added challenge of large climatic variations as well as climate change will (according to most projections) lead to higher temperature (meaning more evaporation) and less rainfall and thereby on the whole an even greater water scarcity.

Paradoxically, these alarming trends have not led to much-need reforms in the water sector in the region (although there are some emerging positive signs). Misguided incentives and subsidies for irrigated agriculture and a weak governance structure plague the water sector. The writing on the wall does not seem to instigate comprehensive and efficient attempts of multilateral cooperation over transboundary water resources in the region. There are possibilities for increased coordination and improved cooperation in the region such as linking water and energy as drivers for improved cooperation. Waxman et al[81] even go to the extent of arguing along a functionalist line that increasing integration of water and energy in the region could, to some degree, mimic the EU Coal and Steel Union. Water and renewable energy (which is rapidly developing in the region primarily in relation to solar energy) could utilize the interdependence in basins such as the Jordan Basin to nurture increased cooperation, largely driven by tapping into interdependence between the two sectors and also between the countries in relation to these sectors. As outlined in chapter 4, there are already developments linking countries together. Adding the energy aspect to the water situation is something that can promote cooperation over water. Having said this, it needs to be noted that while this is a potential development drawing on functionalist reasoning, the Middle East has, by and large, so far, been characterized by a realist mindset.[82]

An important perspective on water-sharing issues in the region is the one focusing on power asymmetries and hegemony in the basins.[83] Water in the Middle East is inherently political and is, therefore, influenced by, as well as influences, politics. Similarly, food, energy, and migration are also viewed from a security perspective. Thus, when analyzing the relations between countries sharing water resources in the region, it is imperative also to understand general power relations as they are decisive factors in deciding water allocations between riparian states in a river basin or countries sharing a groundwater system. For example, the breakdown of the Israeli-Palestinian peace negotiations and the ongoing Israeli occupation have led to the continued depriving of Palestine of its legitimate right to water.

An analysis of the water relations between Israel and Palestine is illustrative. The parties are still living with the Oslo Declaration of Principles (DOP) from 1993 and the so-called Oslo II from 1995. Both of these accords fall short of providing for the necessary joint management of the shared water resources and also fail to provide Palestine with water rights. While cooperation is provided through the so-called Joint Water Committee (JWC), its way of functioning is basically flawed. It essentially provides Israel with a veto over Palestinian projects in the West Bank since decisions are to be taken by consensus.[84] The situation has led to Palestinians not being able to develop a well-functioning water sector. An analysis by the World Bank of the situation in the Palestinian water sector clearly puts responsibility on Israel and its occupation for this situation. The report discusses obstacles to Palestinian development of its water sector, while highlighting in detail how power is used by Israel at the Israeli-Palestinian JWC.[85] Even if a project gets approved by the committee, there is no guarantee that it will actually be implemented. The civil administration in Israel (in practice, the Israel Military Defense Forces, IDF) has the right to stop water projects on the grounds of security issues and this right is being frequently used as well.[86] Israel can prevent Palestinian projects in the JWC, or can even construct a wall or a safety barrier on top of a major spring.[87] It is worth noticing that these water conflicts are not necessarily violent, but can be rather subtle and take place underneath a facade of cooperation.

The lack of comprehensive and inclusive agreements on transboundary waters in the region means increased pressure on the water relations in the region. The bilateral nature of the (few) agreements that exist and the lack of flexibility to address increased climate variability (larger variations in water flow/availability) are challenges that need to be overcome or else they can serve to further magnify existing conflicts over water. Over and above, power asymmetries in the basin furthermore institutionalize a situation in which progress toward equitable cooperation is hampered.

As a result of the civil war in Syria, severe pressure has been put on the water sector (and societies at large) of the region, in particular, in Lebanon and Jordan as a result of the influx of refugees (see chapter 5). Providing assistance to the refugee population in camps and the increasing demand have put immense pressure on the water supply infrastructure of the countries. The challenges posed by the refugee influx have also affected the sociopolitical stability in the host countries. More water and treatment of water are the need of the hour in the Syrian neighborhood.

The securitization of water resources has been evident in the Middle East for a long period of time. The interstate politics is monopolized by governments, but at the same time there are many other types of actors who interact at the global and regional water arenas on issues of trade, technological, scientific, and cultural exchanges. International relations theory usually refers to such group of actors as "epistemic community."[88] An epistemic community is an international network of knowledge-based professionals in, for example, scientific and technological areas that can have an impact on policy decisions. The formation of joint technical committees along many water basins in the region provides in theory a platform to advance the role of scientific and technical cooperation between riparian countries. In practice, such committees have not been mandated with any decision-making powers, and some of them function more on an ad hoc basis. These can potentially serve as tools for desecuritization. The case of the Joint Water Committee between Israel and the Palestinian Authority reflects power asymmetries since Israel, in principle, can veto any decision. The sanctioned discourse in the region is to treat transboundary water as a core foreign policy and security issue, which hampers the influence of epistemic communities and the way sharing of transboundary water can be discussed and negotiated. The "advice" that epistemic communities can provide is likely to be taken into consideration only when they correspond to the sanctioned discourse, and therefore, a more realistic mindset has the upper hand in the situation.[89]

NEW TRENDS IN THE REGION—THE USE OF WATER AS A WEAPON

Increasingly, water installations and infrastructure are becoming targets in wars and armed conflicts.[90] Though there have been some previous examples, the relatively recent cases in the Middle East are perhaps the first more serious efforts in utilizing water as a weapon in such a direct manner. It has become more evident after the advances of the ISIS to experience how water installations can (and are being) be used as a weapon with a direct or indirect effect on food and water security. The ISIS, has on some occasions, shut water, including drinking water to villages, and on other occasions flooded agricultural plains in Iraq, thus destroying parts of the agricultural yield.[91] When nontraditional actors such as the ISIS gain territorial control, as they did on a significant scale during 2014, it opens up new security challenges with repercussions on water security. There is also the risk of floods, potentially of a catastrophic nature. As such, control over primarily dams becomes a potential weapon in the arms of these actors, a weapon that they seemingly do not shy away from using.

The ISIS gained control over the Tishrin Dam in Syria in November 2012, the Tabqa dam in February 2013, and again in January 2014 after they gained control over Falluja. In April 2014, they closed the Falluja gates to stop supplying water to downstream adversaries.[92] After capturing these water infrastructures, the ISIS did not hesitate to use them both as weapons and in the war strategy, which contributed to the increased vulnerability of the enemy. The capture by ISIS of the major Mosul Dam on August 7, 2014, was an even more serious development.[93] The dam, located on the Tigris River, has around 11 billion cubic meters of flood storage capacity and is important for irrigation in the Nineveh province in Iraq. It also generates 310 MW of energy daily. The fear was not only that the ISIS could use the dam to flood Mosul with a major wave, but also that it would threaten the capital Baghdad. These developments led to swift action by the United States, which supported the Kurdish Peshmerga forces with airstrikes; Kurdish Peshmerga forces, together with Iraqi security forces, were able to retake the dam on August 18.[94] Perhaps, this development can be seen as a situation where water's strategic role (or rather the threat of using water as a weapon to flood Mosul and Baghdad) has moved into hard security considerations.

The seizure of dams and control of water infrastructure in many aspects also seemed to be a trigger for the international community to intervene against the ISIS and join forces with the Iraqi army and the Kurdish Peshmerga forces. As such, water issues (access, risk of flooding etc.) seemed to have been given increasing strategic importance. Already in 2006, a leaked US State Department cable warned that Syria's "emerging water crisis carries the potential for severe economic volatility and even sociopolitical unrest."[95] This clearly shows that the issue of water is increasingly receiving attention from security and foreign policy communities.

CONNECTING TO SECURITY ARCHITECTURE

Water governance is a matter of national security in most countries within the Middle East. The water scarcity in the region has served to move the issue up on the political agenda. The World Bank claims that the per capita availability in the Arab world in 2050 will be half of that 2015. This is a significant decrease from an (in many cases) already low level. While in other regions water issues are dealt with at the political-technical level, water in the Middle East is highly securitized.[96] Decisions on transboundary water allocations are often taken by ministries of foreign affairs and subject to strict security considerations. Securitization of water issues, or any issue for that matter, serves to silence critical voices and to facilitate ruling regimes' promotion of other agendas, in the guise of national security.[97] Efforts to desecuritize the discourse, by expert groups and civil societies, can have positive effects, but arguably this is only the case when the advice is seen as suitable and useful by the regimes (at least in the realm of transboundary waters). In spite of the dire water situation, this has not led to significant improvements in the governance systems for water in the Middle East, as water productivity in the region is still, by far, the lowest in the world.[98]

There is a lack of well-functioning regional mechanisms to address the challenges related to transboundary waters. The League of Arab States and the UN Economic and Social Commission for Western Asia (ESCWA) are organizations mandated to deal with issues in the Middle East (not Israel), but progress is slow primarily as a result of limited investments and engagement in the organizations by the countries. Water is still subordinate to "high politics" in the region[99] and decisions are not made with a focus on water but rather other politically more salient issues take precedent. There are also new and disturbing trends related to water as a weapon in the Syria crisis with the ISIS taking over dams and using it either to partly stop water from flowing (with resulting acute water shortages in the downstream) or in some cases flooding the enemy areas. The military movements against some key water infrastructure in Iraq seem also to have been seen as a "red line" by the international coalition, and significant air support was given to Kurdish Peshmerga forces as well as the Iraqi forces to retake and defend the key water infrastructures.

The conflict in Syria and Iraq is intertwined with the water relations in the region. The complex web of water security includes considerations related to food supply, energy security, and population migration. In many senses, one can notice a globalization of the security considerations in the region. Not only is the international coalition engaged against the ISIS in the region, it also supports the recapturing and defending of dams and other water infrastructures (Mosul dam is a case in point) and is engaged in protecting energy supplies (gas and oil primarily) which are under threat of being interrupted. Dams and energy supplies represent a major source of financing for the ISIS.

Water security discussions in the Middle East have moved from the domain of international relations to broader discussions on governance, political economy, development, and also to debates on the water-food energy nexus. Water is a fundamental precondition for human life and economic activities. However, most of the countries in the Middle East are poorly endowed with natural freshwater supplies, making it the driest region in the world. The lack of water affects almost all aspects of life and the likelihood of one's survival. Due to the extreme link to one's survival, it is also easier for water to mobilize along regional or sectarian lines. The management of water resources in the Middle East is thus often eclipsed by power politics and sectarian rivalry. The importance of water availability keeps further rising as climate change interacts with demographic and economic drivers to increase water scarcity and variability. This poses serious problems for better water governance and leads to tough human security challenges.

The efficient management of scarce water resource plays a critical role for the development and security of countries in the Middle East. Water management issues cut across all sectors of governance and have a critical bearing on any development planning. At bottom, the imperative of adequate water supply and the weakness of the state in this region form a nexus, which demands sophisticated basin-based cooperative planning, for the short as well as long term. These political, economic, social, and environmental interdependencies give water resources in the region a crucial potential in either fostering cooperation among neighbors or exacerbating conflict and political unrest.

NOTES

1. Malin Falkenmark, "Freshwater: Time for a Modified Approach," *Ambio*, 15, 4 (1986): 192–200; Igor A. Shiklomanov, "Global Water Resources," *Nature and Resources*, 26, 3 (1990): 34–43; Ashok Swain, "A New Challenge: Water Scarcity in the Arab World," *Arab Studies Quarterly*, 20, 1 (1998): 1–11.
2. Thomas R. Malthus, *An Essay on the Principle of Population* (London: J. Johnsson, 1798).
3. John K. Cooley, The war over water, *Foreign Policy*, 54, (1984): 3–26. John Bullock and Adel Darwish, *Water Wars: Coming Conflicts in the Middle East.* (London: St. Dedmundsbury Press, 1993). Joyce R. Starr, Water Wars, *Foreign Policy,* 82 (1991): 17–36.
4. Anders Jägerskog, Ana Cascao, Mats Hårsmar and Kyungmee Kim, "Land Acquisitions: How Will They Impact Transboundary Waters?," Report Nr. 30, 2012, Stockholm: SIWI, 2012); Ashok Swain, *Understanding* Emerging *Security Challenges: Threats and Opportunities*, London: Routledge, 2012).
5. Barry Buzan, People, *States & Fear - An Agenda for International Security Studies in the Post–Cold War Era* (Harvester Wheatsheaf, London, 1991).
6. Malin Falkenmark, Anders Berntell, Anders Jägerskog, Jan Lundqvist, Manfred Matz, Håkan Tropp, "On the Verge of a New Water Scarcity: A call for Good Governance and Human Ingenuity," *SIWI Policy Brief* (Stockholm: SIWI, 2007).
7. For an extensive overview of water security please, see Anders Jägerskog, Ashok Swain and Joakim Öjendal, eds., *Water Security*, A Four Volume Set of SAGE Major Works (London: SAGE Publications, 2014).
8. Jan Lundqvist, Jenny Grönwall and Anders Jägerskog, "Water, food security and human dignity – a nutrition perspective," Ministry of Enterprise and Innovation, Swedish FAO Committee, Stockholm, 2015.
9. United Nations Development Program, Human Development Report Office, *Beyond Scarcity: Power, Poverty and the Global Water Crisis* (New York: UNDP, 2006).
10. United Nations General Assembly, *The Future We Want*, Rio+20 United Nations Conference on Sustainable Development, 2012.
11. UN Water, "Water Security and the Global Water Agenda," United Nations University/UNU-INWEH and UN-ESCAP, 2013.

12. UN Water, 2015, at http://www.unwater.org/statistics/en/, (accessed July 20, 2015).

13. UNDP, *Beyond Scarcity: Power, Poverty and the Global Water Crisis.*

14. Falkenmark, Berntell, Jägerskog, Lundqvist, Matz, Tropp, "On the Verge of a New Water Scarcity: A call for Good Governance and Human Ingenuity."

15. The food supply chain is discussed in more detail with a focus on the Middle East region in the Food Security chapter in this volume. Jan Lundqvist, Charlotte de Fraiture and David Molden, *Saving Water: From Field to Fork – Curbing Losses and Wastage in the Food Chain*, SIWI Policy Brief (Stockholm: SIWI, 2008); Lundqvist et al, "Water, food security and human dignity – a nutrition perspective."

16. Anders Jägerskog, Ashok Swain and Joakim Öjendal, "Water Security – Origins and Foundations, Volume I," Anders Jägerskog, Ashok Swain and Joakim Öjendal, eds, *Water Security, A Four Volume Set of SAGE Major Works* (London: SAGE Publications, 2014).

17. Aaron T. Wolf, *Hydropolitics along the Jordan River: Scarce Water and its Impact on the Arab–Israeli Conflict* (Tokyo: United Nations University Press, 1995); Aaron T. Wolf, Annika Kramer, Alexander Carius and Geoffrey D. Dabelko, "Managing water conflict and cooperation," in *State Of the World: Redefining Global Security* (Washington DC: World Watch Institute, 2005).

18. J. A. Allan, 2011. *Virtual water: tackling the threat to our planet's most precious resource* (London: I. B. Tauris, 2011).

J. A. Allan, *The Middle East Water Question: Hydropolitics and the Global Economy* (London, I.B. Tauris, 2001).

19. Anton Earle, Anders Jägerskog and Joakim Öjendal, eds., *Transboundary Water Management: Principles and Practice* (London: Earthscan, 2010).

20. Mark Zeitoun and Naho Mirumachi, "Transboundary Water Interaction I: Reconsidering Conflict and Cooperation." *International Environmental Agreements*, 8, 4 (2008): 297–316.

Mark Zeitoun and Jeroen Warner, "Hydro-Hegemony a Framework for Analysis of Transboundary Water Conflicts," *Water Policy*, 8 (2006): 435–60.

21. IPCC Fifth Assessment Report, *Climate Change 2014: Impacts, Adaptation, and Vulnerability, 2014.*

22. Ashok Swain, "Global Climate Change and Challenges for International River Agreements," *International Journal on Sustainable Society*, 4, (2012): 72–87; Malin Falkenmark and Anders Jägerskog, "Sustainability of Transnational Water Agreements in the Face of Socio-Economic and Environmental Change," in *Transboundary Water Management: Principles and Practice*, eds., Anton Earle, Anders Jägerskog and Joakim Öjendal (London: Earthscan, 2010).

23. Jägerskog et al, "Land Acquisitions: How Will They Impact Transboundary Waters?."

24. Earle et al, *Transboundary Water Management: Principles and Practice.*

25. Anders Jägerskog, "Challenges and Opportunities related to Transboundary Waters in the EU's Broader Neighbourhood," in *The European Union's Broader Neighbourhood: Challenges and Opportunities for Co-operation beyond the European Neighbourhood Policy*, eds., Siegliende Gstöhl and Erwann Lannon (London: Routledge, 2015).

26. Green water is the water in the topsoil layer.

27. Joyce R. Starr, "Water Wars," *Foreign Policy*, 82 (1991).

28. Egypt heads the list among the externally water-dependent countries in this region, whose 97 percent of the total water flow originates outside of its border. It is followed by Syria (79%), Sudan (77%), Iraq (66%), Jordan (36%), and Israel (21%). A large part of Israel's water supply comes from the disputed territories. World Resource Institute, *World Resources, 1991–1992* (New York: Oxford University Press, 1991).

29. Anton Earle, Ana Cascao, Stina Hansson, Anders Jägerskog, Ashok Swain and Joakim Öjendal, *Transboundary Water Management and the Climate Change Debate*, (London: Routledge, 2015).

30. John Waterbury 2002, *The Nile Basin: National Determinants of Collective Action* (New Haven, CT and London: Yale University Press, 2002); Swain, "Global Climate Change and Challenges for International River Agreements."

31. David Phillips, Marwa Daoudy, Stephen McCaffrey, Joakim Öjendal and Anthony Turton, "Transboundary water cooperation as a tool for conflict prevention and broader benefit sharing," Global Development Studies No. 4, Stockholm: Swedish Ministry for Foreign Affairs, 2006; Ashok Swain, "Challenges for Water Sharing in the Nile Basin: Changing Geo-Politics and Changing Climate," Hydrological Science Journal, 56, 4 (2011): 687–702; Earle et al, *Transboundary Water Management and the Climate Change Debate*.

32. Swain, "Challenges for Water Sharing in the Nile Basin: Changing Geo-Politics and Changing Climate."

33. Earle et al, *Transboundary Water Management and the Climate Change Debate*.

34. Huiyi Chen and Ashok Swain, "The Grand Ethiopian Renaissance Dam: Evaluating Its Sustainability Standard and Geopolitical Significance," *Energy Development Frontier*, 3, 1 (2014): 11–19.

35. The section on the Jordan River draws largely on Jägerskog, "Why states cooperate over shared water: The water negotiations in the Jordan River Basin."

36. These figures are highly contested and different accounts exist. Greg Shapland, *Rivers of Discord: International Water Disputes in the Middle East*, (London: Hurst & Co., 1997), p. 9 shows that figures for the inflow to Lake Tiberias/Kinneret vary between a low figure of 500 mcm per year and a high figure of 790 mcm per year. This is typical of all the figures presented in this conflict.

37. John Kolars, "The spatial attributes of water negotiation: the need for a river ethic and advocacy in the Middle East," in *Water in the Middle East: A Geography of Peace*, eds., Amery A. Hussein and Aaron T. Wolf (Austin, TX: University of Texas Press, 2000); Falkenmark and Jägerskog, "Sustainability of Transnational Water Agreements in the Face of Socio-Economic and Environmental Change."

38. Kolars, "The spatial attributes of water negotiation: the need for a river ethic and advocacy in the Middle East."

39. Greg Shapland, *Rivers of Discord: International Water Disputes in the Middle East* (London: Hurst & Co, 1997).

40. Ashok Swain, *Managing Water Conflict: Asia, Africa and the Middle East* (London & New York: Routledge, 2004).

41. Personal communication with Jordanian official, June 9, 2015.

42. Anders Jägerskog, "Why states cooperate over shared water: The water negotiations in the Jordan River Basin," (PhD Dissertation, Linköping University, 2003); Jan Selby, "Dressing up domination as 'co-operation': the case of Israeli-Palestinian water relations," *Review of International Studies*, 29, 1 (2003): 121–38; Mark Zeitoun, *Power and water in the Middle East: the hidden politics of the Palestinian-Israeli water conflict* (London: IB Tauris, 2006).

43. Shapland, *Rivers of Discord: International Water Disputes in the Middle East*; Munther J. Haddadin, *Diplomacy on the Jordan: International Conflict and Negotiated Solution* (Boston: Kluwer Academic, 2001). See also Treaty of Peace between the State of Israel and the Hashemite Kingdom of Jordan, at http://www.kinghussein.gov.jo/peacetreaty.html (accessed June, 2014).

44. Jägerskog, "Why states cooperate over shared water: The water negotiations in the Jordan River Basin."

45. Aysegul Kibaruglu and Tugba E. Maden, "An Analysis of the causes of the water crisis in the Euphrates-Tigris River Basin," *Journal of Environmental Studies,* 4 (2014): 347–53.

46. Peter Beaumont, "The Euphrates River: An International Problem of Water Resources Development," *Environmental Conservation*, 5, 1 (1978): 35–43.

47. Nouar Shamout and Glada Lahn, *The Euphrates in Crisis – Channels of Cooperation for a Threatened River* (London: Chatham House, 2015).

48. Aysegul Kibaruglu and Waltina Scheumann, "Evolution of Transboundary Politics in the Euphrates-Tigris River System: New Perspectives and Political Challenges," in *Global Governance*, 19 (2013): 279–305.

49. Shamout and Lahn, *The Euphrates in Crisis – Channels of Cooperation for a Threatened River.*

50. Kibaruglu and Scheumann, "Evolution of Transboundary Politics in the Euphrates-Tigris River System: New Perspectives and Political Challenges."

51. Kibaroglu and Maden, "An Analysis of the causes of the water crisis in the Euprates-Tigris River Basin."

52. Kibaroglu and Scheumann, "Evolution of Transboundary Politics in the Euphrates-Tigris River System: New Perspectives and Political Challenges."

53. Shamout and Lahn, *The Euphrates in Crisis – Channels of Cooperation for a Threatened River.*

54. Ashok Swain, "Constructing Water Institutions: Appropriate Management of International River Water," *Cambridge Review of International Affairs*, 12, 2 (1999): 214–25.

55. For a link to an unofficial translation of the agreement, see http://international-waterlaw.org/documents/regionaldocs/Disi_Aquifer_Agreement-English2015.pdf

56. Cooley, The war over water; Bullock and Darwish, *Water Wars: Coming Conflicts in the Middle East*; Starr, "Water Wars"; Ashok Swain, *Managing Water Conflict: Asia, Africa and the Middle East* (London & New York: Routledge, 2004).

57. Earle et al, *Transboundary Water Management and the Climate Change Debate.*

58. IPCC, *Climate Change 2014: Impacts, Adaptation, and Vulnerability.*

59. Stephen McCaffrey, "The need for flexibility in freshwater treaty regimes," *Natural Resources Forum*, 27, 2 (2003): 156–62; Itay Fishhendler, "Legal and institutional adaptation to climate uncertainty: a study of international rivers," *Water Policy*, 6, 4 (2004): 281–302; Falkenmark and Jägerskog, "Sustainability of Transnational Water Agreements in the Face of Socio-Economic and Environmental Change."

60. Kibaroglu and Scheumann, "Evolution of Transboundary Politics in the Euphrates-Tigris River System: New Perspectives and Political Challenges."

61. Fishhendler, "Legal and institutional adaptation to climate uncertainty: a study of international rivers"; Falkenmark and Jägerskog, "Sustainability of Transnational Water Agreements in the Face of Socio-Economic and Environmental Change."

62. Earle et al, *Transboundary Water Management and the Climate Change Debate*.

63. Erik Berglöf and Shanta Devarajan, "Water for development: Fulfilling the promise," in *Water for Development; Charting a Water Wise Path*, eds., Anders Jägerskog, Torkil J. Clausen, Torgny Holmgren, Karin Lexén, SIWI Report Nr. 35. (Stockholm: SIWI, 2015).

64. Håkan Tropp and Anders Jägerskog, "Meeting the Water Scarcity Challenges in the Middle East and North Africa," *Arab Journal of Water*, 1, 2 (2008).

65. Berglöf and Devarajan, "Water for development: Fulfilling the promise."

66. Ellie Elhadj, "Dry Aquifers in Arab Countries and the Looming Food Crisis," Middle East Review of International Affairs, 12, 4 (2008).

Ellie Elhadj, "Saudi Arabia's Agricultural Project: From Dust to Dust," Middle East Review of International Affairs, 12, 2 (2008).

67. Berglöf and Devarajan, "Water for development: Fulfilling the promise."

68. "Saudi Scraps Wheat Growing to Save Water," *Reuters*, January 8, 2008.

69. Berglöf and Devarajan, "Water for development: Fulfilling the promise."

70. For more info on the project, see http://web.worldbank.org/WBSITE/EXTERNAL/COUNTRIES/MENAEXT/EXTREDSEADEADSEA/0,,contentMDK:218274 16~pagePK:64168427~piPK:64168435~theSitePK:5174617,00.html, (accessed May 10, 2015).

71. See: http://chartsbin.com/view/1455, (accessed September 30, 2015).

72. Berglof and Devarajan, "Water for development: Fulfilling the promise."

73. C. Hausmann and S. Patrick, "Contingency planning: Trade's role in sustainable world food security." *Aquatic Procedia* 1 (2013): 20–29.

74. Anders Jägerskog and Kyungmee Kim, "Land acquisition as a means to mitigate water scarcity and reduce conflict?" Accepted in *Hydrological Sciences Journal* (2015).

75. UNCTAD, Report on UNCTAD assistance to the Palestinian people: Development in the Economy of the Occupied Palestinian Territories, UN, Geneva, July 6, 2015.

76. ICRC, *Bled Dry: How War in the Middle East is Bringing the Region's Water Supplies to Breaking Point* (Geneva: International Committee of the Red Cross, 2015).

77. UNEP, *Virtual Water Graphics – An Overview of the World's Fresh and Marine Waters*, 2nd Edition (Nairobi: UNEP, 2008).

78. Zaid Sabah, Selcan Hacaoglu, Jack Fairweather, "Water Shortages Unite Iraq, Islamic State Against Turkey," *Bloomberg News*, July 1, 2015, at http://www.bloomberg.com/news/articles/2015-07-01/water-shortages-unite-iraq-islamic-state-against-turkey, (accessed August 2, 2015).

79. Wolf et al, "Managing water conflict and cooperation"; Jägerskog, "Why states cooperate over shared water: The water negotiations in the Jordan River Basin"; Jägerskog et al, *Water Security.*

80. Wolf et al, "Managing water conflict and cooperation"; Transboundary Freshwater Dispute Database (TFDD), at http://www.transboundarywaters.orst.edu/database/, (accessed on February 5, 2014).

81. Jessye B. Waxman, Munqeth Mehyar, Gidon Bromberg, Nader Khateb, and Michael Milner, "A Water and Energy Nexus as a Catalyst for Middle East Peace," *International Journal on Water Governance*, 3, 1 (2015): 71–92.

82. Earle et al, *Transboundary Water Management and the Climate Change Debate;* Anders Jägerskog, "New threats? Risk and Securitisation Theory on Climate and Water," in *Coping with Global Environmental Change, Disasters and Security – Threats, Challenges, Vulnerabilities and Risks*, eds., Hans Günter Brauch, John Grin, Czeslaw Mesjasz, Patricia Kameri-Mbote, Bechir Chourou, Pal Dunay, Jörn Birkmann, Hexagon Series on Human and Environmental Security and Peace, vol. 5 (Berlin: Springer-Verlag, 2011).

83. Zeitoun, *Power and Water in the Middle East: The Hidden Politics of the Palestinian-Israeli Water Conflict;* Jägerskog, "Why states cooperate over shared water: The water negotiations in the Jordan River Basin"; Jan Selby, "Cooperation, domination and colonisation: The Israeli-Palestinian Joint Water Committee," *Water Alternatives*, 6, 1 (2013): 1–24.

84. Selby, "Cooperation, domination and colonisation: The Israeli-Palestinian Joint Water Committee."

85. World Bank, "West Bank and Gaza: Assessment of restrictions on Palestinian water sector development," Sector Note, April 2009. Middle East and North Africa Region - Sustainable Development. Report No. 47657-GZ (Washington, DC: World Bank, 2009).

86. World Bank, "West Bank and Gaza: Assessment of restrictions on Palestinian water sector development."

87. Zeitoun, *Power and water in the Middle East: the hidden politics of the Palestinian-Israeli water conflict.*

88. Peter M. Haas, "Do Regimes Matter? Epistemic communities and Mediterranean pollution control," *International Organization*, 43, 3 (1989): 377–403.

89. Jägerskog, "Why states cooperate over shared water: The water negotiations in the Jordan River Basin"; Allan, *The Middle East Water Question: Hydropolitics and the Global Economy.*

90. Peter H. Gleick, "Water and conflict: Fresh water resources and international security," *International Security*, 18, 1 (1993): 99–104.

91. Strategic Foresight Group, *Water and Violence: Crisis of Survival in the Middle East* (Mumbai: SFG, 2014); Kibaroglu and Scheumann, "Evolution of Transboundary Politics in the Euphrates-Tigris River System: New Perspectives and Political

Challenges"; Sabah, Hacaoglu and Fairweather, "Water Shortages Unite Iraq, Islamic State Against Turkey."

92. Strategic Foresight Group, *Water and Violence: Crisis of Survival in the Middle East*.

93. Ahramonline, "Kurdish official confirms Islamic State controls Iraq's biggest dam," August 8, 2014, at http://english.ahram.org.eg/NewsContent/2/0/108049/World/0/Kurdish-official-confirms-Islamic-State-controls-I.aspx, (accessed August 31, 2015).

94. "Iraqi and Kurdish Forces recapture the Mosul Dam," *Al Jazeera,* August 19, 2014, at http://www.aljazeera.com/news/middleeast/2014/08/kurdish-forces-claim-control-mosul-dam-2014818174534291467.html, (accessed August 31, 2015).

95. Mukkad Al Jabbari, Norman Ricklefs and Robert Tollast, "Rivers of Babylon: Iraq's water crisis – And what Turkey should do," in *Foreign Policy,* August 23, 2015.

96. Phillips et al, "Transboundary water cooperation as a tool for conflict prevention and broader benefit sharing."

97. Zeitoun & Warner, "Hydro-Hegemony a Framework for Analysis of Transboundary Water Conflicts."

98. Berglöf and Devarajan, "Water for development: Fulfilling the promise."

99. Jägerskog, "New threats? Risk and Securitisation theory on climate and water."

Chapter 4

Energy Security and its Changing Dynamics in the Middle East

Energy is closely linked to human well-being and progress across the world. From cars to computers, house heating to air conditioning, energy constitutes a critical part of our daily life. Energy provision is a critical component of increased social and economic development.[1] Besides our regular dependence for domestic use, agriculture, manufacturing, transportation, construction, and health and social services also depend on the access to energy. The crucial role of energy in the societal development was also highlighted in the Rio+20 conference[2] that access to sustainable modern energy services helps to eradicate poverty, saves lives, improves health, and supplies basic human needs. There is a significant correlation between an inadequate supply of energy and economic underdevelopment. It is estimated that more than 1.3 billion people, approximately one in five globally, still lack access to electricity, and almost all of them live in developing countries.[3] Nearly 2.6 billion people rely on solid fuels such as wood, coal, and charcoal for subsistence; therefore, it is important that access to electricity must be environmental and socially sustainable.[4] Population growth, urbanization, and increasing demands for more food, goods, and services have put further challenges to energy supplies and energy structure, which are presently dominated by fossil fuels.

The world found a new and powerful source of energy, oil, with its discovery in 1859 in the United States. The exploitation of oil became a precondition for industrialization and economic development. It also brought a significant change to the way wars were being fought on the ground, in the air, and on and under the surface of the seas. Thus, oil fast transformed into being a vital factor for nation-states to achieve their economic and military security.[5] However, oil like water is unevenly distributed around the world, which gives oil-producing nations a very significant strategic importance.

Table 4.1   Fuel Shares of Total Primary Energy Supply of the World

Fuel type	1973 (6,106 Mtoe)	2012 (13,371 Mtoe)
Natural gas	16.0%	21.3%
Nuclear	0.9%	4.8%
Hydro	1.8%	2.4%
Biofuels and waste	10.5%	10.0%
Geothermal, solar, wind, heat, etc.	0.1%	1.1%
Coal (includes peat and oil shale)	24.6%	29.0%
Oil	46.1%	31.4%

Source: International Energy Agency (iea.org). Mtoe, million tons of oil equivalent.

The most plentiful oil reserves in the world are clustered in one part of the Middle East, primarily in the Arabian Gulf region.

Since the 1950s, many petroleum geologists working in the Middle East have authoritatively concluded about the richness of oil in that region.[6] In public perception, "Middle East" and "oil" are images easily connected and oil reserves and production in the region have a huge significance for the health of the global economy. However, the oil reserves also are not evenly distributed among the countries in the region. A large portion of reserves is, in fact, found in an area 800 kilometers by 500 kilometers around the Arabian Gulf, a small part of the Middle East. Some countries in the region also have the advantage of size, while some others get the benefit of their locations. A country like Saudi Arabia, with an area of almost five times the size of Iraq, is home to oil reserves of 268 billion barrels or nearly twice the volume of Iraq's oil reserves of 140 billion barrels. By having one tenth of the size of the territory compared to Syria, Kuwait, because of its close location to the optimal petroleum geology of sedimentary basins, has oil reserves of 104 billion barrels, while Syria's reserves are only 2.5 billion barrels.[7]

In 1960, oil reserves of the Middle East were estimated to be 183 billion barrels, which was approximately 60 percent of the then world's total. The estimated oil of the region increased to 343 billion barrels in 1970, 362 billion barrels in 1980, 661 billion barrels in 1990, 697 billion barrels in 2000, and 766 billion barrels in 2010, accounting for about one-half of the world's

Table 4.2   Regional Shares of Crude Oil Production

Regions	1973 (2,869 Metric Tons)	2013 (4,117 Metric Tons)
Middle East	36.7%	31.8%
Non-OECD Europe and Eurasia	15.7%	16.6%
Asia	5.1 %	9%
Non-OECD Americas	8.5%	9.5%
Africa	10.1%	10.1%
OECD	23.9%	23.0%

Source: International Energy Agency (iea.org).

Table 4.3 Stock of Proved Reserves of Crude Oil and Natural Gas in the Middle East Region

Country	Stock of Proved Reserves of Crude Oil in Barrels (bbl) on January 1, 2014	Stock of Proved Reserves of Natural Gas in Cubic Meters (cu m) on January 1, 2014
Saudi Arabia	268,400,000,000	8,235,000,000,000
Iraq	140,300,000,000	3,158,000,000,000
Kuwait	104,000,000,000	1,798,000,000,000
UAE	97,800,000,000	6,089,000,000,000
Qatar	25,240,000,000	25,070,000,000,000
Oman	5,500,000,000	849,500,000,000
Egypt	4,400,000,000	2,180,000,000,000
Yemen	3,000,000,000	478,500,000,000
Syria	2,500,000,000	240,700,000,000
Bahrain	124,600,000	92,030,000,000
Israel	11,500,000	285,000,000,000
Jordan	1,000,000	6,031,000,000
Lebanon	0	0
Palestine	NA	NA

Source: The World Factbook, Central Intelligence Agency.

proven oil reserves.[8] Besides technological developments, political and economic considerations have also influenced the reporting of oil reserves by different countries. Countries in the region also have a history of manipulating oil reserve data to influence global oil price and/or inflating their strategic importance.[9]

Oil is a finite and unevenly distributed resource and until other energy sources and technologies are developed to successfully replace oil, there will always be increased demands on existing reserves of oil by nations aspiring to secure supplies. Although this demand and supply factor leads to cooperation between some countries in the Middle East region with the world's powerful industrialized countries, it also contributes to tension and violent conflicts. For over a century, the security of oil supplies has figured prominently in the strategies of modern economies and armies. In the 1970s when most Arab members of OPEC along with a few non-OPEC decided to cut the supply of oil to the United States and other Western powers, the fragility of the global oil supply system was exposed. Decades have passed by, but the oil production in the world is still very much concentrated in the Middle East. This makes the region and its oil transport routes exceedingly vulnerable.[10] The general discourse on energy is characterized often by the use of terminology such as oil weapons, energy independency, and energy choke points. The conceptualization of energy as a security threat is gradually being perceived as escalating geopolitical tensions in oil-producing regions, particularly in the Middle East in relation to an increasing energy consumption and demand in rising Asia, together with a global over-dependency on oil and an expected depletion of oil fields.[11]

Though many countries in the Middle East have large oil reserves, there are new issues affecting the development of fuel and energy sectors in the region. Due to new technological advances, previously inaccessible reserves of fossil fuels are becoming potential energy deposits for disposal. This can have potential implications on regional power relations and also on the global energy security arena. States in the Middle East that are large consumers of oil and natural gas and are dependent on imports have been experiencing increased worries about future supplies. Not only importing states, but exporting countries are also facing increased anxiety. Their economies are highly vulnerable to global price fluctuations.[12] Some of them are exploring to diversify energy options and to adopt flexible strategy to avoid risks and achieve long-term energy security.[13] The energy security structure of the region is so complex that the possible threats can no longer be dealt with in isolation from each other. Some countries plan to address the possible energy security challenges comprehensively by taking into account availability and affordability of alternate energy sources and by securing climate goals, but to date, these have not been clearly translated into workable mechanisms for their national energy governance.[14]

EXPORTERS OF CRUDE OIL AND NATURAL GAS

The share of oil in world energy consumption has declined from more than 46 percent in 1973 to about 31 percent at present. This decline is due to improved energy efficiency, switching to other energy sources like natural gas; a yearning to decrease dependency on foreign oil; and recent apprehensions about global warming and climate change.[15] However, the Middle East still dominates the world's oil market, and crude oil- and gas-exporting countries in the region rely on oil income to fund a major share of their economies.[16] While the oil-exporting countries in the region have a relatively strong economy, the oil importers largely face economic hardship. The Middle East also claims to have nearly half of the world's conventional natural gas reserves. The region presently represents about 40 percent of the global LNG trade,[17] and the global market for the gas is growing fast.

Saudi Arabia, having 16 percent of the world's proven oil reserves, is the largest holder of crude oil reserves in the world. In 2014, Saudi Arabia produced on an average around 12 million barrels a day of the total petroleum liquids, and it is estimated that its export of crude oil was nearly 8 million barrels a day during that year. Most of its oil exports go to Asia and the United States.[18] Saudi Arabia holds a huge influence over the global oil market.

According to Telhami,[19] "Saudi Arabia's trump card remains its spare production capacity, which allows it to affect the market significantly by withholding or increasing supply. No other country commands such a capacity, and therefore such power, in the global energy market." The domestic consumption of petroleum of Saudi Arabia is also one of the largest in the region as the country consumes a huge amount of energy for power generation and transportation.[20] Presently, the oil consumption rate is around 3 million barrels of oil a day, and there are projections that the domestic oil demand will reach more than 8 million barrels a day by 2030 if nothing is done to achieve energy efficiency.[21] The country is investing heavily in its atomic energy program, which is aimed to reduce dependence on oil for electricity production.

With the world's fourth largest natural gas reserves, Saudi Arabia at present has modest production levels.[22] It does not import or export natural gas; all consumption needs, therefore, is met by domestic production. To be able to meet increasing demands in the country, which is needed for more desalination plants, increased power generation, etc., continued use of the oil reserve is warranted. However, all planned gas supplies at present are specifically earmarked for domestic purposes. Natural grass production is not only limited but also heavily subsidized in the country.[23] However, Saudi Arabia intends to increase its electricity generation capacity to 120 GW by 2032 and plans to reduce its overdependence on oil and natural gas and to diversify fuel use, with the aim of releasing larger amounts of oil and natural gas for export.[24]

Iraq has one of the world's largest proven crude oil reserves and is also the second largest producer of crude oil within OPEC. In spite of huge proven reserves, only a fraction of the fields have been developed, the reason—wars and political instability for a considerable period of time. The country's crude oil production was around 3.4 million barrels a day in 2014. This is a major leap from 2010, when production had almost gone down to 2.4 million barrels, from its peak of 3.5 million barrels before the Saddam Husain regime's Kuwait invasion in 1990.[25] However, the country has failed to achieve its expected growth in recent years due to infrastructure bottlenecks in its southern parts, supply disruptions in the north, and ongoing violent civil wars in the heartland. Due to ISIS' offensives, supply of oil through the Iraq-Turkey pipeline has been regularly disrupted since 2014. Though the country has vast oil reserves, they are not divided equally over the territory. This also promotes ethnic animosity and political instability as the reserves lie in the Shia-dominated southern part (75 percent) and in the Kurdish-dominated northern part (17 percent), while they are significantly less within the Sunni-dominated central region (8 percent).[26]

Iraq also possesses one of the largest supplies of natural gas in the world today. Iraq's Western Desert, which currently has no proven reserves of oil resources, is also believed to contain large amounts of natural gas deposits but least explored. However, more than half of the supplies of the natural gas of Iraq are vented and flared. Venting is the direct release of natural gas into the atmosphere, while flaring is the burning of natural gas in an open flame. Therefore, the country is planning to take steps to reduce wastage and adjust the usages of its natural gas resources for power generation. Every day, approximately 20 million cubic meters of natural gas is currently being flared in the southern part of the country mostly due to insufficient pipelines and poor infrastructure for transport for export and import. Iraq at present produces approximately 66 billion kilowatthours (kWh) of electricity and imports nearly 8 billion kWh from Iran and Turkey. Though Iraq has planned to be self-sufficient in electricity production by 2016, the delays in development of oil fields are causing electricity expansion plans to fall behind schedule.[27]

Bahrain is the first among the Gulf states to discover crude oil.[28] In 2013, Bahrain produced almost 48,000 barrels of crude oil daily and its only oil field, Awali, peaked long ago at about 75,000 barrels per day. The country also has a shared production of the Abu Safah field with Saudi Arabia and its refining capacity exceeds the domestic crude oil production today. A new pipeline is being constructed to transport 350,000 barrels of crude oil from Saudi Arabia to Bahrain's refinery in Sitra from 2017.[29] In the early 1990s, a border dispute between Bahrain and Qatar involving the Hawar Islands was referred to the International Court of Justice (ICJ) and the verdict was given in 2001. It is the only territorial dispute in the region, which has been peacefully resolved by the ICJ.[30] Bahrain got the islands but has not found any oil or gas deposits near Hawar yet, which was the prime incentive for the dispute to take shape. Moreover, the country and its oil industry infrastructure are also highly vulnerable to rising sea levels due to global warming.[31]

Oman's total oil production in 2013 was approximately 945,000 barrels per day, but the country is still not an OPEC member.[32] The country has huge oil reserves. Oil accounts for the country's 71 percent of total primary energy production, while the share of natural gas is the rest, around 29 percent. Oman is also experiencing increased energy consumption. Its oil production has declined recently; however, the country has been able to recover to a large extent by using enhanced oil recovery (EOR) techniques.[33] EOR technology generally involves the injection of a fluid that increases the recovery of oil from a reservoir compared to conventional water flood or pressure maintenance by gas injection. Most of Oman's oil exports go to Asia, particularly to China. The country is also the fifth largest dry natural gas producer in the region and this sector is developing fast. Oman's future natural gas development depends on the production of its tight natural gas reservoirs, which are geologically complex and difficult to retrieve than regular natural gas reserves where gas flows easily.[34]

The United Arab Emirates (UAE) is one of the largest oil producers in the world. Besides being an influential member of OPEC, the country is today one of the world's most important financials centers as well as a central trading center in region. UAE is a federation of seven emirates and each emirate is responsible for the oil industry within its border. The country has proven oil reserves of 97.8 billion barrels, with approximately 94 percent of them located in Abu Dhabi.[35] The most important policy body to manage oil resources in Abu Dhabi is the Supreme Petroleum Council (SPC). There are several other institutions involved in the oil, gas, and petroleum sector, such as the Abu Dhabi National Oil Company (ADNOC), the operations and implementation agency of the SPC. Within the emirate of Dubai, the Dubai Supreme Council of Energy (DSCE) is in charge of energy policy development and coordination.

The country has not been able to witness any substantial recent discoveries of crude oil. However, at present UAE is producing 2.7 million barrels per day and has set a crude oil production target of 3.5 million barrels by 2020 through the use of EOR techniques in Abu Dhabi's existing oil fields.[36] UAE has a number of domestic pipeline networks to transport oil from processing plants to export terminals. With most of its oil exports going to Asia, UAE needs safe access to global energy markets. The newest pipeline is the Abu Dhabi Crude Oil Pipeline, which gives the country a direct link between its energy-rich oil fields in the west to the Gulf of Oman, thus getting the advantage of not having to use the Strait of Hormuz.

UAE also has the seventh largest proven reserves of natural gas in the world. Despite this, the country has become a net importer of natural gas since 2008. A reason for this is that the UAE has an inefficient but rapidly expanding electricity grid, and it relies heavily on electricity produced from natural gas-fired facilities. Thus, the country imports gas from Qatar with the help of the Dolphin Gas Project's pipeline and is also dependent on LNG trading to meet the growing electricity demand. The Dolphin Gas Project is the first major interstate pipeline project of its kind in the region.[37] The country's demand for natural gas is increasing further due to energy used for desalination and to fuel the EOR operations to increase oil production. However, the UAE also intends to diversify its source for electricity generation beyond fossil fuel and is scheduled to get its first nuclear reactor in 2017 and the second in 2021. Power shortages have prompted the UAE to explore nuclear power as an alternate energy source and it collaborates with the International Atomic Energy Agency for technology transfer on carbon-free nuclear energy.[38]

Kuwait is one of the world's largest petroleum producers and its economy is highly dependent on energy production and export revenues, accounting for approximately 60 percent of the country's GDP. Kuwait's petroleum production is nearly 3 million barrels per day and it plans to produce crude oil of 4 million barrels by 2020.[39] Around half of its crude oil production comes from the country's southeast region, mostly from the Burgan field. The country with its "Project Kuwait" aims at attracting foreign investment for planned increase of production capacity by exploiting its northern Ratqa field.[40] Kuwait has recently become a net importer of natural gas and this has prompted the authorities to expand natural gas exploration and development to meet the increasing domestic demand.[41]

In terms of area and population, Qatar is the smallest OPEC member country. Most of the country's crude oil production capacity comes from three of its oil fields, and the Al Rayyan field was the last major discovery that took place in 1994. Most likely, the country might not have any new major source for crude oil supply; however, increased production can come from increased output from the existing fields.[42] However, with the world's third largest natural gas reserves, Qatar is the region's largest producer of gas and has had the strongest growth in production and exports.[43] With a relatively low domestic energy demand for the electricity and water desalinization sectors, Qatar manages to export nearly all of its natural gas production. The country has huge reserves of natural gas in the world, but nearly all of the reserves are in its north field. Qatar has spent years to develop its natural gas resources and is at the forefront of gas-to-liquids (GTL) technology. Like many other countries in the region, Qatar's economy is highly intertwined with its energy sector. Qatar has one of the world's fastest growing economies and this factor has increased the demand for energy use on the domestic front. All of the country's power generation capacity comes from natural gas.

Yemen is not a large producer of oil or gas compared to its neighboring countries in the region. The country has, however, a strategic location for international shipping and this makes Yemen important for international energy trade.[44] Yemen has 3 billion proven oil reserves, but still oil production has decreased since the peak in 2001, due to the decline in the country's aging fields as well as increasing political instability. Attacks of militant groups on oil pipelines have seriously affected Yemen's exports. In 2013, Yemen had exported around 124,000 barrels of crude oil, mostly to Asia. It intends to increase the use of natural gas for electricity generation as the majority of the country's population do not have access to electricity.[45] Deterioration in the domestic political situation has brought serious doubts about the future development of the country's oil and natural gas sectors.

IMPORTERS OF CRUDE OIL AND NATURAL GAS

Unlike the countries around the Gulf, the countries in the Marshek region are not well endowed with natural oil and gas resources. Jordan is heavily dependent on energy imports from other countries in the region. Since Jordan does not possess any significant energy resources of its own, the country is highly dependent on imports of natural gas, particularly from Egypt. Jordan's energy imports cover up to 90 percent of the country's energy demand and imports account for more than 40 percent of the country's budget.[46] The Arab Gas Pipeline from Egypt to Jordan is the primary source of Jordanian natural gas imports. Imports have been seriously affected by the growing political instability in the Sinai Peninsula and Syria. In January 2015, Egyptian jihadists bombed a pipeline in the Sinai that provides gas to Jordan in response to Jordan's role in the US-led offensive on the ISIS.[47]

In September 2014, Jordan signed a Memorandum of Understanding (MoU) with Israel to purchase natural gas worth $15 billion from the newly explored Tamar field, and if the deal comes through, it will be the largest collaboration between the two countries and Israel will replace Egypt as the chief supplier of natural gas to Jordan.[48] Besides protests at home, the legal challenges facing oil companies in Israel have brought uncertainties about the future of this deal.[49] This has put the Jordanian authorities in a fix as the Jordanian prime minister Abdullah Ensour admitted during the Jordan International Energy Summit in early 2015: "Jordan will increase its focus on the energy sector during the period as demand on electricity is expected to grow 5.5–6.5 percent during the next decade."[50]

Israel has over 11.5 million barrels of proven reserves of oil, but by the end of the last decade, only 12 percent of Israel's energy came from local resources, the rest were imported.[51] Due to low domestic reserves and increasing demand for electricity consumption, Israel traditionally emphasized on building coal power plants to improve energy security. In 2004, the Israeli Energy Master Plan proclaimed the country's need to manage its unique energy position in the Middle East and recognized the need for a new energy reserve. The master plan aimed to substitute coal with natural gas from Egypt and offshore of Gaza.[52] The consumption of natural gas has continued to expand after Israel signed a natural gas deal with Egypt in 2008. The gas pipeline connects El Arish in Egypt's Sinai to the port of Ashkelon in Israel. However, Israel is almost like an "energy island" due to its low energy infrastructure connectedness with its neighboring states.[53]

Until recently, Israel was seen as largely dependent on imported energy resources, making the state highly vulnerable to external circumstances and events. Natural gas became a part of Israel's energy mix as late as 2004, with the gas supplied by a domestic gas field in Yam Tethys. The Mari-B field, which was discovered in 2000, is now in its final stages of depletion, though the field continues to meet the country's natural gas demand up to 40 percent.[54] Thanks to the recent discoveries of vast offshore reserves of natural gas, Israel seems on its way to become a large player in the energy market in the region. The new discovery of Leviathan and Tamar fields proved that reserves of natural gas are at 10.1 trillion cubic feet (tcf).

Palestine consumes around 25,000 barrels of oil per day, and in terms of natural gas, there has not been any consumption or production. It has no proven hydrocarbon reserves and domestic refining capacity. However, in 2012, Palestine signed a natural gas supply deal with Egypt, in which the latter agreed to convert its generating capacity to natural gas–fired facilities. During 2014, Israel agreed that the Palestine territories will have been supplied gas from the newly explored Leviathan field by 2016 or 2017. The electricity generation in the territories is able to meet only 10 percent of the demand and the rest is supplied by Israel.[55]

Syria has 2.5 billion barrels of proven oil reserves, and the country had a production of around 400,000 barrels per day before the ongoing civil war. The current conflict has brought severe damage to Syria's energy infrastructure and has brought down production to 25,000 barrels per day. Most of Syria's proven oil reserves are near the border with Iraq and there are some minor fields in the central part of the country. Nearly 50 percent of country's electricity comes from oil, much of which has to be imported. Thus, Syria had an ambition to shift its generation strategy to gas-fuelled power plants. However, Syria's level of proven gas reserves has also remained constant over the last two decades.[56] Syria was importing gas from Egypt through the Arab Gas Pipeline (AGP) since 2008, till terror groups started targeting it since 2011. The AGP is being used to export Egyptian natural gas to Israel, Jordan, Syria, and Lebanon, and there are plans to expand the pipeline to Turkey and in the long run to Europe, but this is unlikely to materialize in the near future.

Syria might not have enough oil and natural gas deposits in its territory; however, it is a strategic location for energy trade. In 2009, Qatar proposed to build a pipeline from its north field, close to Iran's South Pars field, through Saudi Arabia, Jordan, Syria, and on to Turkey, with the aim to supply energy to European markets. This plan was aimed to end Russia's distinction of being Europe's top supplier of natural gas. However, Syria, instead of going along with the Qatari proposal, pursued another pipeline proposal with Iran under which Iran would supply gas to Europe from its South Pars field, and signed an MoU with Iran in July 2012. In early 2013, Iraq also joined this pipeline plan. However, this gas pipeline politics has further aggravated rivalry and complicated geopolitics in the region.[57]

Lebanon is one of the major energy importers in the region. It is highly dependent on import of oil products to meet more than 97 percent of its total primary energy supplies. In 2013, Lebanon's oil imports amounted to more than \$5 billion, representing more than 11 percent of its GDP.[58] The government is pushing for developing oil and natural resources; however, due to disputes between Lebanon and Israel over the shared maritime boundary, there are delays in exploration of hydrocarbon resources in the Levant Basin. Lebanon's exclusive economic zone (EEZ) forms part of the this basin, and there were some initial estimates that Lebanon's seabed could contain up to 30 trillion cubic feet (tcf) of natural gas and 660 million barrels of oil. However, a recent survey has brought down this figure to some extent and estimates the recoverable offshore gas reserves at only 25.4 tcf. Clearly, these different estimates bring some uncertainty to the future exploration processes of the reserves.[59]

Egypt is one of the largest consumers of energy in the region. Oil is mostly used in the transportation sector, whereas natural gas is used for power generation.[60] Since 2010, the country's oil consumption has surpassed its own oil production, as the demand has increased at an annual average by 3 percent during the past 10 years. Egypt, with 1.2 percent of the world's proven gas reserves, is relatively a minor player in the global natural gas industry. However, Egypt supplies all the natural gas used in Lebanon, most of the natural gas consumed in Jordan, and a large portion of natural gas consumed in Israel.[61] The country has experienced significant natural gas discoveries in the Mediterranean Sea and other areas, but these reserves have not been properly developed yet. Moreover, the increasing domestic demand and a terror attack on the AGP have also reduced the capacity of Egypt to export its gas to other countries. For some time, Egypt has had an important role in supplying natural gas to its neighbors, perhaps most notably Israel. However, Israel, with its new discoveries, is now set to become a competitor in the supply of natural gas.[62]

Egypt's Suez Canal, connecting the Mediterranean to the Red Sea, is a major route for global energy trade. However, there is a gradual decrease in oil cargo flows through the canal in recent years. The canal has been closed twice in its 145-year history, first for 17 months during the 1956 Suez Crisis and then for nearly eight years after the 1967 Arab-Israeli War. In those times, it used to be the route for 60 percent of Europe's oil supplies, while this figure has come down to 15 percent at present.[63] Any closing down of the canal will still have an immediate significant impact on the global energy sector.[64] However, the Arab Spring and the political instability afterward in Egypt did not have any noticeable effect on the oil transits through the Suez Canal.

NEW CHALLENGES AND NEW DISCOVERIES

Technological developments have made it possible to access new reserves of natural gas, which was hitherto inaccessible and the process not financially feasible. Natural gas is now replacing oil for the purpose of electricity generation and some oil-exporting countries have also started allocating gas for domestic energy supply. Moreover, gas also brings as much export revenues as oil does, though the economically profitable gas export needs large and long-term infrastructure expenses. The present development in the region indicates a clear interest toward profiting from natural gas use and export, more recently due to the huge discoveries in the Mediterranean. For many years, the Levantine countries of Syria, Lebanon, and Israel, including Palestine, have been engaged in the exploration of oil and gas. Israel's precarious energy security situation has long been a matter of serious concern for the country's strategic planners. With limited domestic production of hydrocarbon, Israel has always been dependent on oil and gas imports.[65] Thus, the country made it a priority to reduce its dependence on energy imports and it achieved some success with the discovery of some modest gas fields off its coast in 1999 and 2000.

Natural gas exploration in the Levant Basin in the Mediterranean has important consequences for the energy security of the region. The outlook for gas production has completely transformed since 2009 when Israel made a series of large offshore discoveries in the Eastern Mediterranean. Though the discoveries are not on the same scale as some of the world's larger natural gas–producing countries, they are enabling Israel to see itself in a position where it can become self-sufficient in the domestic market as well as open up possibilities for exports to neighboring countries.[66] The discoveries in the East Mediterranean, also claimed by Cyprus, Lebanon, and Palestine, create a number of geopolitical, regulatory, and commercial challenges which need to be resolved since they could potentially undermine the development of gas deposits in the basin all together. Thus, the disputes over ownership might not be overcome in the short term, which means that the development will be largely driven by local political dynamics and energy policies within the countries.[67]

In the Eastern Mediterranean, the Tamar field was discovered in January 2009 at a depth of 1650 meters near the city of Haifa, Israel. And in June 2010, the Leviathan offshore was discovered, also located off the coast of Haifa.[68] Thus, after the discoveries off the Tamar and Leviathan fields, Israel plans to achieve a diverse energy mix.[69] It is estimated that these fields, together with several smaller gas field discoveries, will result in the production of around 950 BCM of natural gas, which can support almost two-thirds of the total energy demand of Israel from 2020 to 2070, unless this much quantity is exported.[70] Securitization of energy politics is common and this has not escaped Israeli discourse toward its future natural gas policy, which emphasizes on urgency and depicts the issue as existential and paramount for the state of Israel.[71] Israel treats energy policies from the perspective of national security and has classified data relating to energy consumption and publishes information and trends on energy only over a four-year time period. Also, Israel does not give out official data on strategic reserves.[72]

With the new discoveries of gas reserves in the Eastern Mediterranean, Jordan is also configuring how to secure for itself a more diversified energy mix for the future. A potential deal with Noble Energy, a company that owns a major share in the Leviathan natural gas field in Israel, to supply Jordan's National Electric Power Company (NEPCO) with gas for a period of 15 years, starting from 2017, for a cost of $15 billion, is being hotly debated. There is popular opposition in Jordan for any deals that might make it dependent on Israel for its energy security. The opponents of the deal argue that Jordan should not make a deal that will make it come "under the control of the Zionist entity." Some also oppose in principle any gas that is stolen from Palestine.[73] Political disagreements and legal challenges have put the brakes on the proposed deal.[74] The issue of gas in the Eastern Mediterranean is embroiled in many challenges like the modus operandi of reaching the market, identifying the markets to be served, and the means of transporting the gas, challenges arising out of the unstable geopolitics of the region.[75]

There has been very limited cooperation and development of energy networks for gas and oil at the regional level. Partly, it is because of the long distances, the vast desert landscape, as well as a limited regional market, not to mention regional political rivalries and violent disputes. Not only does the region lack sufficient infrastructure, but frequent terror attacks, delays in investments and payments, etc. cause supply disruptions, resulting in many development challenges for the regional energy sector. However, there are two significant infrastructures for gas supply in the region—the AGP and the Dolphin Pipeline. The AGP connects Egypt, Jordan, Syria, and also Israel and the Dolphin Pipeline connects Qatar, UAE, and Oman. The Dolphin Pipeline was to be extended to connect Kuwait and Bahrain in order to supply these two countries low-cost gas. However, the border disputes have prevented this plan from being executed and Kuwait has opted for importing Russian LNG. The AGP has also experienced some difficulties; besides terror attacks, the availability of gas has become undependable due to erratic supplies from Egypt where shortages have become frequent.[76] There are other regional pipeline plans as well. In 2013, Iraq and Iran signed an agreement to fuel Iraqi power plants in Baghdad and Diyala. The security situation delayed the construction of the Iran-Iraq pipeline;[77] however, the project is almost complete now.[78] Before the Gulf War, Iraq used to export natural gas to Kuwait and it is presently considering whether or not to use this pipeline. There is also a grand plan to build a transcontinental pipeline to export natural gas to Europe from the region.[79]

The Middle East exports crude oil mostly to the Asian market. Almost 83 percent of Japan's crude oil imports in 2012 came from the region. China has

also increased its oil imports from the region and is becoming highly dependent on it. In 2012, half of its total crude oil imports came from the region.
India's crude oil imports are also mostly from the Middle East, with nearly 70
percent originating from the region in the fiscal year 2011/2012.[80] The region
is also the main supplier to the Asia-Pacific as there is a reduction in North
American demands and there is increasing oil consumption in the emerging
economies of Asia. As per the present trend, where crude oil is being refined
is also changing with the available refining capacity in different parts of the
world. Not only have North American imports from the Middle East declined
due to increase in domestic production, but also the refining facilities in the
Middle East have become expensive.[81]

The total proven oil reserves in the Middle East accounts for more than 45
percent of the total reserves in the world.[82] However, the cost of production
of heavy oil is increasingly becoming higher and it also takes a lot of natural
gas for heating to extract heavy fuel. In the Middle East, the natural gas business is booming, with new natural gas reserves being found in more countries
every year. In 1991–2011, the region's proven gas reserves increased by more
than 80 percent.[83] Globally, the natural gas demand is expected to grow in
the next two decades by an average of 1.9 percent annually, which is twice
as much as oil demand is predicted to be. The region is predicted to be the
largest contributor to supplying natural gas to meet this increasing global
demand.[84] This has obviously affected the region's geopolitics and has started
creating a new dynamic for energy relations within the region.

Member countries of the GCC are facing increasing demands for electric-
ity. To meet this challenge, the GCC countries, Kuwait, Qatar, Bahrain, Saudi
Arabia, and Oman, have commissioned a regionwide power grid.[85] The countries in the Marshek region have started the Eight Country Interconnection
Project involving Egypt, Iraq, Jordan, Libya, Lebanon, the Palestine, Turkey,
and Syria since 1989. Bilateral interconnection lines like Turkey-Syria,
Syria-Jordan, Jordan-Egypt, and Egypt-Libya have been built, while the
Syria-Lebanon, Syria-Iraq, and Jordan-Palestine lines are only in the planning
stages.[86] The extraordinary political situation is partly to be blamed for the
long delay of this interconnection project. If successful, such collaborative
projects will not only strengthen energy security but also contribute to the
reduction of the overall environmental pollution in the region.[87]

A number of Middle Eastern countries like Saudi Arabia, Jordan, and
Egypt have also been planning the construction of nuclear power plants. In
the case of Saudi Arabia, the construction is argued to be essential due to the
country's increasing demand for electricity as well as desalinated water.[88] The
energy situation within the countries of the region is gravely unsustainable at
various levels. They seriously suffer from systemic inefficiencies in the patterns of both energy consumption and production. This is clearly evident in

their increasing reliance on oil or gas-fuelled desalination to address the high water scarcity in the region.[89]

The challenges for energy security in the region are immense. The commonalities between the majority of the countries are the problems imposed by high energy subsidies, which not only cause economic losses and create unsustainable consumption patterns but also hinder the adoption of alternate energy solutions to fully develop the market potential and integrate the energy market into the global market. Most of the countries are experiencing an increasing demand for energy and they need to diversify their electricity generation and improve infrastructure to sustain generation capabilities. An important factor that is diminishing the diversification to alternate energy sources and investments is that there is an easy access to relatively low-cost oil in the region. Adding to this are vast energy subsidization programs which have transformed the countries in the region to be one of the world's largest oil consumers per capita.[90] The Arab Region is highly dependent on subsidy for fossil fuels. In some of the Gulf countries, the subsidization ranges up to 90 percent of the original price. The use of subsidies has transformed some former oil-exporting countries, such as Egypt and Syria, to become importers. There is an increasing demand within and outside the region for restructuring taxation and to phase out fossil fuel subsidies.[91]

Regimes in the region justify low energy prices in the name of promoting diversification and industrialization for the purpose of increasing employment, creating opportunities, and enhancing the economy. They also use this low price as a tool to keep inflation down. However, the use of energy subsidies poses a challenge to investments in renewable energy sources. The subsidies also have a negative environmental impact since they encourage wasteful consumption of fossil fuels. High energy subsidies can also be counterproductive in the sense that they can result in misallocation of resources, which, in turn, could lead to underinvestment in some sectors, fuel shortages, and large-scale cross-border fuel smuggling.[92]

MOVING OUT OF THE OIL AND GAS TRAP

The Middle East is experiencing a huge demographic expansion with young people under 25 years representing some 60 percent of the population. This makes the region the most youthful in the world.[93] A number of development challenges stare in the face of the Middle East, one of them being employment. The projections of an increasing demand of natural gas and oil suggest that production would pull forward the employment sector to some extent. The revolution of hydraulic fracturing in the United States in recent years has resulted in ending the rather expensive methods used for oil and natural gas extract. However, because of financial viability as well as opening a way for commercial production of shale oil, which is trapped in shale rock formations, fracturing has given the United States a fundamental relevance on the global energy market. In the Middle East, there is also now an equally important factor affecting the energy development of the region—the unconventional drilling technology that is reexamining reserves that were considered inaccessible.[94] However, the oil and gas-fuelled energy industry is not manpower extensive, which leads to employment only for a few locals and does not generate opportunities for a majority of the population.[95]

The countries in the Middle East have one of the highest greenhouse gas emissions (GHGs) in the world. In 2011/12, the region experienced a trend of increasing emissions by four percent each year. The primary reason for the extremely high rate of increasing GHGs is the region's dependence on the fossil fuel-driven electricity generation industry. There are two major risks for the countries associated with fossil fuel dependence. First, the finite nature of fossil fuel resources means that countries that are reliant on fossil fuels are increasingly vulnerable to volatile international markets and regional political uncertainties. Second, the continued use of fossil fuels increases the negative effects and risks of climate change. Fossil fuels are the main sources of carbon dioxide emissions into the atmosphere.

More than 97 percent of all electricity generation in the Middle East comes from fossil fuels.[96] The increasing demand for electricity and low energy prices poses a huge challenge to combating climate change.[97] The region is experiencing, and will continue to experience, increasing effects of climate change. The future consequences of rising temperatures will have profound effects on the region with increased risks of reduced water levels in rivers, desertification, and sea water intrusion. The adverse effects of the climate will directly and indirectly force millions of people to move out and become "climate refugees."[98]

Thanks to climate change, in the Middle East, the increasing temperatures will most likely be significant due to high solar radiation and the heat absorbent soils in the region, which will increase the probability of elevated temperatures. Projections show that the changes in temperature during 2011–2041 will be within the range of 0 and 2°C, according to their maximum and average scenarios. However, farther in the future, perhaps between 2041 and 2070, there will be differences between the maximum and average scenarios, the former scenario exhibiting temperature changes rising by up to 3–4°C and the later scenario indicating changes of 1–2°C.[99] The region has been already identified as the first one globally to run out of fresh water supplies, which makes the issue more serious in relation to climate change.[100] At the same time, the region is already heavily dependent on desalination to meet its water demand. However, desalinization is highly energy intensive and also subsidized, which leads to overuse and waste. In Saudi Arabia, around half of the potable water comes from desalinization.[101] According to the IPCC, the key risks for the most parts of this region vary between flooding in urban and coastal areas, leading to damage to infrastructure and livelihood, and increased drought-related water and food shortage.[102]

Many hope to slow down the pace of global warming by reducing the consumption of fossil fuels and increasingly shifting to renewable sources of energy.[103] For the energy industry in the Middle East to meet the challenges of climate change, it needs to take effective steps to reduce emissions and provide cleaner energy.[104] Due to increased energy demand, nuclear energy has gained some momentum in some of the Gulf countries like Saudi Arabia and the UAE. However, besides the sizable initial investment costs, the other hidden costs like national and regional political instability and the future disposal of nuclear waste have prohibited the nuclear energy sector to become a viable alternate energy source.[105] The dominant use of oil and gas for electricity generation continues because these fuels are considered to be cheaper than the available renewable energy technologies.[106] Renewable energy is "energy gained from resources that are replenished by natural processes in a relatively short time," whereas nonrenewable energy is "energy from resources that can be depleted and are not replenished by natural processes within a human time scale."[107]

The cost advantages of nonrenewable fossil fuels over renewable sources for power generation wane in the long run, and other risks are considered. Adapting to renewable energy sources can become an instrument for improving energy security and a way to mitigate greenhouse gas emissions. In the long term, renewable sources can improve reliability of electricity supplies while reducing energy costs. It is, therefore, not surprising that there has been an increasing interest globally to switch from the traditional fossil fuel–based power generation to renewable energy sources. In recent times, the cost of renewable energy technologies has declined significantly, globally installed capacity and production of all renewable technologies has increased extensively, and policies that are essential to shift to renewable energy technologies have continued to spread throughout the world.[108] Globally, renewables are increasingly perceived as crucial to achieving future energy demands. It not only helps to abate global climate change; it also has a number of associated benefits. These include improved economic and energy security, unlimited sources of energy, decreased fossil fuel dependence, and increased job opportunities.[109]

As energy is the driver for development, renewable energy is the stimulus for sustainable development. The importance of renewable energy has also been emphasized in the Rio+20 summit.[110] The UN initiative "Sustainable Energy for All" focuses on "access to energy, energy efficiency and renewable energies" and with the hope that this will help to eradicate poverty and lead to sustainable development and global prosperity. The Action Plan of Agenda 21 also emphasizes that renewable sources of energy should be encouraged to change consumption patterns. The distinguishing feature of renewable energy is that it is inexhaustible and thus a critical part of sustainable development.[111]

RELYING ON RENEWABLES

In 2013, the League of Arab States adopted the "Pan-Arab Strategy for the Development of Renewable Energy Applications: 2010–2030," which is the first milestone for the region in expressing interest in renewable energy alternatives. The strategy has its focus on electricity generation, which is a major concern for the region due to increasing demand.[112] For the first time, a broad political consensus was reached in the region on long-term renewable energy targets. The strategy aims to increase the amount of renewable energy sources through setting guidelines and providing tools to create national renewable energy action plans as well as to enhance regional cooperation. The target level of the agreed strategy is to increase the renewable energy power capacity from around 12 GW in 2013 to 75 GW by 2030.[113]

Many countries in the region have a huge potential for renewable energy sources, particularly from solar, wind, and water. In 2014, the League of Arab States, together with the International Renewable Energy Agency (IRENA) and the Regional Center for Renewable Energy and Energy Efficiency (RCREEE), launched an implementation roadmap study, which proposes country-specific as well as regional-specific suggestions that would support the region's renewable energy development.[114] The study, titled "Pan-Arab Renewable Energy Strategy 2030: Roadmap of Actions for Implementation," suggests that regional interventions are needed as national policies are not enough. Globally, there is a decrease in renewable energy costs and at the same time there is an increasing interest in renewables to compensate for declining fossil fuel reserves, which provide the opportunity for renewable energy market in the Middle East to grow. In this context, the study recommends the promotion of manufacturing and services of renewable energy in Arab countries, the conduct of research studies for assessment of the potential of opportunities for financial cooperation on renewable energy projects, and the launch of technical and financial assistance programs in order to support Arab countries in the formulation of national renewable energy action plans.[115]

There are many challenges in the way of speedy implementation and generation of renewable energy solutions in the Middle East. The region lacks a coordinated and integrated energy planning system. Besides high

Table 4.4   Renewable Energy Production in the Middle East Region

Country	Year	Solar	Wind	Hydropower	Bioenergy
Egypt	2013		550 MW	2,800 MW	
Israel	2013	420 MW			11.15 MW
Iraq	2013			2,514 MW	
Jordan	2013	1.6 MW	1.5 MW	12 MW	3 MW
Lebanon	2013			282 MW	
Syria	2013			900 MW	
Palestine	No Data				
Yemen	2013				
Bahrain	2013		0.5 MW		
Kuwait	2013	0.5 MW			
Oman	2013				
Qatar	2013	3.2 MW			25 MW
Saudi Arabia	2013	25 MW			
UAE	2013	133 MW			

Source: International Renewable Energy Agency (irena.org).

subsidization of electricity prices, there are very limited support mechanisms. The capacity of the electricity networks to integrate with large networks for renewable energy generation is less.[116] Renewable energy constituted only 1 percent of the region's total primary energy supply in 2010. However, in recent years, there has been increased investment in renewable energy sectors, particularly in the solar market.[117]

Among the renewable energy sources, hydroelectric power is one of the most important one that can be used for large-scale production to achieve environmental, social, and economic development.[118] The World Summit on Sustainable Development in 2002 recommended that hydropower be promoted and developed to increase the use of renewable energy all over the world.[119] Hydropower has a wider scale range of electrical output and much higher efficiency compared to other renewable energy sources.[120] Thus, it can play a critical role in renewable energy promotion. Besides, hydropower can be effectively stored and is less climate dependent and less unpredictable than other renewable energy sources. However, besides a few countries like Egypt, Syria, Iraq, and Lebanon, others do suffer from topographical disadvantage in opting for hydropower generation.

Hydropower is the third largest energy source for Egypt. The majority of the hydropower generation of the country comes from the Aswan High Dam and Aswan Reservoir Dams along the Nile River. However, Egypt's New and Renewable Energy Authority (NREA) has started shifting focus from hydropower and pursuing other renewable energy alternatives such as solar wind power as the Nile's hydropower potential has already been largely exploited. The same is the case for Iraq and Syria. In the case of Syria, the conflict and the upstream dams in Turkey have reduced the hydropower production of the country from 1505 megawatts in 2007 to 900 megawatts in 2013. In Iraq, the ongoing conflict has moved the focus away from hydropower development, which is part of the long-term strategy to develop gas and oil-fired power plants in a short duration.[121]

Egypt is one of the countries in the region that has established several institutions to enable the local renewable energy industry to develop. The Renewable Energy and Environment Protection Program supports renewable energy generation initiatives financially and technically, provides information, and conducts feasibility studies to assess technical capabilities.[122] Egypt's plan is to double the share of renewable energy in the country's total power generation to 20 percent by 2020. Currently, Egypt generates wind power from farms located on the western coast of the Gulf of Suez and there are a number of projects developed and financed in cooperation with Germany, Denmark, Spain, and Japan. In 2014, Egypt also announced a plan to invest $1 billion in developing solar projects.[123]

The UAE is also investing in renewable energy solutions and technologies and desires to produce 7 percent of its total power generation from renewable sources by 2020.[124] According to the International Renewable Energy Agency (IRENA), the UAE shows a realistic potential for achieving higher renewable energy production. The installations of solar photovoltaic (PV), wind and landfill gas, as well as solar heating, are "low-hanging fruits" for the UAE. However, solar energy is in the essential scheme of things in the UAE and different types of solar energy could account for 90 percent of the total renewable energy use. In 2012, the UAE produced 20 megawatts of solar power, while in 2013, the production jumped to 133 megawatts. The costs for renewable energy solutions also continue to decline, whereas natural gas costs are rising. Renewables like solar PV have already become cost competitive compared to even high-efficiency natural gas plants, and the PV is already cheaper than LNG.[125]

Due to a great number of advantages, the solar has become the fastest growing resource to produce energy in the world as well as in the Middle East. The benefits of solar energy are that solar panels are eco-friendly, reduce fossil fuel dependence, and are easy to move and expand. In some countries, these benefits have been combined with increased tax breaks and increased subsidies for solar developers. Another advantage of solar energy is that solar cells emit no greenhouse gases, although they are not carbon free, because fossil fuels are used to transport and produce the cells. But, these emissions are small in comparison with those resulting from the use of fossil fuels. Furthermore, solar energy can be easily taken to the rural regions, which are not connected to an electrical grid. At the same time, the costs of electricity generation from solar PV have fallen sharply over the last two decades.[126] However, there are also some disadvantages associated with solar energy, and these include the need for getting access to the sun and having electricity storage or backup systems. Also, solar-cell power plants could disrupt desert ecosystems. However, the Middle East provides an extremely suitable environment for the development of solar energy with its very large open areas with large amounts of daily sunlight.

The League of Arab States framed an Arab Guideline in 2010, which asked member states to prepare a three-year National Energy Efficiency Action Plan (NEEAP). In 2014, the International Energy Agency (IEA), the Regional Centre for Renewable Energy and Energy Efficiency, the European Bank for Reconstruction and Development, and the Arab League participated in a roundtable conference hosted by the Jordanian Ministry of Energy and Mineral Resources, where energy efficiency and regional challenges were presented. Though implementation of policies is ongoing, there are still challenges that countries in the region are facing like their poor capacity to enforce regulatory policies, lack of coordination across ministries, and inability to develop and implement energy-efficiency projects.[127]

Significant increases in the share of renewable energy in the regional energy mix can be achieved more expeditiously through cooperation between various stakeholders. It is essential that authorities develop policies that will encourage investment and promote an environment that ensures investment security.[128] A well-designed policy instrument can reduce the cost of renewable electricity substantially.[129] Investment in solar energy technology in the region can also be an effective means for authorities to stimulate growth and accelerate economic recovery, particularly while recovering from violent conflicts.[130] To increase stakeholder confidence and secure long-term investment and future interest in projects, a clear political and societal commitment toward renewable energy is needed. The successful transition to a low-carbon energy future needs to be a priority for policy makers in the countries of the region. Investments in high-cost low-carbon technologies, especially solar, can be largely motivated by public policy.[131] To achieve effectiveness with regard to installed solar capacity, a sufficiently high policy support level and a perceived long-term stability of policy framework are paramount.[132] The existence of alignments of interests between different stakeholders can influence the state of affairs, which will result in changes to governmental policy or in the behavior of the energy market.

EVALUATING THE REGION'S ENERGY SECURITY SCENARIO

The world's demand for energy is increasing dramatically. A few countries in the Middle East control a large part of the world's oil reserves and a substantial share of the global oil production due to their geological advantage. In spite of experiencing wars, international interventions, civil conflicts, revolutions, and growing terror activities, the region still continues to act as a main supplier of oil to global markets.[133] However, the major oil-producing countries in the region possess primitive political systems, weak or nonexistent political institutions, and regimes with very little political legitimacy.[134] It can be argued that oil and gas have helped empower nondemocratic authoritarian regimes in the region.[135] Most of these regimes have smartly used increased oil and gas revenue to nullify public opposition and buy loyalties at home through lavish spending and low taxes and cultivating friends and partners outside.[136]

Oil and gas revenue has changed the balance of power between state and society in most parts of the region.[137] It has brought a false sense of economic security in the policy making of many countries. Regimes have used the money from oil and gas to suppress civil society and prevent popular institutions from putting checks on their authority. However, the lack of basic democratic rights increases possibilities for violent revolutions in the region. While the regime and a few elites control the rich oil resource, the rapidly increasing population in the region suffers from poverty, unemployment, and worsening conditions for human development. There is no doubt that the regimes in the region are highly unstable. The prevailing political instability raises questions about the long-term oil production capacity of the region due to external sanctions, ethnic unrests, and the changing investment environment.

The Middle East being one of the highest energy consumers per capita in the world, environmental pollution and carbon emission have been major challenges facing the region. For several decades now, many countries in this part of the world have been living beyond their ecological means. The world is not the same as it was in 1970s, and the concept of energy security has broadened to include other sources of energy, though oil still occupies a critical place in the policy debate.[138] Oil and gas are no longer cheap and plentiful, and their highly fluctuating prices regularly create havoc for both exporting and importing economies. Discoveries of oil and gas fail to keep up with increasing demand, and competition for the scarce fossil fuels has been complicating regional and international tensions. Countries in the Middle East need to seriously reevaluate their energy strategy, prioritize investment in renewable energy, and achieve energy efficiency. As Sawin and Moomaw[139] argue,

> Efficiently delivered energy service that use natural energy flows will protect the global climate, strengthen the economy, create millions of new jobs, help developing countries reduce poverty, increase personal and social security in all the countries, reduce international tensions over resources, and improve the health of people and ecosystems alike.

The renewable energy industry creates more jobs than the oil and gas-fuelled industry, both in terms of installed capacity and the cost involved.[140] It has been estimated that the solar energy industry alone could possibly generate more than 100,000 jobs in the GCC countries.[141] Thus, it is important for the countries to look beyond the current short-term energy glut and seriously start creating roadmaps of how to expand energy production to the renewable sector and improve the efficiency of energy sector technology. Strong political will backed by substantial investment in the renewable energy sector can be the key in meeting the challenges of energy security of the region in the long term. However, the countries in the Middle East have a long way ahead in adopting renewable energy options. Large deposits of fossil fuel in the region and high subsidies on them are some of the most important obstacles for the countries in the region to move to renewable energy production. Moreover, the countries have no cooperation at the regional level in the area of renewable energy generation, and as Mari Luomi[142] argues, no "silver bullet" solution is out there at present for an increased regional cooperation.

The regional geopolitics on energy has undergone a significant transformation in recent decades due to new discoveries, changing regimes, and political realignments. The globalization of energy trade has also added further challenges to regional energy security. To meet the growing domestic energy demand due to increasing population and a growing economy and the international obligations necessitated by the urgency of climate change, the region needs to follow the path to sustainable energy future. The need of the hour for this highly volatile and fragmented region is to invest in technological development and to prioritize the use of renewable energy sources in order to achieve sustainable energy security. This will have immense potential benefits and create a more cooperative rules-based society of reduced poverty and increased human development. In many respects, a smart energy policy will play a pivotal role in shaping the future of this region and improving its ties with the rest of the world.

NOTES

1. Michael Toman and Barbora Jemelkova, "Energy and Economic Development: An assessment of the State of Knowledge," *The Energy Journal*, 24, 4 (2003): 93–112.

2. United Nations General Assembly. *The Future We Want*, Rio+20 United Nations Conference on Sustainable Development, 2012.

3. International Energy Agency. *Energy for all, Financing access for the poor, special early excerpt of the World Energy Outlook 2011* (Paris: International Energy Agency, 2011).

4. World Bank. *Energy-the facts*, (Washington, DC: World Bank, 2013).

5. SIPRI, *Oil and Security* (Stockholm: Almqvist & Wiksell, 1974).

6. A.S. Alsharhan, and A.E.M. Nairn, *Sedimentary Basins and Petroleum Geology of the Middle East* (Amsterdam: Elsevier, 2003). Z.R. Beydoun. *Arabian Plate Hydrocarbon Geology and Potential: A Plate Tectonic Approach* (Tulsa, OK: AAPG Studies in Geology #33, 1991).

7. Rasaul Sorkhabi, "How Much Oil in the Middle East?," *GeoExPro*, 11, 1 (2014).

8. Sorkhabi, "How Much Oil in the Middle East?."

9. Collin Campbell and Jean Laherrere, "The End of Cheap Oil," *Scientific American*, (March 1998): 78–84.

10. Aleh Cherp and Jessica Jewell, "The three perspectives on energy security: intellectual history, disciplinary roots and the potential for integration," *Environmental Sustainability*, 3 (2011): 202–12.

11. Itay Fischendler and Daniel Nathan, "In the Name of Energy Security: The Struggle over the Exportation of Israeli Natural Gas," *Energy Policy,* 70 (2014): 152–62.

12. Cherp and Jewell, "The three perspectives on energy security: intellectual history, disciplinary roots and the potential for integration."

13. Cherp and Jewell, "The three perspectives on energy security: intellectual history, disciplinary roots and the potential for integration."

14. Cherp and Jewell, "The three perspectives on energy security: intellectual history, disciplinary roots and the potential for integration"; Aleh Cherp, Jessica Jewell and Andreas Goldthau, "Governing global energy: systems, transitions, complexity," *Global Policy*, 2, (2011): 75–88.

15. Bright E. Okugu, "Middle East to Dominate World Oil for Many Years," *Finance and Development*, 40, 1 (2003).

16. Ian Talley, "Middle East Oil Producers Could See $300 Billion Export Loss," *The Wall Street Journal*, 21 January 2015.

17. Toni Johnson, "Global Natural Gas Potential," *CFR Backgrounder*, Council on Foreign Relations, 24 August 2011.

18. US Energy Information Administration, 2014a, *Country Analysis Brief: Saudi Arabia,* at http://www.eia.gov/beta/international/analysis_includes/countries_long/Saudi_Arabia/saudi_arabiapdf, (accessed May 29, 2015).

19. Shibley Telhami, "The Role of the Persian Gulf Region," in *The Contemporary Middle East*, ed., Karl Yambert (Boulder, CO: Westview Press, 2006), 173.

20. *The Guardian*, January 22, 2015.

21. US Energy Information Administration, 2014a, *Country Analysis Brief: Saudi Arabia,* at http://www.eia.gov/beta/international/analysis_includes/countries_long/Saudi_Arabia/saudi_arabia.pdf, (accessed May 29, 2015).

22. Toni Johnson, "Global Natural Gas Potential."

23. US Energy Information Administration, 2014a, *Country Analysis Brief: Saudi Arabia,* at http://www.eia.gov/beta/international/analysis_includes/countries_long/Saudi_Arabia/saudi_arabia.pdf, (accessed May 29, 2015).

24. US Energy Information Administration, 2014a, *Country Analysis Brief: Saudi Arabia,* at http://www.eia.gov/beta/international/analysis_includes/countries_long/Saudi_Arabia/saudi_arabia.pdf (accessed May 29, 2015).

25. Lawrence Kumins, "Iraq Oil: Reserves, Production, and Potential Revenues," Congressional Research Service Report for Congress, April 13, 2005.

26. Center on Global Energy Policy, *Issue Brief: Iraq's Oil Sector*, Columbia, SIPA, June 14, 2014.

27. U.S. Energy Information Administration, *Country Analysis Brief: Iraq*, 2015, at: http://www.eia.gov/beta/international/analysis_includes/countries_long/Iraq/iraq. pdf (accessed May 28, 2015).

28. *The Telegraph*, March 16, 2011.

29. US Energy Information Administration, 2014b, *Bahrain – Analysis*, at http://www.eia.gov/beta/international/analysis.cfm?iso=BHR (accessed May 25, 2015).

30. Krista E. Wiegand, "Bahrain, Qatar, and the Hawar Islands: Resolution of a Gulf Territorial Dispute," *The Middle East Journal*, 66 (2012): 79–96.

31. Elasha B. Osman, *Mapping of Climate Change Threats and Human Development Impacts in the Arab Region*, Research Paper Series, 2010, UNDP, RBAS.

32. The Organization of the Petroleum Exporting Countries (OPEC) was established in September 1960 and the founder members of the organization were Iran, Iraq, Kuwait, Saudi Arabia, and Venezuela. Other members of the OPEC are Algeria (1969), Angola (2007), Ecuador (1973), Libya (1962), Nigeria (1971), Qatar (1961), and the United Arab Emirates (1967).

33. US Energy Information Administration, 2014, *Countries: Oman*, at http://www.eia.gov/beta/international/analysis_includes/countries_long/Oman/oman.pdf, (accessed May 29, 2015).

34. Justic Dargin, *The Dolphin Project: The Development of a Gulf Gas Initiative* (Oxford Institute for Energy Studies, 2008).

35. US Energy Information Administration, 2015, *International energy data and analysis: United Arab Emirates*, at http://www.eia.gov/beta/international/analysis_ includes/countries_long/United_Arab_Emirates/uae.pdf, (accessed May 27, 2015).

36. US Energy Information Administration, 2015, *International energy data and analysis: United Arab Emirates*, at http://www.eia.gov/beta/international/analysis_ includes/countries_long/United_Arab_Emirates/uae.pdf, (accessed May 27, 2015).

37. Justic Dargin, *The Dolphin Project: The Development of a Gulf Gas Initiative* (Oxford Institute for Energy Studies, 2008).

38. World Economic Forum, *The United Arab Emirates and the World: Scenarios to 2025*, World Scenario Series, 2007.

39. US Energy Information Administration, 2014d, *Countries: Kuwait*, at http://www.eia.gov/beta/international/analysis_includes/countries_long/Kuwait/kuwait.pdf, (accessed May 27, 2015).

40. *The Times* (Kuwait) Issue No. 687, April 20–26, 2014.

41. *Middle East Online*, December 24, 2014.

42. A. Al-Siddiqi and R. R. Dawe, "Qatar's Oil and Gas fields: A Review," *Journal of Petroleum Geology*, 22 (1999): 417–36.

43. Toni Johnson, "Global Natural Gas Potential."

44. Mark N. Katz, "Yemeni Unity and Saudi Security," *Middle East Policy*, 1 (1992).

45. US Energy Information Administration, 2014, *Countries: Yemen*, at: http://www.eia.gov/beta/international/analysis_includes/countries_long/Yemen/yemen.pdf, (accessed May 28, 2015).

46. US Energy Information Administration, 2014, *Country Overview: Jordan*, at http://www.eia.gov/countries/country-data.cfm?fips=JO, (accessed May 29, 2015).

47. *The Jordan Times*, March 4, 2015.

48. Marissa Newman, "Israel signs $15 billion gas deal with Jordan," *The Times of Israel*, September 3, 2014.

49. *The Times of Israel*, January 4, 2015.

50. *The Jordan Times*, March 4, 2015.

51. Fischendler and Nathan, "In the Name of Energy Security: The Struggle over the Exportation of Israeli Natural Gas."

52. Fischendler and Nathan, "In the Name of Energy Security: The Struggle over the Exportation of Israeli Natural Gas."

53. Brenda Shaffer, "Israel - New Natural Gas Producer in the Mediterranean," *Energy Policy*, 39 (2011): 5379–87.

54. US Energy Information Administration, 2014, *Israel – Analysis*, at http://www.eia.gov/countries/country-data.cfm?fips=IS, (accessed January 21, 2015).

55. Shaffer, "Israel - New Natural Gas Producer in the Mediterranean."

56. Manfred Hafner, Simone Tagliapietra and El Habib El Elandaloussi, *Outlook for Oil and Gas in Southern and Eastern Mediterranean Countries*, MEDPRO Technical Report No. 18, October 2012.

57. Nafeez Ahmed, "Syria intervention plan fueled by oil interests, not chemical weapon concern," *The Guardian*, August 30, 2013.

58. Mirna Chami, "Lebanon's Trade Activity in 2013 Highlights a Hectic Year," *Blominvest Bank, 2014*.

59. Bassam Fattouh and Laura El-Katiri, "Energy subsidies in the Middle East and North Africa," *Energy Strategy Reviews*, 2 (2013): 108–15.

60. US Energy Information Administration, 2014, *Country Analysis Brief: Egypt*, at http://www.eia.gov/countries/analysisbriefs/Egypt/egypt.pdf, (accessed April 24, 2015).

61. Michael Ratner, *Implications of Egypt's Turmoil on Global Oil and Natural Gas Supply*, Congressional Research Service Report for Congress, May4, 2011.

62. Andrea Clabough, "Beyond Oil: The New Energy Geopolitics of the Middle East," *Georgetown Security Studies Review*, December 10, 2013.

63. Marsoft, *Marsoft Flash Report: New Suez Canal Crisis?*, February 2011.

64. Michael Ratner, *Implications of Egypt's Turmoil on Global Oil and Natural Gas Supply*, Congressional Research Service Report for Congress, May 4, 2011.

65. Natan Sachs and Tim Boersma, *The Energy Island: Israel Deals with its Natural Gas Discoveries*, Foreign Policy at Brookings, Policy Paper, No. 35, February 2015.

66. Hakim Darbouche, Laura El-Katiri and Bassam Fattouh, *East Mediterranean Gas: what kind of game-changer?* (Oxford: The Oxford Institute for Energy Studies, 2012).

67. Darbouche, El-Katiri and Fattouh, *East Mediterranean Gas: what kind of game-changer?*.

68. Shaffer, "Israel - New Natural Gas Producer in the Mediterranean."

69. Fischendler and Nathan, "In the Name of Energy Security: The Struggle over the Exportation of Israeli Natural Gas."

70. Eugene Kandel, "Remark of the Head of the Israeli National Economic Council during Tzemach Committee public hearings," 11 June 2012.

71. Fischendler and Nathan, "In the Name of Energy Security: The Struggle over the Exportation of Israeli Natural Gas."

72. Shaffer, "Israel - New Natural Gas Producer in the Mediterranean."

73. Merza Noghai, *Friday march planned against Israel gas deal, The Jordan Times*, May 10, 2015.

74. Sharon Udasin, *Jordanian parliament member announces pause in gas negotiations with Israel, 2015,* at: http://www.jpost.com/Middle-East/Jordan-suspends-talks-with-Israel-over-15-billion-natural-gas-deal-386600, (accessed May 30, 2015).

75. John Roberts, "Energy in the Eastern Mediterranean: Promise or Peril?," in *A Eurasian Energy Primer: The Transatlantic Perspectives,* ed., David Koranyi (Washington DC: Atlantic Council, 2013) 25–36.

76. Hisham Khatib, "Oil and natural gas prospects: Middle East and North Africa," *Energy Policy*, 64, (2014): 71–77.

77. US Energy Information Administration, *Country Analysis Brief: Iraq*, 2015, at: http://www.eia.gov/beta/international/analysis_includes/countries_long/Iraq/iraq.pdf, (accessed May 28, 2015).

78. Islamic Republic News Agency, *Iran-Iraq gas pipeline 95% complete,* February 25, 2015.

79. US Energy Information Administration, 2015. *Country Analysis Brief: Iraq*, at: http://www.eia.gov/beta/international/analysis_includes/countries_long/Iraq/iraq.pdf, (accessed May 28, 2015).

80. International Energy Agency, 2014, "Energy efficiency outreach focuses on regional priorities," at http://www.iea.org/ieaenergy/issue6/energy-efficiency-outreach-focuses-on-regional-priorities--.html, (accessed June 9, 2015).

81. International Energy Agency, 2014, "Energy efficiency outreach focuses on regional priorities," at http://www.iea.org/ieaenergy/issue6/energy-efficiency-outreach-focuses-on-regional-priorities--.html, (accessed June 9, 2015).

82. BP, *BP Statistical Review of World Energy June 2014.* British Petroleum (BP).

83. Khatib, "Oil and natural gas prospects: Middle East and North Africa."

84. Khatib, "Oil and natural gas prospects: Middle East and North Africa."

85. US Energy Information Administration, 2014. *Countries: Qatar*, at: http://www.eia.gov/beta/international/analysis_includes/countries_long/Qatar/qatar.pdf

86. Al-Shalabi Abdulaziz, Nocolas Cottret and Emanuela Menichetti, "EU-GCC Cooperation on Energy," in *Bridging the Gulf: EU-GCC Relations at a Crossroads,* ed., Silvia Colombo (Rome: IAI, 2014), 158–222.

87. The Arab Fund for Economic and Social Development. 2014, *Projects and Operations: Electricity*, at http://www.arabfund.org/default.aspx?pageId=454, (accessed June 9, 2015).

88. Ali Ahmad and M.V. Ramana, *"Does Middle East really need nuclear power?," Al Monitor*, September 25, 2014.

89. ESCWA, "Energy in the Arab Region: *Regional Coordination Mechanism (RCM)," Issues Brief for the Arab Sustainable Development Report* (2015): 1–16.

90. UNEP, UNROWA, and ESCWA, "Sustainable Consumption and Production in the Arab Region," *Regional Coordination Mechanism (RCM): Issues Brief for the Arab Sustainable Development Report*, (Nairopbi: UNEP, 2015), pp. 1–15.

91. UNEP, UNROWA, and ESCWA, "Sustainable Consumption and Production in the Arab Region," *Regional Coordination Mechanism (RCM): Issues Brief for the Arab Sustainable Development Report*, (Nairobi: UNEP, 2015): 1–15.

92. Fattouh and El-Katiri, "Energy subsidies in the Middle East and North Africa."

93. UNDP, *Arab Human Development Report 2009.* (United Nations Development Program; Regional Bureau for Arab States, Lebanon, 2009).

94. Clabough, "Beyond Oil: The New Energy Geopolitics of the Middle East."

95. Khatib, "Oil and natural gas prospects: Middle East and North Africa."

96. International Energy Agency, 2014, "Energy efficiency outreach focuses on regional priorities," at http://www.iea.org/ieaenergy/issue6/energy-efficiency-outreach-focuses-on-regional-priorities--.html, (accessed June 9, 2015).

97. Fattouh and El-Katiri, "Energy subsidies in the Middle East and North Africa."

98. UNDP, *Arab Human Development Report 2009.*

99. UNEP 2015, *Second Session for the High-Level Forum on Sustainable Development: RCM Documents - Climate Change in the Arab Region.* at http://www.escwa.un.org/information/meetingdetails.asp?referenceNum=3572E, (accessed June 9, 2015).

100. UNEP, *Second Session for the High-Level Forum on Sustainable Development: RCM Documents - Climate Change in the Arab Region.*

101. Khatib, "Oil and natural gas prospects: Middle East and North Africa."

102. IPCC, *Climate Change 2014: Impacts, Adaptation, and Vulnerability - Summary for Policymakers.* Intergovernmental Panel on Climate Change. IPCC, 2014.

103. Michael I. Klare, "Climate Change Blowback: The Threats to Energy Security," *SAIS Review of International Affairs*, 35, 1 (2015): 61–72.

104. International Energy Agency, 2014, "Energy efficiency outreach focuses on regional priorities," at http://www.iea.org/ieaenergy/issue6/energy-efficiency-outreach-focuses-on-regional-priorities--.html, (accessed June 9, 2015).

105. Aarti Nagraj, "Nuclear Power: Boon or Bane for the GCC?," *Gulf Business*, April 19, 2014.

106. Bastian Becker and Doris Fischer, "Promoting renewable electricity generation in emerging economies," *Energy Policy,* 56 (2013): 446–55.

107. Tyler G. Miller and Scott E. Spoolman, *Living in the environment* (Eighteenth edition) (Stamford: CT: Cengage Learning. 2015), 42.

108. Ren21, *Renewable 2014: Global Status Report. Key Findings:* Renewable Energy Policy Network for the 21st Century, Paris, 2014.

109. Miller and Spoolman, *Living in the environment* (Eighteenth edition) (Stamford: CT: Cengage Learning, 2015).

110. United Nations General Assembly, *The Future We Want*, Rio+20 United Nations Conference on Sustainable Development, 2012.

111. Huiyi Chen and Ashok Swain, "The Grand Ethiopian Renaissance Dam: Evaluating Its Sustainability Standard and Geopolitical Significance," *Energy Development Frontier*, 3, 1 (2014): 11–19.

112. IRENA, League of Arab States, and RCREEE, *Pan-Arab Renewable Energy Strategy: Roadmap of Actions for Implementation*, (IRENA, League of Arab States, RCREEE, 2014).

113. IRENA et al, *Pan-Arab Renewable Energy Strategy: Roadmap of Actions for Implementation.*

114. IISD, *Arab Forum Launches Renewable Energy Strategy, 2014*, at http://energy-1.iisd.org/news/arab-forum-launches-renewable-energy-strategy/, (accessed June 9, 2015).

115. IRENA, League of Arab States, and RCREEE, *Pan-Arab Renewable Energy Strategy: Roadmap of Actions for Implementation*, 66.

116. IRENA, League of Arab States, and RCREEE. *Pan-Arab Renewable Energy Strategy: Roadmap of Actions for Implementation.*

117. United Arab Emirates, IRENA and REN21, *MENA Renewables Status Report 2014*. Paris: REN21, 2014.

118. Botin Zhang, 2011. Debate: Hydropower. Accessed November 17, 2013, from China.org.cn: http://www.china.org.cn/environment/2011-06/07/content_22725492.html (accessed November 17, 2013).

119. Kristin Schumann, Lau Saili, Richard Taylor and Refaat Abdel-Mark, "Hydropower and Sustainable Development: A Journey," International Hydropower Association, 2010, http://www.worldenergy.org/documents/congresspapers/392.pdf, (accessed November 17, 2013).

120. Chen and Swain, "The Grand Ethiopian Renaissance Dam: Evaluating Its Sustainability Standard and Geopolitical Significance."

121. UNIDO and ICSHP, *World Small Hydropower Development Report 2013: Iraq*, United Nations Industrial Development Organization (UNIDO) and International Center on Small Hydro Power, 2013.

122. United Arab Emirates, IRENA and REN21, *MENA Renewables Status Report 2014.*

123. US Energy Information Administration, 2014h, *Country Analysis Brief: Egypt*, at http://www.eia.gov/countries/analysisbriefs/Egypt/egypt.pdf (accessed April 23, 2015).

124. US Energy Information Administration, 2015b, *International energy data and analysis: United Arab Emirates*, at http://www.eia.gov/beta/international/analysis_includes/countries_long/United_Arab_Emirates/uae.pdf (accessed on May 28, 2015).

125. IRENA, 2015. *REmap 2030 Executive Summary Renewable Energy Prospects: United Arab Emirates, at* http://irena.org/remap/IRENA_REmap_UAE_summary_2015.pdf (accessed May 25, 2015).

126. Ren21, *Renewable 2014: Global Status Report. Key Findings:* Renewable Energy Policy Network for the 21st Century.

127. IEA, *Regional Energy Efficiency Policy Recommendations: Arab-Southern and Eastern Mediterranean (SEMED) Region,* International Energy Agency, 2014.

128. Andrea Masini and Emanuela Menichetti, "The impact of behavioural factors in the renewable energy investment decision making process: Conceptual framework and empirical findings," *Energy Policy*, 40, 1 (2012): 28–38.

129. David de Jager and Max Rathmann, *Policy instrument design to reduce financing,* Utrecht: IEA - Renewable Energy Technology Deployment, 2008.

130. Stephen Spratt, Wenjuan Dong, Chetan Krishna, Ambuj Sagar and Qi Ye, *"What drives wind and solar energy investment in India and China,"* (Brighton: Institute of Development Studies, 2014).

131. Sonja Lüthi and Rolf Wüstenhagen, "The price of policy risk — Empirical insights from choice experiments with European photovoltaic project developers," *Energy Economics*, 34, 4 (2012): 1001–11.

132. Masini and Menichetti, "The impact of behavioural factors in the renewable energy investment decision making process: Conceptual framework and empirical findings."

133. Bassam Fattouh, "How Secure are Middle East Oil Supplies?," Oxford Institute for Energy Studies, September 2007.

134. Gideon Rose, "Energy Security in the Middle East," in *International Security Challenges in a Changing World,* eds., Kurt R. Spillmann and Joachim Krause (Bern: Peter Lang, 1999), 235–42.

135. Michael Ross, "Does Oil Hinder Democracy?," *World Politics*, 53, (2001): 325–61.

136. Richard Youngs, *Energy: A Reinforced Obstacle to Democracy*, CEPS Working Document No. 299, July 2008.

137. Marry Ann Tetreault, "The Political Economy of Middle Eastern Oil," in *Understanding the Contemporary Middle East*, 3rd Edition, eds., Jillian Schwedler and Deborah J. Gerner (Boulder, Col: Lynne Rienner Publishers, 2008), 255–79.

138. Daniel Yergin, "Ensuring Energy Security," *Foreign Affairs*, March/April 2006.

139. Janet L. Sawin and William R. Moomaw, "An Enduring Energy Future," in *2009 State of the World: Into a Warming World* (New York: W.W. Norton & Company, 2009), 131.

140. Laura El-Katiri and Muna Husain, *Prospects for Renewable Energy in GCC States: Opportunities and the Need for Reform*, OIES Paper MEP 10 (Oxford: Oxford Institute for Energy Studies, 2014).

141. IISD-RS, *Irena Bulletin*, 187 (16), January 24, 2015.

142. Mari Luomi, *The International Relations of the Green Economy in the Gulf: Lessons from the UAE's State-led Energy Transition*, OIES Paper: MEP 12 (Oxford: The Oxford Institute for Energy Studies, 2015).

Chapter 5

Managing Large Population Migration

The number of refugees and internally displaced people in the world has reached almost 60 million, roughly the equivalent of the total population of Italy. The world has never witnessed such a large number of people being pushed out of their homes since World War II. After some years of improved stability in the post–Cold War period, as the Australia-based Institute for Economics and Peace's Global Peace Index suggests, the world has been increasingly becoming more violent for the last eight years. Many of these displaced people are in the Middle East and in particular in Iraq and Syria, where ongoing civil wars have driven a large number of people from their homes.[1] Syria has now become the main refugee-producing country, overtaking Afghanistan, which had held the number one position for more than thirty years.[2] The mass movement of people has come at a huge social, economic, and political cost.

However, migration is a very complex term, which includes issues ranging from chosen to coerced movements of a population.[3] A number of demographic, economic, sociocultural, and psychological issues guide the character, shape, and course of voluntary human migration, while forced migrations are the result of civil war, political unrest and ethnic oppression, food scarcity, environmental destructions, and climate change.[4] A large volume of research on voluntary migration stresses the economic motives, arguing that people migrate to take advantage of better economic prospects in terms of employment and income. The neoclassical economic framework, with its "equilibrium model of migration," conceptualizes population movement as the geographical mobility of workers who respond to imbalances in the spatial distribution of land, labor, capital, and natural resources.[5] Throughout history, people have been forced to move because the land on which they lived could no longer support them due to deforestation, desertification, and

125

drought. However, what is a more recent phenomenon is that more people are being forced to leave their homes because of irreversible destruction of the environment and climate change impacts.[6] People are moving within and across international borders and from the rural areas to urban centers in large numbers due to economic and environmental reasons, something also discussed in the water and food security chapters (in this volume) in relation to the Syrian crisis.

While the clarification of voluntary migration is dominated by the economic approach, the causes of forced migration are usually attributed to political factors. Leon Gordenker[7] provides four political reasons for the forced movements: The first one is international war; the second, internal disturbances; the third, deliberate changes within the social structure because of political transformation; and the final one involves international political tension. Proponents who cite political reasons for forced migrations dub forced migrants "refugees," and their interpretation of forced migration seems to have been guided by the legal definition and the universal treatment of "refugees."[8]

The Middle East has an interstate migratory history dating back to the collapse of the Ottoman Empire. However, voluntary migration in a major scale began in 1970s only to the oil-rich countries. After independence, suffering from a small and untrained local population but having some of the largest endowment of oil and gas, the Gulf countries depended upon their fellow Arab countries in the region to get foreign workers. In 1971, Egypt even openly encouraged its nationals to migrate and linked the policy with the country's economic development.[9] Since 1980s, though a major part of the labor force of the oil-producing Gulf countries has moved to South Asia, labor migration from the Arab countries is high due to geographical proximity and cultural, religious, and linguistic closeness.

The Middle East has also witnessed large-scale labor migration to different places. Many migrants, particularly from the non-Gulf state, have also migrated permanently to other parts of the world, particularly from Lebanon. To compensate on the home front, Lebanon also attracts labor migrants from other neighboring countries. However, most of the countries in the region are primarily remittance-receiving countries. Remittances represent an important source of income for many countries, particularly for Egypt, Lebanon, and Jordan. In the case of Lebanon, remittances have helped improve its creditworthiness and facilitate access to international capital markets. Thus, the economy of the region is very much connected to the vagaries of the global economy.

The region not only has voluntary migrants, but it is also a source or host of a large number of forced migrants, refugees, and internally displaced persons. Since 1948, the region has been hosting a large number of Palestinian refugees and its number is more than 5 million at present.[10] Besides the

Palestinian conflict, the other long-standing issue affecting the Middle East is the Kurdish issue. The Kurds, much like the Palestinians have been, are a nation without a state. Besides, Iraq and Syria, the other two neighboring regional powers, Turkey and Iran, have substantially large Kurdish minorities. The long-standing separatist struggle of Kurds has also contributed to large-scale population displacement in the region. However, the number of refugees in the region has jumped significantly in recent years due to the ongoing violent conflict in Iraq and Syria.

Large-scale forced migration has many facets and it induces conflict between host and home states in the region.[11] In some cases, refugees, after settling in the host country, indulge in antiregime activities against their home government. Antiregime activities against their home government by Iraqis after settling in Syria or in Iran have become a major source of tension in the region, having implications for regional security. Kurdish militants' frequent use of the host state's territory against homeland regimes is very common, and security is problematic in the region as well. There is no doubt that large population displacements on account of the Israel-Palestinian conflict, Iraq War, and the Syrian Civil War have also posed a structural threat to many refugee-receiving countries in the region. Competition with the local population over resources has become a serious law and order concern. In some cases, particularly in Jordan and Lebanon, the refugees are increasingly seen as a serious threat to the host regimes. The region is increasingly getting worried about the threats posed by large-scale Syrian migration.

According to the United Nations,[12] the number of persons living outside their country of birth in the world has increased from 76 million in 1960 to 232 million in 2013 (which accounts for 3.2 percent of the world population). However, the figure represents only a small percentage of people involved in the migration and transnationalism. In today's globalized world, an increased mobility of people fuelled by better transportation and communication systems has contributed to the erosion of state boundaries and promoted globalized migrant communities, who have become an active and potentially crucial link between their countries of origin and the migrant-receiving countries. As such, studies on the role of migrant communities in either contribution to development and peace or conflict escalation have been catapulted to the forefront. The complex nature of migrants is such that in some cases they promote peace, while in others they support conflicts, depending on the various opportunity costs.[13] Migrant communities' involvement in homeland politics is not a new phenomenon. As a consequence of globalization, migrants have built vast transnational networks, with a potential to contribute to peace, reconciliation, and development. In recent decades, remittances received from migrants have become an invaluable form of economic support for the homeland.

IMPORTANCE OF REMITTANCES AND
CHALLENGES OF FOREIGN WORKERS

Remittances are generally considered as the flow of funds from migrant workers back to their home countries. Remittance is not only an important source of income in many developing economies, but it is also a critical element for development, with increasingly enormous aggregate cash flows and number of stakeholders. The huge international flows of remittances have significantly increased in recent years, so their impact is "only beginning to be understood."[14] According to the World Bank's estimation, officially recorded remittance flows to developing countries have been $436 billion in 2014.[15] Remittances are an important source of both family and national income in many developing countries, representing in some cases up to a third of GDP for recipient countries and accounting for about a third of the total global external finance. Moreover, the flow of remittances constitutes a higher percentage of national income in poorer and smaller countries and is more stable than other forms of external finance. Developing countries in total receive nearly double from remittances than they get from official development assistance.[16] As part of a larger stream of financial transfers between migrant communities and their homelands, remittances are thought to play an important role in preventing conflict,[17] reducing the effects of wars,[18] and contributing to postconflict reconstruction.[19]

Monetary remittances are sent through different ways, depending on cost, speed, and convenience. A variety of flows, from the migrants themselves or from their descendants, are sent as financial transfers to support their relatives or friends in their country of origin or to finance economic investment. Besides, remittance flows are transferred by individuals or as collective philanthropic support to development projects. However, remittances can also be considered to cover in-kind gifts, value transfers, domestic financial transfers (in case of internal migration), as well as financial flows to developed economies. The presence of millions of migrant communities who are regularly connected to their homelands in the Middle East, as well as the impact that these connections have on local economies and on various dynamics, including development, is not negligible. Interestingly, migrant communities interact in complex global networks with mixed identities and loyalties with their country of origin, while also adapting and identifying in varying degrees with the host country. Remittances are considered the tool of choice by which most migrants assist the development process in their homelands.[20] The effectiveness of remittances as a tool in a country's development process is due in part to the fact that they are stable, countercyclical, and augment the recipient's income more directly than official aid could. Remittance is extremely important if a country is smaller in size and economically weak.

Though migrant communities have always transferred remittances to their homelands for several generations, their contributions have largely been ignored in the past. However, in recent years, evidence showing the role of remittances in stimulating the economies of developing countries has catapulted their relevance to the forefront and caught the attention of the international community. Fragile countries susceptible to conflict situations and crisis management are especially dependent on remittances as a tool to resolve conflicts, build infrastructure, reduce poverty, and promote broad-based economic development.[21] Remittances can help promote economic recovery and thus consolidate the foundations of stability and peace. Private sector investments through remittances can contribute to building the kinds of institutional mechanisms and services needed in poor and fragile countries. On the other hand, remittances are used primarily for consumable goods, not for a long-term sustainable growth of country's economy. Remittances can be politicized and thereby contribute in creating tensions. Person-to-person remittances are important for families, but they do not have as direct an impact on the society or state as business remittances do. Moreover, remittance capital can be termed a "coward," since it does not stay where it is risky. Thus, the hope of receiving remittance capital might force countries to maintain political order. Tourism remittances, although romantic in nature, since they come "home" every summer or winter, need a peaceful environment to thrive.

Table 5.1   Remittance Inflows as a Share of the Middle Eastern Countries' GDP

Country	Remittances as a Share of GDP in 2013	Remittance Inflows in 2014 (in USD Millions)	Remittance Outflows in 2013 (in USD Millions)
Bahrain	-		2,166
Egypt	6.6%	19,612	-
Iraq	0.1%	271	-
Israel	0.3%	901	5,025
Jordan	10.8%	3,757	457
Kuwait	0%	4	15,242
Lebanon	17.7%	8,899	4,659
Oman	0%	39	9,104
Palestine (West Bank and Gaza)	-	2,294	10
Qatar	0.3%	496	11,281
Saudi Arabia	0%	272	34,984
Syria	-	1,623	-
UAE	-	-	17,933
Yemen	9.3%	3,455	333

Source: The World Bank (worldbank.org).

Nearly 13 percent of the total global remittance (inward and outward) comes from the Middle East. Saudi Arabia is second and UAE is sixth among the top 10 remittance-sending countries in the world. A large share of remittance sent from these two countries also goes to other countries in the region. Around 70 percent of the total remittance sent and received in the Middle East is from Saudi Arabia and UAE. Middle East is the third largest hub of migration in the world and its oil-rich Gulf countries have been hosting more than 15 million foreign labor force. The six member states of the GCC, Bahrain, Kuwait, Oman, Qatar, Saudi Arabia, and the UAE, pay out more than $100 billion in worker remittances to migrant workers living within their borders.

With increased oil production in 1970s, demand increased for skilled and unskilled labor in the Gulf states. Once the oil-producing countries in the region started raising oil prices, oil-importing states began sending migrant workers there. Currently, Saudi Arabia is the largest recipient of migrant workers, with the UAE close behind with over two-thirds of its population classified as migrant workers. Remittance transfers from permanent migrants usually diminish over a period of time, as linkages between migrants and their country of origin weaken over time. The second-generation migrants might culturally and emotionally remain connected with their parental homeland, but they more or less distance themselves from any economic activities and obligations. The policies of the Gulf countries give priority in providing short-term work permits to the young migrant workforce and bar them from settling permanently. So, most of the foreign workforce in Gulf countries are temporary migrants, and this factor encourages them to continue sending most of their savings as remittances.

Remittances carry an extremely important value for the economic development of the non-oil-exporting countries of the Middle East. More than 2.7 million Egyptian migrants are working abroad, and approximately 70 percent of them are living in Arab countries. For a country like Egypt, remittances are three times more than the foreign exchange revenues from the Suez Canal or incomes from tourism or even from direct foreign investment in the country. Remittances represent the largest source of foreign exchange after exports and a critical source of household income in Egypt. According to the World Bank, in 2014, Egypt was the biggest recipient of remittances in the region, an estimated $19.6 billion, representing approximately 6.6 percent of the national GDP. However, the remittance share used to be 10 percent of the country's GDP in 2008, before the advent of the global financial crisis and the Arab Spring. The absence of favorable investment opportunities, high interest rates, and highly cumbersome exchange transactions also act as disincentives for migrant Egyptian workers to send home remittances.

The high increase in oil prices in the mid-1970s led to large-scale labor emigration from Egypt to the oil-producing Arab states. Before this surge,

Egyptians were already working in the Gulf countries but only in small numbers and mostly as professionals and skilled workers. In the 1980s, Iraq hosted the largest number of Egyptian unskilled workers of nearly 1 million. As the Iraqi army was drafting a large number of Iraqi men of working age to fight the war with Iran, Egyptian workers were needed in the country.[22] In the 1990s, because of economic sanctions in Iraq, Saudi Arabia, Kuwait, and the UAE became the major destinations of Egyptian migrant workers.

Besides Egypt, the economies of Lebanon, Jordan, and Yemen are very much dependent on their received remittances. Jordan received $3.757 billion in remittances from its citizens working overseas in 2014. This figure represents only officially recorded remittances and it does not include remittances in kind and unrecorded ones. Jordan is a small country with a very limited resource base. Remittances are the biggest source of foreign exchange for this oil-importing country and a major pillar of economic frame. Most of the remittance-sending Jordanians are living in the oil-producing countries in the Gulf.[23] The issue of remittance has worked as a double-edged sword for Jordan. No doubt, it has a made a very significant contribution to the country's income, but at the same time it has brought high inflation from outside, particularly in the real estate sector, and has led to a serious shortage of certain domestic skills. Moreover, the country's economic health is highly dependent on the Arab economies.

Lebanon has received $8.899 billion as remittances for 2014, which is approximately 17.7 percent of the country's GDP. In receiving remittances, Lebanon comes second in the Middle East, only behind Egypt. Historically, Lebanon has experienced several migration waves. From 1850 to World War I, a third of the country's population migrated mainly to North and South America. Though migration continued after the end of World War II, a large number of Lebanese again left the country to escape its long civil war, which started in 1975 and continued till 1990. Lebanese overseas diaspora is estimated to be 14 million, more than three times the size of the country's domestic population of about 4 million. However, the major portion of remittances to Lebanon primarily comes from recent migrants who have been working in the Gulf countries. Lebanese migrants working in Arab Gulf countries provide more than two-thirds of the country's total remittances.[24] Remittances constitute a major pillar of the Lebanese economy and play a critical role in poverty alleviation in this politically volatile country. However, Lebanon's overdependence on foreign financial inflows tends to contribute to an increase in consumption, which, in turn, has not led to the setting up of productive industries that are needed for sustained and long-term broad-based growth.[25] Moreover, Lebanon not only receives remittances, it has also been a source of remittances for some neighboring countries, particularly for Syria. There were nearly 300,000 Syrian workers in Lebanon before the Syrian crisis.[26]

Yemen, one of the poorest countries in the region, where a third of its 25 million people live on less than $2 a day, received $3.455 billion as remittances in 2014, almost 9.3 percent of the country's gross domestic product. Nearly, one million Yemenis work in Saudi Arabia, sending an estimated $1.4 billion for their families back home. Since the 1970s, Yemen's economic health has been very much tied to remittances received from the oil-rich countries of the Persian Gulf. Wages sent home from the Yemeni workers turned the country's agricultural economy into an unsustainable hub for the importation of consumer goods. The Saudi government expelled a large number of Yemeni workers in 1990 in retaliation for Sanaa's support for Iraq after it invaded Kuwait, and this caused a serious economic crisis in Yemen and contributed to some extent to the country's 1994 civil war.[27] A similar crisis occurred in 2013, when Saudi Arabia, in order to reduce black market in labor and facilitate Saudi citizens to find jobs, started mass expulsion of migrant workers, including a large number of Yemenis. The deportation of Yemeni workers came to a halt in late March 2015, following the intensification of violent conflict in Yemen, in which Saudi armed forces were involved.

Due to political unrest, civil wars, and falling crude oil price, remittances to many countries in the region have declined during the last few years. The future projection is not very promising, though the inflow of remittances is more reliable than other external resources available to the region. Saudi Arabia, the major provider of remittances to countries in the Middle East, is gradually enforcing restrictive labor laws as the oil-rich kingdom is seeking to increase the numbers of Saudi nationals working in the private sector through nationalization policies like the Nitiqat program. This has affected most of the remittance-receiving countries in the region, particularly Egypt and Yemen. Nearly 300,000 Egyptians were asked to leave the kingdom, which is the destination for about 37 percent of Egyptian migrants, in the second half of 2013.[28] The ongoing crisis in Syria is highly problematic in terms of access to payment systems and remittances. Most of the remittances that used to be sent in to the country are now needed to be sent to Syrian refugees in their host countries. Moreover, the procedure of sending whatever remittances going into Syria has become exceedingly difficult as Syrian banks no longer allow transfers from some Gulf states.

With the oil boom of the 1970s, most of the Gulf countries, including Saudi Arabia, imported cheap labor from Asia, Africa, and also from the neighboring countries in the Middle East. Saudi Arabia has continued to accept millions of these foreign workers, with most in lower-income jobs. In recent years, this practice has created serious problems for the country's economy. Saudi citizens have witnessed high levels of unemployment as it peaked in 2011 at 12.4 percent.[29] Besides the global economic slowdown, Saudi workers face stiff competition from lower paid foreign workers. Moreover, the dependence on cheap foreign workforce has resulted in the country not investing enough to train its own nationals in order to be integrated into the labor market.

As the kingdom grappled with declining oil revenue, high unemployment among its nationals, and the lingering threat of domestic unrest, Saudi authorities began streamlining the process of recruiting foreign workers through the Nitaqat policy which aims at "Saudizing" the workforce. From November 2013, Saudi authorities started deporting "illegal" foreign workers in a nationwide campaign after years of lax law enforcement. The crackdown by the interior ministry on those foreigners who had been residing illegally, which resulted in violation of labor laws, forced one million to leave the kingdom in 2013 alone. This has created some challenges for the authorities to finding trained workforce within the country to fill in the positions vacated by the foreign workers. However, as 30 percent of Saudi Arabia's population are immigrants from other countries, changes in the Saudi labor laws affect not only the workers but also their families around the world. Most of the deported foreign workers were from South and South East Asia, and also a sizable number were from Egypt and Yemen. With Saudi Arabia being the first source of remittances for many Arab and Asian countries, such deportations may have significant economic consequences on their fragile economies.[30]

Over the past few decades, the UAE has become a popular destination for temporary labor migrants, both low- and high-skilled, particularly from Asia and the Middle East. Despite a drop in oil prices and the global financial crisis of 2008, the UAE still attracts a large number of foreign workers due to its economic attractiveness, relative political stability, and modern infrastructure. The country now hosts the fifth largest international migrant stock in the world. To meet its labor demand, the UAE introduced the Kafala Sponsorship System in 1971, which allows nationals, expatriates, and companies to hire migrant workers. This guest workers' program has posed some challenges for the UAE authorities. There is growing resentment within the country over the lack of job opportunities for UAE nationals.

Foreign workers usually get lower wages than UAE nationals, and they have shown willingness to work in adverse conditions and for long hours. These have been the reasons for foreign workers dominating the private sector by cornering more than 98 percent of the positions available.[31] Responding to public concerns about foreign workers, the UAE government has occasionally used restrictive immigration measures and even imposed temporary bans on migrants from certain labor-sending countries. Moreover, there have been widespread concerns about the appalling treatment of foreign workers in the UAE, who constitute 80 percent of the population and 95 percent of the workforce.[32] Under the kafala system, foreign workers are excluded from national labor laws, and their labor complaints are primarily dealt with only by police.

Moreover, since 2004, UAE has created a system of preferences for its own nationals in the labor market. This *Emiratization* policy includes a set of rules that protect its own nationals, known as Emirati, from open competition with foreign workers in both the public and private sectors. Due to increasing popular unrest, the UAE government launched a new "Absher Initiative" in 2012, which aims at further improving Emiratis' chances in the job market. These restrictive policies against foreign workers of a major host country, of course, create new challenges for remittance-receiving countries in the region.

Labor migration flows to Gulf countries have posed a critical public policy challenge in the region. The UAE, which is relatively more open than other Gulf countries and at least makes some cosmetic attempts in addressing human rights concerns of the migrants, still tries to balance labor market needs with native-born employment. Qatar, which is slated to host the FIFA World Cup in 2022, has brought in a large number of migrant workers under the kafala system to build its stadiums and other infrastructure. However, the country has attracted huge international condemnation as it has failed to make much progress in improving migrant workers' rights, partly due to pressure from native workforce and social groups. Other Gulf countries like Bahrain and Oman with large numbers of migrant workers are also struggling with similar challenges and have taken several measures to regulate temporary labor migration over the past several years. Some have restricted migration inflows and carried out deportation of "illegal workers," while others have undertaken policies of providing positive discrimination to increase the native-born share of their workforces. In 2013, Kuwait announced to reduce by a million the number of migrant workers in the country over a ten-year period.[33] In the Gulf, policies aimed at forcing more locals into the job market have accelerated in recent years due to the fear that high native-born unemployment, in particular among youth, might lead to political unrest similar to what took place in countries that experienced the Arab Spring.

While the rich oil-producing countries in the Middle East are imposing restrictions on the entry of new migrant workers and are even deporting those who are there already in a bid to prevent social unrest at home, there is the possibility that this policy would create economic hardships and political uncertainties in those countries in the region that send workers to the rich countries. Remittances from the Gulf countries not only provide a major source of foreign direct investment to the fragile economies of Egypt, Jordan, Lebanon, and Yemen, but also supply aid and relief via family-to-family transfer in times of hardship. The large financial transfers play a significant role in preventing conflict in these vulnerable societies and also contribute to postconflict reconstruction and economic recovery. Migrants are also an important source of tourism in these Middle Eastern states where collapsing infrastructure and fear of terror attacks otherwise discourage it. By providing support for the livelihood of those who stay behind, remittances reduce the scope of further forced migration from these countries. And by supporting basic services such as health care and education in these poor Middle Eastern countries, remittances sustain the structures that foster social network and interpersonal trust and provide a basis for future economic recovery. The adverse impacts of restrictive migrant-receiving policies in the oil-rich Gulf states are now being felt by the rest of the countries in the Middle East.

THE MIDDLE EAST: THE REGION OF AND FOR REFUGEES

International interventions and civil wars have created a serious refugee crisis in the region. The massive number of people being forced out of their homes in the region has created unprecedented humanitarian crisis, which has become serious international concern. Most of the displaced people have remained inside the region, and the host states for these "conflicts migrants" are not the oil-rich Gulf countries, but primarily their poorer neighbors. The refugee crisis is not new to the region as it has experienced two large waves of forced migration in the last century and two more in the short time period of this century. The two long-term refugee crises involve Kurdish and Palestinian displacement and the new ones are originating from Iraq and Syria.

Kurds are living in an area of 230,000 square miles spread into the territories of several countries in the Middle East, which are Turkey, Iraq, Iran, Syria, and also in Armenia. There is a considerable Kurdish immigrant population close to nearly half a million living in European countries. Kurds are mostly Sunni Muslims and speak Kurdish which is related to Persian and not to Arabic or Turkish. Most of the Kurdish people (approximately 45 percent) live in Turkey, while in Iraq the figure is 20 percent, in Iran it is 20 percent, in Syria 5 percent, and the rest in Armenia and in other countries.[34] However, it is not easy to accurately determine the exact numbers of Kurdish population as the states in the Middle East regularly downplay the numbers of their minority population for political reasons; the Kurdish groups usually provide inflated numbers to shore up their political importance.[35]

After the fall of the Ottoman Empire, post–World War I treaties created the Middle Eastern countries of Syria and Iraq, but refused to create a Kurdish state. Even the Treaty of Lausanne, which recognized the formation of the Turkish Republic, did not keep any provision for allowing Kurdish autonomy. Turkey, Syria, Iraq, and Iran joined hands to restrict the Kurdish aspiration for a separate state and this led the Kurds to rebel way back in the 1920s. In recent decades, violent movements of the Kurdish Workers Party (PKK) in Turkey and the Turkish response have led to the loss of over 30,000 lives and massive permanent and periodic forced migration. In the late 1980s,

Saddam Hussein's Anfal Campaign against Kurds in Iran reportedly led to at least 50,000 deaths and forced displacement of a large population, with many of them fleeing to Turkey.[36] However, when a major outflow of Kurds from northern Iraq took place in the Gulf War in 1991 after their rebellion was crushed by Iraqi troops, Turkey refused to admit them, so the US-led coalition forces created a "safe haven" for them inside Iraqi territory in the north. However, only after the Second Gulf War in 2003 did the Kurds in Iraq receive some kind of autonomy. In Syria and Iraq, there have been several attempts to crush Kurdish ethnicity as well. Overall, the political condition of the Kurdish minority had improved in Turkey and Iraq in the last decade.

However, the recent ISIS crisis has exposed the Kurds in these two countries to greater uncertainties, while a large number of Kurdish refugees are still living in various countries within and outside of the Middle East. The ongoing civil war in Syria has the potential to increase conflict among Kurdish groups within Turkey. In the 1980s and 1990s, Syria used to provide base and other kinds of support to the PKK in its armed struggle against Turkey.[37] In 1998, after making a deal with Turkey, Syria expelled the PKK from its territory and started supporting Turkey in its military operations against Kurdish groups. However, with the intensification of the civil war, the Syrian authorities withdrew troops from the northern Kurdish area and left it to be run by the dominant Syrian Kurdish political party, Democratic Union Party (PYD). This party has strong ideological links with the PKK, which has led Turkey to suspect that the increased autonomy of Kurds in Syria will strengthen the demands of its own Kurdish population. Though Turkey has started to develop diplomatic relations with the Kurdistan Regional Government (KRG) in Iraq for some years now in the hope of getting access to its energy resource, it is still apprehensive about the Kurdish groups in Syria due to its historical closeness with the PKK. Turkey even withheld humanitarian aid to the Syrian Kurdish area for some time in 2013[38] and also in late 2014, when ISIS militants seized the Kurdish town of Kobane on the Turkey-Syria border.[39] Developments during this year have led to the breakdown of the truce between the PKK and the Turkish government, and the fighting has intensified. At the same time, Turkey has also started to attack the ISIS.

As a byproduct of the civil war, the given autonomy to Syria's Kurdish majority areas has provided some opportunity for Kurds in the region to come closer politically and militarily in their fight for a separate statehood. Though it has fueled the rise of Kurdish nationalism across the northern Middle East, Kurds in Syria do not possess enough political or military muscle to determine the outcome of the conflict or their own future trajectory. The domestic politics within Syria, Iraq, Turkey, and Iran and regional geopolitics will be crucial factors in deciding the aspirations of the Kurds. Thus, it is very hard to foresee the early resolution of this nearly 100-year-old separatist insurgency and end of the hardships of the large displaced Kurdish population.

The other long-term refugee crisis, which is affecting this region and the world, is the case of Palestinian refugees. The UN General Assembly established the United Nations Relief and Works Agency for Palestine Refugees in the Near East (UNRWA) to provide humanitarian assistance to more than 700,000 Palestinians who were displaced as a result of the 1948 Arab-Israeli war. In 1967, the six-day war also displaced another large number of Palestinians. For the past 67 years, millions of displaced Palestinians have been living as refugees in West Bank and Gaza and in the surrounding host countries—mostly in Jordan, Lebanon, and Syria. In 2014, there were more than 5.5 million Palestinian refugees living in refugee camps.

The refugee issue has been one of the most difficult and complex issues in Israeli-Arab relations.[40] Israelis and Palestinians do not even agree on the reasons of displacement in 1948. While Palestinians say that they were expelled by Israeli forces, Israelis argue that Palestinians fled as Arab commanders encouraged them to do so in a war that was foisted upon a newly born Israel by Arab neighbors. Similarly, Israel also blames Arab host states for their failure to resettle the refugees, while Palestinians blame the international community for failing to make Israel agree for refugee return. Moreover, both the parties even fail to agree on whom to consider a refugee: while Israel argues for the narrow definition covering only first-generation refugees displaced by the 1948 and 1967 wars, Palestinians ask for a broad and inclusive definition covering family members.[41] During the last decades, critical Israeli historians such as Benny Morris[42] have analyzed the Arab-Israeli wars, including providing accounts of how most Palestinians were actually expelled by the Jewish army.

Table 5.2   Palestinian Refugees in the Middle East in 2015

	Jordan	Lebanon	Syria (Working Estimate)	West Bank	Gaza Strip	Total
Registered refugees (RR)	2,117,361	452,669	528,616	774,167	1,276,929	5,149,742
Other registered persons	95,556	40,465	63,164	168,017	72,544	439,746
Total registered persons (RP)	2,212,917	493,134	591,780	942,184	1,349,473	5,589,488
Increase in RP over previous year (%)	2.7	2	3.9	3	3	3
Official camps	10	12	9	3	8	58

Source: The United Nations Relief and Works Agency for Palestine Refugees (UNRWA), unrwa.org.

The majority of displaced Palestinians are located in Jordan, hosting around 2.2 million refugees within its borders in 10 refugee camps. Jordan's relationship with Palestinian refugees is extremely precarious. The demographic character of this small kingdom went through a metamorphosis after the influx of a large number of Palestinian refugees in 1948 and 1967. With Jordan's claim over the West Bank, Palestinians in Jordan outnumbered the local population. Besides the demographic imbalances, the large presence of Palestinian refugees in Jordan has transformed its political, economic, and sociocultural life. In 1970, in what is termed "Black September," the Palestinian Liberation Organization (PLO) unsuccessfully attempted to overthrow the Jordanian regime and capture power. This led to a violent reaction from the regime, and the PLO was expelled to Lebanon. In the pursuit of preserving national identity and also due to an Arab consensus to recognize the PLO as the sole representative of the Palestinian people, Jordan formally renounced all legal claims to the West Bank in 1988.[43]

Jordan sees the Palestinians as a "demographic threat" and is constantly striving for a solution to this problem. Palestinian refugees face discriminatory policies by the host state, particularly in getting employment in the government sector and in playing a very marginal role in the country's politics. But at the same time they constitute the backbone of Jordan's economy. The perceived mistreatment of Palestinians inside Jordan is a ticking bomb waiting to explode.[44] The situation is almost similar for Palestinian refugees in neighboring Lebanon. After being expelled by Jordan due to its misadventure in 1970, the PLO established itself in southern Lebanon. Influx of a large number of Sunni Muslim Palestinians threatened to upset the precariously poised Christian-Muslim balance in this highly segmented country. When Lebanon got entangled in a civil war in 1975, the PLO played a part in it; however, it fled to Tunisia after the Israeli invasion of south Lebanon in 1982. In the late 1980s, the Syrian-backed, Shia militia group, Amal Movement, launched several attacks on Palestinian refugee camps in Lebanon to drive out the remaining pro-Arafat PLO militants.[45] Even the violent conflict between Hizbullah and Israel in July-August 2006 brought a lot of miseries to mostly Palestinian refugees in the south of Lebanon.[46] Since 1975, many Palestinian refugees in Lebanon have been displaced, some of them several times.[47]

There are more than 450,000 Palestinian refugees living in Lebanon. The Lebanese government brackets all Palestinians who have arrived after 1948 as "illegal residents" and restricts their entry into the job markets and prevents them from even owning and inheriting properties. Palestinian refugees in Lebanon are highly discriminated and Lebanon has placed several legal restrictions, denying them political, social, and civil rights. However, the condition of Palestinian refugees in Syria was relatively better before the country plunged into the ongoing civil war and also when compared to their counterparts in Jordan and Lebanon. Syria had housed approximately 590,000 Palestinian refugees. Though they were not given citizenship and voting rights, they had the rights to employment, commerce, and national service and also access to a special travel document. However, the ongoing conflict has created an extremely difficult situation for Palestinians living in refugee camps in Syria.

In spite of the raging civil war, the UNRWA estimates that approximately 95 percent of the refugees still live in its camps inside Syria and are in continuous need of humanitarian support. Though the neighboring countries of Syria, Jordan, and Lebanon have accepted a large number of Syrian refuges, they have closed their borders to Palestinian refugees. So, the escaping Palestinian refugees are being forced to take more unsafe routes through Turkey. Moreover, Palestinian refugees are extremely vulnerable in the new host countries since they do not have any legal status nationality or civil registration number.[48] The civil war in Syria has brought extreme damage to the Palestinian refugee camps in the country. The combatants are committing severe human rights violations and are using heavy weapons with targeted attacks on civilian areas. The direct attacks on Palestinian refugee camps have displaced more than 50 percent of the Palestinians within the country.[49]

Prior to the Syrian crisis, the condition of Palestinian refugees in Lebanon was quite hazardous. The Syrian conflict has resulted in a further influx of 44,000 Palestinian refugees to Lebanon, and they have become extremely vulnerable due to their irregular legal status and limited social protection services as well as available livelihood opportunities. All these refugees are being given a very short time period to regularize their residential status. Moreover, they are highly concentrated in peripheral regions and in some of the poorest areas of Lebanon. The housing of Syrian refugees exacerbates the already difficult living conditions of poor host communities and has generated increased tensions.[50] From 2013, Lebanon has severely restricted the entry of Palestinian refugees from Syria and there are only rare cases of allowed entry into the country. The condition of the Palestinian refugees escaping the Syrian civil war to Jordan is also fairly similar. Only Palestinians who have Jordanian national documents are allowed to enter Jordan from Syria. This has forced many to take irregular and unsafe routes into the country, and they are living under constant uncertainty and risk. There are around 15,000 Palestinian refugees from Syria who have approached the UNRWA for assistance in Jordan. Due to Jordan's restrictive policy, the majority of Palestinian refugees from Syria have not been able to receive any assistance from other humanitarian agencies operating in the country, besides the UNRWA.[51]

Quite similar to the present situation in Syria, Palestinian refugees in Iraq also suffered harsh treatment and dual displacement in the post–Saddam period.[52] Approximately 15,000 Palestinian refugees were living in Iraq.

These "Sunni" refugees were receiving subsidies and other privileges under Saddam Hussein's regime. However, after the US invasion in 2003, the Palestinian refugees were subjected to an anti-Sunni backlash, as Shias suspected them for supporting the Sunni insurgency. Palestinians repeatedly received death threats and were attacked by insurgents. When these Palestinians wanted to move to Jordan or Syria, they were not allowed on legal grounds and were kept in the refugee camps at the border. The predicament of Palestinian refugees, wherever they are in the region, seems to be continuing even after being displaced for nearly seven decades.

Besides the long-running refugee situation concerning Kurdish and Palestinian displacements, the region has been also exposed to new waves of refugee crises. In the last decade, a major refugee crisis started with the displacement of Iraqis after the United States launched its attack against Iraq in 2003. In the immediate aftermath of the fall of the Saddam regime, there were some Saddam loyalists who left the country, but the number was not significant. However, the civil war in the country, which took a serious turn after the attack on the Samarra Shrine in 2006, produced a serious humanitarian crisis by displacing a large number of people. Many left the country, and also a very substantial number of the displaced population moved to "safe" areas within Iraq. By March 2007, according to the UNHCR estimates, more than 2 million Iraqis became refugees and 1.9 million were internally displaced. Most of the Iraqi refugees landed up in neighboring Jordan and Syria. The international community was underprepared to meet these challenges as it had not anticipated the outbreak of civil war after the removal of the Saddam regime in Iraq.

The large Iraqi displacement during 2006–2007 became a serious regional challenge. Many feared that the large-scale population migration from Iraq might spread instability to the rest of the region by enhancing not only economic challenges but also sectarian differences. Of the 2 million Iraqi refugees in 2007, it is estimated that more than 700,000 were in Jordan. After the 1991 Gulf War, Jordan had received a sizable number of Iraqi refugees, but

Table 5.3   Forced Migration from Iraq in 2007

Receiving Country	Iraqi Refugees
Syria	1,000,000
Jordan	700,000–800,000
Egypt	130,000
Lebanon	40,000–50,000
Iran	54,000
Turkey	5,000
Iraq (internally displaced people)	1,900,000

Source: Kristéle Younés, The World's Fastest Growing Humanitarian Crisis (Washington DC: Refugee International, 2007).

many of them were doctors, academics, and economically sound people.[53] Approximately, 250,000 to 300,000 Iraqis were already living in Jordan before the 2003 US-led invasion of Iraq.[54] Immediately after the fall of the Saddam regime, the demographics of Iraqi refugees going to Jordan were similar to those of the post–1991 group. From 2003 to 2006, Jordan accepted Iraqis with few restrictions and several Iraqi political activists also took sanctuary in Jordan. However, with the spread of the civil war, poorer unskilled Iraqis began to arrive in Jordan and this led Jordan to impose new border restrictions and hinder the flow of Iraqi refugees.[55]

Most of the Iraqis escaping to Jordan were Sunni Muslims with links to the Saddam regime. This caused concern to the Jordanian authorities and they feared the rise of Sunni Islamic militancy in the country. However, being a Sunni majority country, Jordan was much more concerned about the arrival of Shias, though it never officially accepted this. The arrival of a large number of poor and unskilled workers also compounded the economic and ecological vulnerabilities of the country. Apart from facing the challenges of coping with the huge unemployment crisis and rising inflation, Jordan found it difficult to even provide food and water to an increasing population.[56]

As it was in the case of Jordan, the first Iraqi wave to enter Syria following the US invasion consisted of professionals and also politically active members of the Baath Party. However, the fighting in Falluja in November 2004 created a major exodus of common Iraqis, but they were still mostly Sunnis, to Syria.[57] However, the civil war pushed more and more Shias to Syria. In 2007, the official number of Iraqi refugees in Syria was estimated to be one million, in a country of approximately 18 million population. Though Syrians were more considerate toward Iraqi refugees, the country's law did not allow them to work legally, which led to their further deprivation and vulnerability. As the number started growing, the resentment and hostility against poor Iraqi refugees became apparent on the streets of Syrian cities. From late 2007, Syrian authorities started restricting the entry of Iraqis following the similar policy of its neighbor Jordan. Though a relatively small number of Iraqi refugees moved to Lebanon, their situation was most vulnerable. Most of the refugees were Shias and lived in Beirut's southern suburbs. However, unlike Jordan and Syria, and Egypt, the Lebanese state did not avail any social support for refugees.

Iraqi refugees prioritized the countries where they chose to go to along sectarian lines. A large majority of Iraqi refugees in Jordan were Sunnis, while Shia Iraqis went to Jordan and Lebanon. In spite of this, by 2008, the host countries of Iraqi refugees in the region became extremely restrictive in accepting any more migration and wanted Iraqis to return as soon as possible to avoid political instability. Even the Iraqi government wanted the neighboring countries to close their borders in order to assert its control in the border areas. Growing poverty and lack of possibility to find work in the host countries also led many refugees to think of going back to their own country. There was also some improvement in the security situation in Iraq, which facilitated the process of refugees to return.

However, this return has not been smooth. Though highly stressed, host country capacities and the incentives offered by the Iraqi government and the international community expedited the process of refugee returns, but this also led to further tensions at the place of their resettlement. The formal end of conflict did not take away all of its manifestations and left behind intentionally created ethnically and religiously homogeneous societies. Sectarian control of neighborhoods because of civil war made it very unsafe for many returnees and they became internally displaced again. The situation became further volatile after the escalation of armed conflict in the central parts of Iraq after the rise of the ISIS. This led to new displacements across central Iraq and also in the northern Kurdistan region. Though by December 2014, the number of Iraqi refugees receiving international assistance came down to nearly 370,000, the number of internally displaced Iraqis went up close to 4 million.[58] This high internal displacement is due to a rapidly changing security situation in the country, thanks to rapid ISIS expansion. The ISIS has made it a goal to specifically target different religious and ethnic communities in the country such as Christians, Shia Muslims, Druze, Yazidis, Kurds, and Turkomen, and the displacement is to survive and escape abductions, massacres, forced marriages, and sexual enslavement.[59]

Syria has been the source of the latest refugee crisis in the region, which has triggered the largest humanitarian challenge since World War II. The same Syria, which used to host the second largest number of refugee population in 2008 (after Pakistan), has turned out to be the largest refugee producer since 2012. In 2011, the so-called Arab Spring came to Syria, and the violent clampdown on the protests by the regime led to increased political unrest, and by mid-2012, the country faced an ugly civil war. The fight did not remain limited to the Free Syrian Army, led by generals who defected from the Syrian army and forces loyal to the regime. Terror groups linked to the al-Qaeda also became a party to the conflict. The civil war dragged on, contributing to the growing regional instability and turning extremely serious with the advance of the ISIS across large areas of Syria. The conflict severely impacted civilians, resulting in large-scale displacement and migration both inside Syria and also to the neighboring countries of Turkey, Lebanon, Jordan, and Iraq.[60] A large number of Syrians entered Turkey, which has become the main destination for refugees in the world.

The total number of people in need of humanitarian assistance in Syria reached more than 11.5 million by December 2014, approximately 7.6 million who were internally displaced.[61] Syria, in such a short time period, has earned the dubious distinction of having the largest number of internally displaced persons in any country in the world. Till mid-2015, the humanitarian burden of the Syrian crisis was being taken up mainly by Syria's neighbors, with Jordan, Lebanon, and Turkey currently providing shelter to most of the displaced Syrians. The region, which is already hosting millions of Palestinian and Iraqi refugees for years and which is grappling with a huge flow of fresh refugees from Syria, is stretching the limits of its economic and social resources.[62]

For many decades before the Syrian refugee crisis, the world had not witnessed such a large refugee population originating from a single conflict. Neighboring countries hosting Syrian refugees have almost reached their saturation points, particularly Lebanon, Jordan, and Turkey. With the growing influx of refugees, local communities are under growing pressure in terms of livelihood resources, such as food, water, education, health services, and employment. The impact created by these refugees challenges the already precarious stability of the host country in general and host communities in particular. Tensions caused by economic difficulties, social issues, and changing ethnic and sectarian balances have resulted in conflicts between the host country nationals and the Syrian refugees.[63] Thus, the neighbors have stepped up border restrictions and controls as well as security measures in and along areas bordering Syria. Jordan has almost closed the border, so a large number of asylum seekers have been stranded in no-man's land at the border. In the Kurdish region of Iraq, which hosts a significant number of Syrian refugees, there are serious doubts about the capacities of institutional infrastructure to meet the challenge.

The continuing large exodus from Syria and almost saturation in neighboring countries' capacity to host more have forced hundreds of thousands of people to seek shelter in Europe now. This has created a serious public policy challenge for the countries in Europe. However, the number of migrants passing through the Balkans and across the Aegean and Mediterranean to reach Europe account for less than 10 percent of the total Syrian refugees, as most of them are still confined inside the neighboring countries in the region.[64]

Though the focus of the international community is on the Syrian displaced population moving out of the country, particularly reaching European borders, the plight of more than 7.6 million internally displaced people does not receive much attention. In the Syrian civil war, the gross human rights violations by all the groups in the conflict are the foundational driver of this huge number of internal displacements. There is an indiscriminate use of weapons, aerial bombardments, and attacks on civilian locations. Not only are civilians targeted in Syria, there are also indications that human rights and humanitarian law violations are discriminatory in nature, in that these are directed at people belonging to a specific geographical origin and at those with religious, political, or other affiliations. This has been the major cause for this large human displacement.[65] Nearly half of the Syrian population have become refugees or internally displaced since the outbreak of the Syrian conflict.[66]

The other ongoing violent conflict in the region, which has recently displaced a large number of people, is the civil war in Yemen. The total number of internally displaced people in Yemen is 1,439,100.[67] Yemenis are being displaced as the result of the growing socioeconomic and humanitarian crisis in the country. However, there are several conflicts in the country: the Shia al-Houthi movements in the north causing violent insurgency, the civil unrest in the central and southern parts of the country, and the clashes between government forces and militants associated with the Southern Separatist Movement and Ansar al-Sharia, which is an offshoot of the al-Qaeda in the Arabian Peninsula.[68] The increasing intervention of external forces, particularly Saudi Arabia, has made the conflict in Yemen increasingly complicated as people are being forced to flee more than once, resulting in complex displacement patterns. According to an IDMC estimation, approximately 96 percent of the internally displaced people in Yemen are staying in urban settings and are not seeking shelter in relief camps due to the cultural perceptions of the environment being promiscuous.[69]

Besides a large number of refugees, the region has also produced internally displaced people (IDP) on a massive scale. Though the conditions of the IDPs have been the same as those of refugees, the only difference is that the former have stayed inside their home countries under the "protection" of a regime which is mostly responsible for their plight and which considers them as its enemy. Those who have been unable to leave the war zones of the Middle East due to fragmentation of society along sectarian lines and security threats have tried to find safety and refuge in a very threatening environment. In most cases, the conditions of the IDPs are worse than refugees as they are generally ignored by the international community. The international community lacks any legal obligation to protect the IDPs, help them return home, or find them a new place to live. The absence of democratic governments, lack of free press, and abundance of sectarian hatred make the condition of IDPs in the Middle East more dangerous than others.

Table 5.4   Internally Displaced Population in the Middle East

Country	Number of IDPs	Time
Iraq	4,000,000	June 15, 2015
Lebanon	19,719	December 2014
Palestine	263,500	July 2015
Syria	7,600,000	October 2014
Yemen	1,439,100	August 2015

Source: International Displacement Monitoring Center, www.internal-displacement.org.

The Middle East has been witnessing huge refugee movement at least since the Palestinian crisis of 1948. The ramifications of that exodus still continue and even have been more complex with violent conflicts in Iraq, Syria, and Yemen. At present, the Syrian conflict and its spillover into Iraq have posed a serious challenge to the refugee situation in the region. Many of the poorer countries in the Middle East have been both the home of, and host to, a large number of displaced population. Oil-rich countries in the region have actively worked to restrict the passage. Though these countries are still striving to recruit foreign workers, they are very reluctant to accept refugee population. International legal obligations, as well as sectarian divisions, are the primary reasons for this policy. In neighboring Europe, developed countries are also trying to restrict refugees from getting to or staying within their borders. The fear that accepting Muslim refugees to Europe may bring changes to European nation's identity and culture promotes domestic political forces that drive nativism, right-wing populism, and anti-immigration policies.

MIGRANTS IN THE MIDDLE EAST: MORE AS PEACE WRECKERS THAN PEACE MAKERS

Most of the non-oil-producing countries in the Middle East have a large migrant community working in the Gulf countries and also in the rest of the world. The lack of economic opportunities at home has forced them to look for jobs outside their own countries. The agriculture sector in these arid countries is heavily dependent upon waters coming through shared rivers, and the increasing water withdrawal in the upstream countries is making the situation worse.[70] Recurring natural disasters like droughts possibly due to climate change have also added to the miseries of the poorer strata of the society, thus deteriorating the economic situation.[71] Not only a difficult economy but also bad politics in the Middle East have displaced a large population and forced them to move within and outside the region since the end of the World War I.

Some of these migrant communities left their countries of origin many decades back, either as refugees or in search of job opportunities, and settled abroad. Jewish groups in general and in some cases Lebanese and Kurdish groups have been able to acquire decent political and economic status. These migrant communities can potentially contribute to peace and development in their home countries by influencing the conflicting parties to engage in negotiations, targeting remittances, and providing human capital at the time of negotiations and postconflict reconstruction. Through lobbying foreign governments and international organizations and aiding processes of transition, these migrant groups can play an important role in achieving political compromise and nonviolent conflict resolution in their homelands. They also can help international mediators to establish contact with the warring group leaders to facilitate the peace process.[72] Their involvement may also provide the much-needed trust and assurance to both the warring parties and the mediators to engage in the peace process. By giving insights into local issues, historical complexities, and personal characteristics of the group leaders, migrants can really provide an invaluable help to the mediators to make right and appropriate moves before and during negotiations.[73] By disseminating moderate perspectives, migrant groups can influence their homeland kin toward supporting nonviolent conflict resolution and democratic development. Unfortunately, these peace-making and peace-building capabilities of the migrants are rarely seen in the Middle East.

There is an ongoing debate about whether the world is getting more violent or more peaceful. But, one need not be under any illusion that the Middle East has become less peaceful over the last decades. There is no dearth of violent conflicts and migrant communities, both old and new, in this part of the world. The era of global interconnectedness has facilitated a range of non-state actors to get involved as parties to conflicts. Most of the violent conflicts fought after the Cold War are civil wars and many of the armed struggles are deterritorialized through the involvement of migrant groups.[74] The forced mass movement of people has huge social, economic, and political costs for the Middle East. But going by the sheer scale of this movement, it is not difficult to see its reverberations extend far beyond the region. Violent conflict and forced migration are two sides of the same coin. Grievances of migrants are born out of conflicts themselves, particularly out of the experience of violence. Hatred, formed during war and displacement, remains embedded in the psyche of the migrants, and such deep animosities motivate them to support conflicts.

As Hall[75] argues, the role of migrant communities has been critical in two explanations given for civil war: one is greed, which sees their financial support as crucial,[76] and the other is new wars, which see political and ideological support to rebels as significant.[77] Collier and Hoeffler[78] have emphasized the importance and influence of migrant communities' remittances and support for promotion of conflicts in their countries of origin. Migrant communities, by sending large remittances as well as channeling huge funds through welfare organizations close to insurgent or terrorist groups, contribute to conflict escalation rather than supporting constructive conflict transformation.[79] To many, migrant groups are extremist, long-distance nationalist communities, who pursue radical agendas taking advantage of the freedom and financial resources that their host countries provide them.[80] As Cochrane[81] points out, the role of migrant communities within the context of violent conflicts has been seen mostly to provide financial support for the continuation of warfare and to have the tendency to spoil negotiations and peace-building efforts.

Financial support during the conflict escalation phase may encourage more bellicosity and create further instability, as mostly observed with the Palestinian, Jewish, and Kurdish migrant groups. Their long-distance involvement in their homeland conflicts mostly manifested through the Internet, email, television, and telephone without direct physical suffering, risks, or accountability. However, the migrant groups originating from Middle Eastern countries not only provide financial support and send remittances to their home countries but also recruit themselves as fighters to wage battles in their homeland. In fact, this is a regular phenomenon.[82] Many migrant communities have provided weapons, training, or even personnel to their home countries. The Kurdish groups based in Europe substantially contribute to conflicts in their homeland by providing financial and military support as well as fighters to rebel groups. Middle Eastern migrant groups based in Europe and North America have played major roles in supporting conflicts in Israel, Palestine, Turkey, Iraq, and Syria. Conflicts in their homeland are often the yardstick for migrant groups' identity, and therefore they have a tendency to keep homeland conflicts even more protracted.[83] In most of the conflict situations in the Middle East, migrants are seen as part of the problem and not as part of the solution.[84]

For the migrant groups, there is always the issue of returning to their homeland. The idea of a potential return encourages them to intervene in homeland policies, and the notion of a "secure homeland," a place to return in time, plays a very important role in their behavior. It is not surprising that the policy priorities put forward by migrant groups do not always coincide with the priorities that are put forward by homeland state policy makers. So, the new wars explanation goes beyond the greed explanation of providing a supporting role in civil wars and instead argues that in some cases, migrant groups are the main motivators of initiating or reviving conflicts.[85] Migrants in their host countries develop networks on the basis of their ethnic identity, and they actually work on keeping nationalist hopes alive, although they live abroad.[86] Such networks could be highly effective when it comes to raising awareness in the hostland or in the global arena, raising funds for the "cause" back at home and developing stronger bonds with their ancestors or among one another. The migrant Jewish, Kurdish, and Palestinian groups are highly networked, well organized, and much more committed to preserve or restore their "nation." The groups have well-developed international organizations, strong financial resources, and a deep-seated awareness of intergenerational ethnonational identity. A majority of them tend to keep their affinity toward their ancestral homeland and give symbolic importance to it, and this creates major challenges for conflicts to come to an end.

Migrant communities' behavior toward the homeland also gets shaped within the framework of the relationship that exists between homeland and hostland. The host states are the ones who lay down rules and constraints for migrant groups who make political attempts to influence conflicts in their countries of origin.[87] There are numerous examples of migrant groups acting politically in a conducive environment in their host countries to support ethnic kin in the homeland. One very good example is the Jewish groups and their activities through the pro-Israel lobby in Washington, the American Israel Public Affairs Committee-AIPAC, which remarkably has been successful in influencing the United States to pursue a pro-Israel stance in the Palestinian issue.[88] The influence of the Iraqi migrants has also been blamed to some extent for the Bush administration's decision to invade Iraq in 2003.[89] In many cases of insurgency, the core leadership, or elements of it, often spend time abroad, or are forced to lead the insurgency from the migrant groups, as in the case of Yasser Arafat and the PLO staging its operations against Israel from Jordan in the 1960s, Lebanon in the 1970s, and Tunisia in the 1980s. In the last decades, most of the Iraqi Sunni leaders and groups were based in Syria to wage insurgency against the home regime.

However, migrant groups from the Middle East are diverse sets of communities spread across state borders and possess a sense of shared identity. While an influential section of them have adopted an extreme view and supported war efforts, there are also some moderates who have advocated and worked for a peaceful resolution of the conflict. In the light of ongoing globalization, climate change, economic crisis, and violent conflict in the Middle East, high levels of transnational migration flows will continue in the foreseeable future. Both migrant-producing and migrant-receiving countries share a strong interest in understanding how these groups may be encouraged to support peace, development, and security rather than foment ethnic nationalism and war. For countries in the region and the international community at large, moderating the behavior of these migrant communities and supporting their positive efforts may help prevent the development of transnational insurgencies and terrorist networks that might otherwise prove difficult and costly to defeat.

NOTES

1. David A. Graham, "Violence Has Forced 60 Million People From Their Homes," *The Atlantic*, June 17, 2015.

2. "The dispossessed," *The Economist,* June 18, 2015.

3. Ashok Swain, *Understanding Emerging Security Threats: Challenges and Opportunities*, (London: Routledge, 2012).

4. Ashok Swain, "Environmental Migration and Conflict Dynamics: Focus on Developing Regions," *Third World Quarterly*, 17 (1996): 959–73.

5. Charles H. Wood, "Equilibrium and historical-structural perspectives on migration," *International Migration Review*, 16 (1982): 298–319.

6. Swain, *Understanding Emerging Security Threats: Challenges and Opportunities.*

7. Leon Gordenker, The United Nations and Refugees in *Politics in the United Nations system, ed.,* Lawrence S. Finkelstein (Durham, NC: Duke University Press, 1988).

8. In the eyes of international law, a refugee is someone who, "owing to a well-founded fear of being persecuted for reasons of race, religion, nationality, membership of a particular social group or political opinion, is outside the country of his nationality, and is unable to, or owing to such fear, is unwilling to avail himself of the protection of that country." at www.unhcr.org, (accessed May 12, 2015).

9. Martin Baldwin-Edwards, "Migration in the Middle East and Mediterranean," A paper prepared for the *Policy Analysis and Research Program of the Global Commission on International Migration*, September 2005.

10. United Nations Relief and Works Agency for Palestine Refugees in the Near East, at www.unrwa.org, (accessed May 14, 2015).

11. Swain, "Environmental Migration and Conflict Dynamics: Focus on Developing Regions."

12. UN Press Release, September 11, 2013.

13. Jonathan Hall and Ashok Swain, "Catapulting Conflicts or Propelling Peace: Diasporas and Civil War," in *Globalization and Challenges to Building Peace,* eds., Ashok Swain, Ramses Amer and Joakim Öjendal (London, New York & Delhi: Anthem Press, 2007).

14. Donald F. Terry and Steven R. Wilson, *Beyond Small Change: Making Migrant Remittances Count* (Inter-American Development Bank, 2005).

15. The World Bank, *Migration and Development*, Brief 24, April 13, 2015.

16. Ninna Sørensen, Nicholas Van Hear and Poul Engberg-Pedersen, "The Migration-Development Nexus Evidence and Policy Options: State-of-the-Art Overview," *International Migration*, 40, 5 (2002): 3–47.

17. Susan F. Martin, "Remittance Flows and Impact," paper prepared for the regional conference on Remittances as a Development Tool, organized by the Multilateral Investment Fund and the Inter-American Development Bank, May 17, 2001.

18. Patricia Weiss Fagen and Mican N. Bump, "Remittances in Conflict and Crises: How Remittances Sustain Livelihoods in War, Crises and Transitions to Peace," *International Peace Academy Policy Paper*, February 2006.

19. Khalid Koser and Nicholas Van Hear, "Asylum Migration and Implications for Countries of Origin," United Nations University/WIDER Discussion Paper No. 2003/20, Helsinki, Finland, 2003.

20. Fagen and Bump, "Remittances in Conflict and Crises: How Remittances Sustain Livelihoods in War, Crises and Transitions to Peace."

21. Richard Adams and John Page, "Do International Migration and Remittances Reduce Poverty in Developing Countries?," *World Development*, 33 (2005): 1645–69.

22. Helen Chapin Metz, ed., *Egypt: A Country Study* (Washington: GPO for the Library of Congress, 1990).

23. Françoise De Bel Air, *Highly-skilled Migration from Jordan: A Response to Socio-political Challenges* (European University Institute Robert Schuman Centre for Advanced Studies, CARIM-AS 2010/12).

24. Al Monitor, November 7, 2014.

25. Lucio Laureti and Paolo Postiglione, "The effects of capital inflows on the economic growth in the Med Area," *Journal of Policy Modeling*, 27, 7 (2005): 839–51.

26. Peter Seeberg and Zaid Eyadat, eds., *Migration, Security, and Citizenship in the Middle East: New Perspectives* (New York: Palgrave Macmillan, 2013).

27. Charles Schmitz, *Building a Better Yemen* (Carnegie Endowment for International Peace, 2012).

28. Tom Arnold, "Mena Remittance Dips 2% Over Foreign Labor Deportations from Saudi Arabia," *The National Business*, April 16, 2014.

29. Saudi Ministry of Labor, 2012.

30. Françoise de Bel-Air, *Demography, Migration and Labor Market in Saudi Arabia*, Gulf Labor Markets and Migration, No. 1/2014.

31. Mouawiya Al Awad, *The Cost of Foreign Labor in the United Arab Emirates*, Institute for Social and Economic Research (ISER) Zayed University, Dubai, Working Paper No. 3, July 2010.

32. David Keane and Nicholas McGeehan, "Enforcing Migrant Workers' Rights in the United Arab Emirates," *International Journal on Minority and Group Rights*, 15 (2008): 81–115.

33. *The Economist*, July 13, 2015.

34. David McDowall, *A Modern History of the Kurds,* LB (Tauris, London and New York, 1996).

Van Bruinessen, 1998. "Shifting National and Ethnic Identities," *Journal of Muslim Minority Affairs*, 18, 1 (1998): 39–52.

35. Ibrahim Sirkeci, "Exploring the Kurdish Population in the Turkish Context," Genus, 56, 1–2, (2000): 149–75.

36. Edward Wong, "Saddam Charged with Genocide of Kurds," *The New York Times*, April 5, 2006.

37. Jordi Tejel, "Syria's Kurds: Troubled Past, Uncertain Future," Carnegie Endowment for International Peace, October 16, 2012.

38. Kart Emine, "Turkey Not Categorically Against Formation of Autonomous Kurdish Entity Inside Syria," *Hurriyet Daily News*, August 16, 2013.

39. Cengiz Gunes and Robert Lowe, *The Impact of the Syrian War on Kurdish Politics Across the Middle East*, Chatham House Research Paper, July 2015.

40. Jacob Tovy, "Negotiating the Palestinian Refugees," *The Middle East Quarterly*, 10, 2, (2003): 39–50.

41. Terry M. Remple, "Who are Palestinian Refugees," *Forced Migration Review*, 26, (2006): 5–7.

42. Benny Morris, *1948 and after: Israel and the Palestinians* (Oxford: Clarendon Press, 1994).

43. W. Andrew Terrill, *Global Security Watch-Jordan* (Santa Barbara: Praeger, 2010).

44. Mudar Zahran, "Jordan is Palestinian," *The Middle East Quarterly*, 19, 1 (2012): 3–12.

45. Jaber Suleiman, "The Current Political, Organizational, and Security Situation in the Palestinian Refugee Camps of Lebanon," *Journal of Palestine Studies*, 29, 1 (1999): 66–80.

46. IDMC, *Lebanon: Displaced return amidst growing political tension*, December 2006.

47. UNRWA, *The Situation of Palestine Refugees in South Lebanon*, August 2006.

48. UNRWA, *UNRWA Syria Regional Crisis Emergency Appeal 2015*, at http://www.unrwa.org/sites/default/files/syria_regional_crisis_emergency_appeal_2015_english.pdf (accessed May 11, 2015).

49. UNRWA, *UNRWA Syria Regional Crisis Emergency Appeal 2015*.

50. ILO, *Assessment Of The Impact Of Syrian Refugees In Lebanon And Their Employment Profile 2013*, (Beirut: International Labor Organization Regional Office for the Arab States, 2014).

51. UNRWA, *UNRWA Syria Regional Crisis Emergency Appeal 2015*.

52. Jill Goldenziel, "Refugees and International Security," in *On the Move: Migration Challenges in the Indian Ocean Littoral*, eds., Ellen Laipson and Amit Pandya (Washington DC: The Henry L. Stimson Center, 2010), 29–42.

53. Hassan M. Fattah, "Uneasy Exiles Await Those Who Flee the Chaos in Iraq," *New York Times*, December 8, 2006.

54. Human Rights Watch, "Iraqi Refugees, Asylum Seekers, and Displaced Persons: Current Conditions and Concerns in the Event of War," *Human Rights Watch Briefing Paper*, February 13, 2003.

55. Jackie Spinner, "Iraqis find travel to Jordan increasingly frustrating," *Washington Post*, January 17, 2006.

56. Nathan Hodson, "Iraqi Refugees in Jordan: Cause for Concern in a Pivotal State," *Research Notes*, The Washington Institute for Near East Policy, Number 13, April 2007.

57. Al-Khalidi Ashraf, Sophia Hofmann and Victor Tanner, *Iraqi Refugees in the Syrian Arab Republic: A Field-Based Snapshot*, The Brookings Institution-University of Bern Project on Internal Displacement, June 2007.

58. UNHCR, 2015 UNHCR Country Operation Profile – Iraq, at www.unhcr.org, (accessed April 29, 2015).

59. IDMC, *Global Overview 2015 - People internally displaced by conflict and violence,* at http://www.internal-displacement.org/assets/library/Media/201505-Global-Overview-2015/20150506-global-overview-2015-en.pdf, (accessed May 10, 2015).

60. Nigel Fisher, "Foreword: the inheritance of loss," *Forced Migration Review*, 47 (2014): 4–5.

61. UNHCR, 2015 UNHCR Country Operation Profile – Iraq.

62. Benedetta Berti, "The Syrian Refugee Crisis: Regional and Human Security Implications," *Strategic Assessment*, 17, 4 (2015): 41–53.

63. Oytun Orhan and Sabiha Senyücel Gündoğar, Effects Of The Syrian Refugees On Turkey, Ankara: ORSAM Report No: 195, January 2015.

64. Samya Kullab, "4 Million More," *The Globe and Mail*, September 10, 2015.

65. United Nations General Assembly, 70th Plenary Meeting, 18 December 2013.

66. IDMC, *Yemen: resolving displacement essential for long-term peace and stability,* 2014, at http://www.internal-displacement.org/middle-east-and-north-africa/yemen/2014/yemen-resolving-displacement-essential-for-long-term-peace-and-stability, (accessed May 12, 2015).

67. IDCM, *Global Overview 2015 - People internally displaced by conflict and violence.*

68. IDCM, *Yemen: resolving displacement essential for long-term peace and stability.*

69. IDCM, *Global Overview 2015 - People internally displaced by conflict and violence.*

70. Ashok Swain, "A New Challenge: Water Scarcity in the Arab World," *Arab Studies Quarterly*, 20, 1 (1998): 1–11.

71. Peter H. Gleick, "Water, Drought, Climate Change, and Conflict in Syria," *Weather, Climate and Society*, 6, 3 (2014): 331–40.

72. Cochrane Feargal, Bahar Baser and Ashok Swain, "Home Thoughts from Abroad: Diasporas and Peace-Building in Northern Ireland and Sri Lanka," *Studies in Conflict and Terrorism*, 32, 8 (2009): 681–704.

73. Bahar Baser and Ashok Swain, "Diasporas as Peacemakers: Third Party Mediation in Homeland Conflicts," *International Journal on World Peace*, 25, 3 (2008): 7–28.

74. Arjun Appadurai, *Modernity at Large: Cultural Dimensions of Globalization* (Minneapolis: University of Minnesota Press, 1996).

75. Jonathan Hall, "Diasporas and Civil War," in *War: An Introduction to Theories and Research on Collective Violence,* ed., Tor G. Jakobsen (New York: Nova, 2011).

76. Paul Collier and Anke Hoeffler, "Greed and Grievances in Civil War," *Oxford Economic Papers*, 56, 4 (2004): 563–95.

77. Mary Kaldor, *New and Old Wars: Organized Violence in a Global Era*, 2nd Ed. (Oxford: Polity, 2006).

78. Collier and Hoeffler, "Greed and Grievances in Civil War."

79. Wolfram Zunzer, "Diaspora Communities and Civil Transformation," Berghof Occasional Paper Nr. 26, Berghof Research Centre for Constructive Conflict Management, September 2004.

80. Joanna Spear, *The Potential Diaspora Groups to Contribute to Peace Building: A Scoping Paper.* University of Bradford, Transformation of War Economies Project's Working Paper, 2006.

81. Feargal Cochrane, "Civil Society beyond the State: The Impact of Diaspora Communities on Peace Building," *Global Media Journal: Mediterranean Edition*, 2, 2 (2007): 19–29.

82. Steven Vertovec, "The Political Importance of Diasporas," *Migration Information Source*, June 2005.

83. Terrence Lyons, "Engaging Diasporas to Promote Conflict Resolution: Transforming Hawks into Doves," Working Paper Presented at the Institute for Global Conflict and Cooperation Washington Policy Seminar, May 2004.

84. Joell Demmers, "New Wars and Diasporas: Suggestions for Research and Policy," *Journal of Peace, Conflict and Development*, 11 (2007).

85. Hall, "Diasporas and Civil War."

86. Terrence Lyons, "Engaging Diasporas to Promote Conflict Resolution: Transforming Hawks into Doves," Working Paper Presented at the Institute for Global Conflict and Cooperation Washington Policy Seminar, May 2004.

87. Eva Ostergaard Nielsen, *Diasporas and Conflict Resolution-Part of the Problem or Part of the Solution?* Copenhagen: DIIS Brief, March 2006.

88. John Mearsheimer and Stephen Walt, "The Israel Lobby," *London Review of Books*, 28, 6 (2006): 3–12.

89. Vertovec, "The Political Importance of Diasporas."

Chapter 6

Conclusion

In Search of Sustainable Regional Security

The aim of this volume has been to outline and critically analyze some of the key emerging security challenges that are not the traditional ones associated with the security discourse in the Middle East. As discussed in the Introduction, the region is characterized by a high level of securitization and a number of intractable as well as new conflicts. Following a flurry of "new wars" and "new conflicts" in the last decades, a lot of rethinking has been done (and certainly will be done) on the causes of regional insecurity. In the evolutions beyond the conventional security paradigm, which is more narrowly focused on state and military security, it has been argued that there has been reason to move beyond the state as the referent object of analysis. The question of *whose* security we are talking about is most important in this context.[1] Before the end of the Cold War, and increasingly so after, many keen observers have been arguing for a widening and deepening of the security concept.[2] Therefore, the question of how security is defined and framed is a vital one. Buzan et al. argues that security is *socially constructed.*[3] They point to an issue area (food, water, or health) as being under threat and with increasing recognition within a society (or international community or both) it becomes securitized. By being securitized, it moves up on the political agenda. However, in this book in which security aspects that are "emerging" have been put under analysis, it is clear that they may not in the first instance appear to be *existential threats* but rather incrementally growing *vulnerabilities* that may indeed become somewhat existential threats if not addressed properly and in a timely manner. An expanded form of security concept also relates to development considerations. The nexus of security and development becomes interesting and worth analyzing in this respect.

The issue of security and development has for the last two decades been one of the most prominent issues on the international agenda, primarily in the context of the work of the international community. The end of the Cold War in Europe meant that the UN Security Council could unite when parties to violent conflicts sought the assistance of the United Nations to monitor peace and to support the peace-building process. While celebrating the fiftieth anniversary of the United Nations, the General Assembly passed a unanimous resolution in October 1995 recognizing the link between security, development, and human rights. In 2005, in his report "In Larger Freedom," secretary general, Kofi Annan, argued that security and development, as well as human rights, are interdependent and mutually reinforcing. A second "arena" for security and development took place at the bilateral level. A number of developed countries established strategies, policies, and/or guidelines for their own engagement in fragile countries or regions. Depending on the strategic importance of the affected countries and whether any given situation could constitute a threat against a donor country's own national security, the emphasis could have been more on a military approach or on a development one. It was, however, accepted that a military solution alone would not guarantee stable and durable peace and security.

Parallel to the developments taking place in the framework of the United Nations and at the bilateral level, the concept of security and development also figured in the discussions of the academic world, which remains more skeptical. Critical voices to the good intentions as well as to the clarity of the concept have emerged. This development-security approach focuses particularly on the re-creation of state capacity to govern, democratization of societies, and the generation of macroeconomic growth in postconflict societies. The guiding assumption has been that the presence of strong state institutions would facilitate macroeconomic growth and provide economic security to its citizens. However, in most cases this development-security strategy fails to include in its framework of analysis the social and environmental factors of fragile societies. As development and security are relational concepts, many ask whose security and whose development this nexus is concerned about. Short-term security considerations of powerful countries increasingly override the long-term developmental challenges of the poor and fragile regions. This approach also poses challenges for long-term and comprehensive engagements necessary for lasting peace and sustainable development. For peace to mature and development to endure, it is vital to balance social, economic, and environmental factors in both security and development policies.

There is no doubt that, while a lot of attention has been paid to understand countries and regions that are in conflict or are emerging from conflict over the last 20 years, there is still not enough knowledge about how to design the best possible framework for fragile countries to not slide into violence and humanitarian crises. It is gradually getting clearer that the ambitions and objectives as well as actions of the states in regard to development, poverty alleviation, environment, and rule of law, are essential factors for maintaining peace and internal stability. However, it is important to strive for a common understanding among all the stakeholders, not least the state themselves, in regard to what are the possible emerging challenges for the security architecture. In the pursuit of this objective, the analysis in this book has made use of an extended security concept, including the new and emerging security challenges not only for the state but also for the society and the region, with a particular focus on water, food, energy, and migration.[4] The concluding chapter draws on key insights from the respective chapters on water, food, and energy security as well as from the chapter on large-scale human migration in the region and contextualizes the findings within the broader security debate on the Middle East.

Many of the conflicts in the Middle East have deep-seated historical roots, and also the region suffers from being an arena in which major powers hold deep interests. So, any security issue is not only a concern to the region itself but invariably attracts international repercussions. Energy, water, and food security, which have all become securitized in the region, are all interlinked with international markets and concerns, either directly or indirectly, the broader world. Migratory flows, be they refugee movement or labor migration, affect Europe, Asia, and beyond. The global impact of the instability in the region is clearly being felt, not least in the second half of 2015, when migration from the region to Europe has occurred in increasing proportions, although it is still far below the level of the flow of refugees from primarily Syria (but also Iraq) to neighboring countries such as Turkey, Jordan, and Lebanon.

The areas covered in this book have received far too little attention in the field of international relations, particularly while discussing security issues in the Middle East, and the "nexus" of relations linking them together is even less well understood.[5] As has been discussed in previous chapters, water, food, energy, and migration issues in the region in general have been highlighted more from a silo approach than from a more holistic framework. The book has made an effort to provide a more coherent and interlinked understanding of the underlying challenges for a secure, sustainable, and peaceful Middle East. In a sense, there has been a sincere attempt at bringing what has been considered "low politics" issues more fully into the security debate, and it can be argued that as a matter of fact these areas, taken together, should be seen as "threats" and not only "vulnerabilities" that can be addressed through merely technocratic approaches. On the contrary, unless the full range of politicization and subsequent "securitization," as Buzan will argue, is taken into account, there will be a certain failure to identify some of the most pressing security (and development) challenges the region is facing.[6]

One could argue that these emerging security *issues* among states *link the states' national security concerns* together. The security framework of the Middle East could also be seen as *sets* of security complexes, or sub-complexes, which all have their own security issues that connect the states together in inextricably entangled relations. However, the almost complete lack of a regionally functioning mechanism for managing the common security concern is striking. The League of Arab States (commonly known as the Arab League) is politically weak and commonly considered as a toothless organization. It was established in 1945 to foster closer relations, politically, economically, culturally, and socially among its member states. In the beginning, the league consisted of six Arab countries: Egypt, Iraq, Lebanon, Saudi Arabia, Syria, and Jordan. Since then, it has become a 22-member club. When the Arab League was formed, two main issues were on its agenda: First, all Arab states were seen as artificial colonial creations that only temporary existed until a pan-Arab state was established. Second, Palestine should be under Arab control and the Jewish Zionist should be prevented from establishing the Israeli State. After 1948, when Israel was established, the Arab League was very much united around its struggle against Israel. However, the pan-Arab unity did not last long, despite Egypt's and Syria's attempt to take the first merging step of forming the Arab Union in 1958. It turned out that national interests were stronger than the pan-Arab sentiments and the union collapsed in 1962. Not only have historic efforts to establish a pan-Arab unity failed, but the subsequent joint policy objectives adopted by the league relating to relevant issue areas have also failed. Efforts at framing joint policies for water, food, energy, and migration have been made, but have far too often remained as documents that have not been implemented. The existing regional power asymmetries, vested interests, loyalties, and alliances are important to understand as they are also reflected in the regional forums to a large extent and also explain why progress is hard to achieve. Joint management and policies aimed at achieving sustainability over scarce resources have almost completely been absent, partly as a result of a weak institutional structure, but also as an outcome of the propensity of conflict in the region that deflects attention away from efforts aimed at a more cooperative development.

From a functionalist perspective, some of the emerging security issues (or being perceived as "low politics" issues) in the region could be a potential leverage for a higher level of cooperation on more salient political matters ("high politics" issues). Scrutinizing the literature on cooperation theory in international relations[7] and social capital theory in development studies,[8] it is not difficult to find a strong argument for the general proposition that cooperation over natural resources between rivaling actors can have positive spin-offs for peace in other contentious areas. The basis for achieving this peace diffusion is that cooperation over natural resources among disputing groups will help remove mistrust and promote regular interactions, creating norms for reciprocity and infusing a broader understanding of the peace.[9] However, in a highly securitized region such as the Middle East, it has been argued while analyzing the water issue in the Jordan Basin that spillover effects of basic regional cooperation over water are not likely to reinforce cooperation in other sectors if the political will to address them as well is not present.[10] Therefore, it is important to understand the new and emerging security issues that have been analyzed in this book through the lens of the regional politics of the Middle East.

From a water security perspective, it is clear that in the countries of the region, water has, during the last decades, moved up the ladder in terms of political priority. The water scarcity, exacerbated by the significant population growth and economic development (craving for more water) as well as climate changes, which will, by in large, mean less rainfall, underpins the perspective that water is a national security consideration. Water has clearly been securitized in the political discourse; however, the responses to this situation have been scattered and have not addressed many of the critical aspects. There is a focus on supply-side solutions as opposed to more demand-side-oriented approaches as can be clearly seen by the planning of the Red-Dead Sea Water Conveyance Project, the focus on building huge desalination plants, etc. In addition, the region suffers, contrary to what one would expect, from the lowest water productivity in the world.[11] Certainly, it suffers from physical water scarcity, but it also needs to focus more on water governance–related aspects. Smart public policy and effective water governance are still considered as challenges in the region. Subsidies for irrigated water do not lead to improvements in efficiency and innovation in agricultural techniques. However, they are more the norm than not in the region. Manipulating elites and lack of transparency are also not factors that will encourage improvements to water productivity. While water has been securitized, it is nevertheless subordinate to perceived higher political priorities.[12]

While deliberate targeting of water installations in an armed conflict is not entirely new, it has become a regular trend in the Middle East in the last few years. The ISIS has been using water installations both as targets while fighting with regime forces in Syria and Iraq and to starve or flood areas under enemy control with water. This strategy of the ISIS has been one of the key motivators for the international community to support the Kurdish Peshmerga forces and the Iraqi army in the summer of 2014 in their efforts to retake the Mosul dam. In that sense, there seems to have been a "red line" for the international community when potentially catastrophic flooding of Baghdad among others appeared as a real risk.

The regional cooperation over water issues is largely fragmented and lacks a functioning multilateral structure. The League of Arab States as a regional organization has yet to reasonably fulfill its assigned role in the area of water governance. In relation to transboundary waters, the existing agreements are often bilateral and cover only parts of the basin. In the Jordan Basin, there are bilateral agreements between Israel and Jordan (which is operational by in large) and between Jordan and Syria (which is not functioning very well). In addition, Israel and Palestine still have road map arrangements, which only address part of the water issue. In the Nile River basin, there are old agreements between Egypt and Sudan as well as new (CFA) that Egypt and Sudan have not signed yet as it is seen as a threat to their water security. Meanwhile, Ethiopia is currently constructing several large dams in the basin unilaterally. On the Euphrates-Tigris, the Syrian crisis has put on hold any ambitious attempts at promoting cooperation, and whatever already exists is disorganized and is primarily on a bilateral level. Thus, a mechanism for regional coordination and cooperation over scarce water resources has yet to be developed. There is a dominant discourse in the region focusing on food self-sufficiency, and as expected, the link between water and food security considerations is strong.

The official rhetoric from the regimes of the region has been one that has emphasized food security through self-sufficiency. However, as it can be seen through the food and water security analysis, the feasibility of this idea in the long term is unrealistic. Egypt even ran out of the water needed for agricultural production to feed its own population way back in the 1970s.[13] The realization that water was not available to produce food to meet the growing demands made analysts predict future wars over water. However, the availability of virtual water on the global market acted as an ameliorating factor and reduced the risk of future water wars in the region. In the Middle East, the linkages between water and food security are obviously strong, as most countries in the region often use over 80 percent of their water for irrigation. It is important to note, however, that while the import of virtual water offers amelioration from the water scarcity, it is also a fact that a large section of the population of the region is either directly or indirectly dependent on agricultural production. Thus, shifting further from agricultural economy may seem logical from a pure water scarcity perspective, but the social adaptive capacity of countries is low, which means that alternate means for employment for a large part of the population engaged in agricultural (or related sectors) is not really there.

The political stability and regime security in the region are also closely related to a stable food price. The importance of subsidization of food (in particular wheat) to keep peace and order in the countries cannot be underestimated. Therefore, when there has been food price hikes at the global markets, it has also led to social tensions in the region. For a market to function well, it is important that the actors in it have a certain degree of trust, and if this is not there, alternate solutions to what the market can provide are likely to be sought. The challenges the food market encountered in 2008–2009 led many Middle East countries to search for alternate and complementary approaches to achieve food security. It has been viewed as increasingly important to reduce vulnerability to global market fluctuations as well as to export barriers (which happened in connection with the food price hikes during 2008–2009). For some Middle East countries (primarily in the Gulf), investing in land abroad for increasing access to food and for reducing vulnerability and dependence on global food markets has been an attractive proposition.[14]

The challenges that the agricultural sector is going to face in the coming years will make food production even more challenging. Climate change, likely to mean less rainfall (and importantly less predictable rainfall), coupled with an increasing population and a growing middle class looking for more water-intensive produce, will place a high burden on the agricultural sector in the region. In addition, the food security in the region is negatively affected by the huge losses in the food supply chain. One telling example is within the fruit and vegetable sector where around 60 percent of the produce is lost from "field to fork."[15] Moreover, the region does not generally possess the adaptive capacity needed to make the societal change of helping people to move from the agricultural sector to another profession. The economies in the region are not diversified enough for such a change.[16] This will add to the challenges in the years to come and this will make the situation even more vulnerable.

The energy security situation in the region is also quite convoluted. In the Gulf states, the abundant availability of oil and natural gas has allowed the countries the access to cheap energy, and has been used by their nondemocratic regimes to counter public opposition. The Gulf states (primarily Saudi Arabia and UAE) continue to be among the world's largest exporters of oil. Meanwhile, the Levant region (Lebanon, Israel, Syria, and Jordan) has been heavily dependent on import of energy. The exploration of new gas fields in the region has brought a new dimension to the energy security scenario.

On the whole, while there is an abundance of energy sources in the region, renewable resources such as water and arable land are sorely missing. In the Gulf countries, the access to cheap energy, apart from helping regimes avoid reform, has also allowed large-scale desalination of seawater. Thus, the water consumption per capita in the Gulf region is among the highest in the world in spite of very low natural availability. The access to "cheap" desalinated water, as well as mining of nonrenewable groundwater (fossil water), has allowed large-scale irrigated agriculture in the name of achieving food self-sufficiency. This shows how access to cheap energy enabled a certain degree of food self-sufficiency in the short term and how strong the food self-sufficiency narrative was (and to some degree still is). The ability to have a large local production of foodstuff made possible by cheap energy was seen as being of strategic importance. While this thinking is still strong, it was realized that the production of wheat using primarily fossil groundwater was not sustainable and would be impossible in the long run. Therefore, other strategies for food security have been taken up, including investment in foreign land for food production.

The challenges for energy security in the region are immense. The countries of the region have put in place a system of high energy subsidies, which causes economic losses and encourages unsustainable consumption patterns. Furthermore, they provide disincentives to alternate renewable energy solutions. In addition, the subsidies distort efforts to create well-functioning energy markets. The subsidies and the availability of cheap oil in the region work against any attempt at energy diversification. Still, more than 97 percent of all electricity generation in the Middle East comes from fossil fuels.[17]

Threats of global climate change pose a growing challenge to the energy security situation in the region. The rest of the world imports huge quantities of oil and natural gas from the Middle East. Due to climate change, not only is the region likely to receive less rainfall and become warmer, but also the world will prioritize alternate sources to burn fossil fuels. Added to this, the process of "fracking" has also made it possible for increasing oil production in other parts of the world. In the United States, the availability of oil that can be accessed through fracking can possibly alter the global energy landscape significantly.[18] Thus, the high reliance of Gulf countries in the Middle East on oil incomes will not be sustainable as the world is increasingly looking at alternatives. Thus, the reliance on oil is, in the long term, a challenge that needs to be overcome.

The Middle East has a long history of both large-scale refugee flows and huge economic migration. A large number of labor migrants from non-oil-producing countries in the region mostly work in the Gulf countries. However, while many skilled Jordanians and Lebanese work in the Gulf, these two countries also host many economic migrants from Egypt who generally have low-skilled jobs. Better economic opportunities in the host country and lack of opportunities in the homeland are encouraging a large number of people to migrate. The Gulf countries, which have received a large migrant labor force from the Middle East and from outside the region to work for their oil-rich economies, have also started facing demands from their own population to restrict migration.

Apart from the economic migrants, there are large refugees' movements within the region as well as from the region to other parts of the world. Due to the unresolved Palestine issue, a large number of Palestinians are still, often in third generation, living as refugees in neighboring countries. The recent and ongoing refugee movements from Iraq, Yemen, and Syria have become a major international concern. Authoritarian regimes, violent armed conflicts, lack of opportunities, and possibly recurring natural disasters have contributed to refugee movements in the region. As the region has been getting less and less peaceful over the last decades, the flows of refugees are likely to continue. This massive forced movement of people has brought negative human, social, political, and economic implications for the region and outside. Some of these migrants are also contributing to the continuation of conflicts in their homelands. Through remittances, these migrants not only help close family members, but also in some cases support rebel forces (politically as well as financially).[19] Mostly, migrants from the region are seen as part of the problem (from a conflict perspective) rather than a solution.[20] While some migrants can exacerbate conflict, there are also moderates who actively contribute toward peaceful solutions to conflict. For those countries that receive refugees (and economic migrants) from inside and outside the Middle East, it is extremely important to see how these migrant communities can support and promote peace and development.

In the Middle East, all these four (water, food, energy, and migration) intertwined, but not so obvious of being violent in nature, emerging security challenges need to be addressed judiciously and promptly. These fast-emerging threats to regional security are all interconnected. Solutions to challenges such as water and food scarcity, energy security, and large population migration cannot be found in isolation. The significance of smart management of economic, social, and environmental factors in achieving not only stable but also sustainable peace is well understood. However, there is a wide gap between understanding and implementation. Short-term narrow security considerations increasingly override long-term developmental challenges. For peace to endure and mature, it is extremely important to balance social, economic, and environmental factors in development policies.

Moreover, a number of scientific projections of climate change have been made in recent years, though agreement on the timing and extent of this change has not been reached. However, there is a sufficient consistency in all these projections that water availability and agricultural productivity in the Middle East will generally decrease as a result of climate change. The less agricultural output will bring more demand to create new agricultural areas within the region and/or to acquire agricultural land abroad to meet growing food demand. Moreover, climate change is predicted to bring further uncertainties to the dwindling water supply of international rivers from the upstream. There is no doubt that the Middle East suffers from huge water stress. There is an ongoing race in the region to gain control of water resources. However, cooperation rather than control is needed to get the best use of scarce water supply. Besides the struggle to acquire more waters from international river systems like the Nile, Jordan, and Euphrates-Tigris, political and legal positioning by countries in the region over transboundary groundwater aquifers is the sticking point. Furthermore, thanks to climate change, the region is predicted to get much hotter, will see more precipitation loss, and will see rise in sea levels affecting its coastal areas. Climate- and weather-related hazards are feared to rise in number and intensity. All these will also force many poor and vulnerable people to move out of their homes and migrate to other areas in search of survival.

FOUR FAULT LINES IN THE REGIONAL SECURITY STRUCTURE

The Middle East is a highly securitized region, which carries many underlying conflicts with deep historical roots.[21] A number of undercurrents which in some cases have already manifested themselves in violence and other forms have not yet been included in traditional security analyses. There are no simple or straightforward solutions to the security dilemmas at hand in the region. Historically, the region gives evidence of limited ability to solve its "internal" security problems. Most of the existing academic works on the Middle East focus on traditional and hard security challenges. However, increasingly the region and its growing population face a highly complex and fragile security system, where the security issues discussed in this volume are critical for peace and stability. The security challenges to the region are too integrated and too complex in order to be understood in traditional ways. The analysis of security nowadays includes a set of issues that are not as easily defined as before. Firmly anchored in this inclusive security perspective, the book tries to understand the Middle East and offer a complementary approach to the more traditional ones that have been the dominant ones in the region. It takes the broadened security concept one step further and argues that that it is not the absence of a military threat that epitomizes security but rather highlights the importance of human rights, sustainable development, good governance, rule of law, and social equity for security. Several aspects included in the concept have largely been brought into the 17 Sustainable Development Goals adopted at the UN General Assembly in September 2015.

While the book as such focuses on new and emerging threats to security, there is no direct preference for a state-centric or human security concept but rather a focus on how they are developing to make the region more vulnerable. From our perspective, the challenges that the areas analyzed in this book are generally not limited to nation-states but, on the contrary, have regional effects. To further underscore this point, it is noted that the issues discussed in the book have many interdependencies. The water-food-energy nexus is one example that has shown how these areas are closely interrelated. Water being the main input in the growing of food and energy is another key element for food production as well as for transport, storage, and cooling; water is the source of energy (hydropower) as well as a user of energy (for pumping water to the place where it is needed in a given country/region, for cooling power plants, etc.). Shortage in one sector will have a bearing on the other. Clearly, there are prospects for improving resource management within the respective sectors through analyzing trade-offs in a better way. From a migration perspective, the linkages to the other sectors are also not difficult to locate. The large refugee flows affect the water, energy, as well as food situation in the country. From a humanitarian perspective, providing food, water, and energy presents a serious challenge.

Furthermore, while linking the extended analytical security framework with the more traditional challenges, some key threads emerge when trying to better understand the region. They relate, in many ways, to the precarious politics of the Middle East and arguably the emerging threats need to be understood and analyzed from this political security perspective. Four main trains of thoughts are being deciphered as a backdrop for analysis. *First* is the divide that in many aspects has been there historically between the two main *sects* of Islam. The Sunni-Shia divide has been increasingly brought out in the open after the 2003 Iraq war and has become a backdrop for forging power alliances in the region. *Second*, the Middle East is a region where high-value resources (oil, natural gas) are plentiful, while livelihood resources (water, arable land, forest) are scarce. The fossil energy resources have been the reasons for the strong international interest in the region and the dependence on regime stability for the provision of these resources to the global market. *Third*, the region suffers from a lack of vibrant social space. Authoritarian regimes, absence of democratic institutions, and a lack of basic fundamental rights have created a society full of fear and mistrust. This has made it more likely that grievances, rather than being addressed in a "normal" way, are either being suppressed or are turning into sudden eruptions of violence as was noticed at the time of the Arab Spring. *Finally*, the international community led by the United States is, by and large, seen as prioritizing issues relating to its strategic interests (regime stability, Israel, oil supply) at the expense of human insecurity affecting the region. It seems that *realpolitik* is still very much the defining perspective through which the region is approached from an international angle.

GLOBALIZATION AND RELIGIOUS SECTARIANISM

There is no denying that the approaches to study regional politics in the Middle East have changed. While "hard security" perspectives continue to dominate the academic work coming out from security studies and international relations, there are increasingly new voices arguing for a broadened analytical framework. One can argue that the Middle East is a good example of a "regional security complex" in the sense that it shares many common features. For example, the long-standing unresolved Palestinian question that affects, to lesser or larger degree, many (if not all) of the states in the Middle East. As a politically salient issue carrying a lot of symbolism, the Palestinian question has also been used in the region as both a rallying point politically and an excuse not to pursue reform agendas. However, there are other power struggles that are going on in the region. As has been discussed in the introductory chapter, the formation of states in the region is relatively new with the states being less than a hundred years. In addition, the state formation process has been one characterized by a process of realignment. Usually, the development and acceptance of regional hegemons take time. From a more traditionalist security perspective, this can also explain the instability of the region as a hegemon usually brings a certain form of stability, and in the absence of a clear hegemon, the struggle for influence continues and leads to confrontations.

As a result of sectarian politics, one of the most difficult problems with the Middle Eastern states is that they are not functioning as strong states in which their populations and civil society are playing their customary roles. The states are not homogenous nation-states but rather multiethno/religious or multinational ones. The region is characterized by a variety of state-building projects, with each state containing several different ethnic or ethnoreligious groups. Due to the direct or indirect Great Power influence in creating "new" states within the region after the collapse of the Ottoman Empire, these groups extend over one or, in most cases, several, territorial borders, and they strive to strengthen and expand their own interests in relation to the dominant ruling elite. This creates a situation where the security concerns of several countries are inextricably linked to each other. The Middle Eastern ruling elites have rather seen themselves as representatives for their own group and not for the "country" as a whole. Most states in the region have a "weak" degree of institutionalization and thereby have managed to gain legitimacy only from sections of its population.

During the Cold War, the region had witnessed the usual power struggle between the United States and the Soviet Union, which had led to their support for various countries at different time periods. The struggle for domination was influenced not only by the quest for power, but also by the need to gain access to the region's rich natural resources. However, in recent years, the power struggle in the region has shifted to the two primary strands of Islam, Sunni, and Shia. More than over a decade this has primarily been played out between Saudi Arabia as the representative for Sunni Islam and Iran as the representative for Shia Islam.[22]

The ancient divide between two most important sects in Islam has always existed. The division between Sunnis and Shias for fourteen centuries over the issue of the rightful successor to Prophet Mohammad has become one dominant prism through which the ongoing violent conflicts in the Middle East are being explained. Sunnis and Shias have been peacefully living together in the region for centuries, sharing faith in the Quran and Prophet Mohammed, though they hold opposing views on rituals and the reading of Islamic law. However, two regional powers that compete for the leadership of Islam, Sunni Saudi Arabia and Shia Iran, have used the sectarian difference to further their political, economic, and geostrategic ambitions in the region, particularly affecting political stability in Syria, Iraq, Lebanon, Bahrain, and Yemen. The differences have always existed between the two sects, but only when it got mixed with regional politics it became really dangerous. The transformation of the Sunni-Shia struggle to the present state can date back to the 1979 Iranian Revolution to some extent, but the real impetus came in 2003, when the United States invaded Iraq and ousted the Saddam regime. Neighboring Iran and Saudi Arabia realized that there would be a power vacuum in Iraq and tried to bring the country under their influence. The Saudi regime, which had long seen Iraq as a counterbalancing power against Iran, tried to destabilize the Shia-led government after the overthrow of the Baathists.[23] The militant group ISIS gained strength in Iraq with the upheaval that ensued and took anti-Shia hatred to new heights. With the expansion of the ISIS into Syrian territory after the Civil War, the violence has reached genocidal levels. These extreme sectarian divisions have been further magnified by the ongoing war in Yemen, with Saudi Arabia leading a coalition of Sunni Arab states against the pro–Iranian Houthi rebels belonging to a part of Shia Islam.[24]

In the last decade, after the fall of the Saddam regime and before the start of the Syrian Civil War, Shia groups supported by Iran managed to get a number of strategic victories in the Middle East. A Shia group dominated the Iraqi parliament and led the post–Saddam government. Hezbollah, the Lebanese Shia group, became the major political force in Lebanon. Similarly, Yemen's political scene also saw domination by a Shia faction. This led to some apprehensions in the minds of Sunni regimes in the region and paved the way to an alliance of regimes on sectarian basis. This, however, in many ways offer a simplistic explanation of the struggle for regional power domination in this manner. There exists a number of multilayer security considerations as well. For example, Iran and Syria have supported Hamas (the Palestinian group consisting of predominantly Sunni Muslims) in its struggle against Israel and the Sunni Muslim Brotherhood in Egypt. The quest for regional hegemony takes various routes. Saudi Arabia has been supporting for decades a specific brand of Sunni Islam often called Wahabism through funding *madrasas* (religious schools) not only in countries in the Middle East but also all over the world. It is described as being very conservative and is largely credited as being a main source of inspiration for terror groups like the al-Qaeda, ISIS as well as the Taliban. Saudi Arabia has been using religion as part of its expansive strategy in its quest for leadership of the Middle East. Shia Iran, on the other hand, has used its relatively moderate oil revenues to support countries that can, to some extent, preempt the Saudi (and generally Sunni) design to exercise dominance in the region. Naturally, this competition has produced and sustained conflicts in the region, promoting various forms of insecurities.

RESOURCE CURSE: TOO MUCH, TOO LITTLE, AND THE CLIMATE CHANGE

The region has a duality in relation to having natural resources. A large part of the region has a rich reserve of high-value natural resources (oil and gas), while there is a striking deficit in relation to availability of renewable resources (notably arable land, water, and forests). Furthermore, while some countries are endowed with plentiful fossil energy resources, other countries are facing energy shortages in spite of some recent discoveries (notably Jordan and Lebanon). The increasing scarcities in water and food supply are expected to get further aggravated due to climate change, which is projected to bring less and more erratic rainfall in large parts of the region. The region is becoming more vulnerable, especially because the higher rate of population growth is bound to result in severe scarcity of all kinds.

The overreliance on income from oil and natural gas has allowed the Gulf countries to economically grow for over four decades. It has helped them achieve spectacular progress in a relatively short period of time and make the quick transition from economies that a few decades back were comparable only to those of the medieval times to those of the twenty-first century. These countries have, however, largely followed a development model where the lack of freedom and social space has been compensated by economic growth. The revenue generated from extractive resources has served to keep the regimes largely immune to political and social opposition and allowed the ruling elites to thrive. It has created and expanded a wealth gap both within countries and between countries in the region. Moreover, thanks to oil resources, many authoritarian regimes in the region have got the ability to spend billions of dollars on arms and weapons systems, to wage wars on its neighbors, and to threaten regional security.

The correlation between oil wealth and authoritarian rule in the Middle East has been established by scholars for some time.[25] Their main finding is that more oil wealth is associated with less democracy. The antidemocratic effect of oil wealth is that it strengthens authoritarian regimes and precludes them from making attempts toward democratization. The rents from these resources also help authoritarian regimes both to avoid and even survive radical threats.[26] Moreover, oil resource wealth restricts the development of state institutions and adversely affects the quality of institutions.[27] The easy availability of a large amount of oil funds leads to rampant corruption and rent seeking on the part of the ruling elites. Overall, the overdependence on oil revenues has actually become the main reason for economic and political underdevelopment in the Gulf. The problem has been further compounded by religious and historical factors, leading to overall institutional decay.

Access to cheap energy has also allowed highly unsustainable practices in both the water and food sectors. For a period of time, Saudi Arabia even used its desert and fossil (nonrenewable groundwater) to grow wheat, becoming the fifth largest wheat exporter in the world. The Gulf countries are also among the highest per capita users of water in the world, despite being one of the poorest (in terms of natural water resources) regions in the world. Water use has been made possible by access to cheap desalinated water as well as overuse of available groundwater. Water scarcity in the region is already extensive and is slated to deteriorate further. The per capita water availability in the Arab world in 2050 will be half of that of 2015. This is a significant decrease considering that most parts of the region are already facing severe water scarcity. While in other regions water issues are dealt with at the political-technical level, in the Middle East water is highly securitized (Phillips et al, 2006). Water is subject to availability of arable land as well as forest cover. Over the last century, the region has lost a significant part of its forests. Forests are important from many perspectives; a significant number of ecosystem services are provided through forests; forests help attract rainfall; they function as carbon storage; and so on. The overuse of land, as well as draining of certain areas, has also meant that important arable land has been lost in the region with adverse implications for agricultural production and subsequently food security.

With new scientific developments in the fossil energy resource extraction sector, particularly with increased use of fracking technology in the United States and the Great Britain as well as in other parts of the world, there is going to be a significant decrease in the global dependence on Middle East oil. Moreover, many high energy-consuming developed and fast developing countries are also gradually shifting to renewable energy use, compounding the challenges for the oil markets of the Gulf countries. As these countries have not significantly utilized their substantial oil and gas revenue to invest in well-functioning markets, innovation, and private sector development, they are increasingly becoming more vulnerable. The *realpolitik*, which has characterized the West's protective approach to the Gulf, may not be a given in the longer term. In this context, the curse of oil will be more apparent and widespread in the region in the near future. Like the overabundance of high-value resources, the scarcities of renewable natural resources (water, arable land, and forest) potentially provide another *curse* that the challenges they bring may prove overwhelming for the region, particularly with the growing threat of climate change.

LACK OF POLITICAL FREEDOM AND
REDUCED SOCIAL CAPITAL

In most countries in the Middle East, political participation is extremely limited due to restrictions imposed by authoritarian regimes.[28] In one of its reports in 2004, the UNDP[29] clearly described lack of freedom and social space in the Middle East as one of the serious challenges for the region. Though the report attracted a lot of criticism from regional elites, its findings became more obvious after the Arab Spring. The report was a forerunner, as the former foreign minister of Jordan, Marwan Muasher, rues that the warning was not heeded by the regime of the region.[30] This warning had come well before the Arab Spring and had outlined many issues of serious concern for the region. The report was unambiguous about the lack of freedom of speech, the massive violations of human rights (particularly in Palestine but also broadly within the region), the restrictions imposed on people's participation in meaningful political activity, and the discrimination of women in the region. The report stated that "the elites of political society need to develop a constructive discourse and reject policies of exclusion."[31] In the absence of this, the report had projected:

> If the repressive situation in Arab countries today continues, intensified societal conflict is likely to follow. In the absence of peaceful and effective mechanisms to address injustice and achieve political alternation, some might be tempted to embrace violent protest, with the risk of internal disorder. This could lead to chaotic upheavals that might force a transfer of power in Arab countries, but such a transfer could well involve armed violence and human losses that, however small, would be unacceptable. Nor would a transfer of power through violence guarantee that successor governance regimes would be any more desirable.[32]

Thus, the UNDP report (with "The Impending Disaster Scenario" as a headline) had shown the "writings on the wall" much in advance of the arrival of the Arab Spring. Though Arab Spring came as a pleasant surprise to many within and outside the region, its success was of a very short term and mostly counterproductive.

Protest reflects the type of relationship that exists between the state and society.[33] When the state fails to meet the demands and expectations of various competing social groups, it may lead to anger and take the shape of a protest movement. However, the type of regime structure sharply affects the character of protest. Democracies experience more protests but less violent ones than those in authoritarian regimes.[34] Authoritarian regimes generally rely more on coercive control, which increases the relative utility of rebellion for challengers. Ronald A. Francisco's study finds that protesters react violently to extremely harsh coercion.[35] An authoritarian regime most often oppresses any dissent that challenges its authority. However, to divert the attention of the opposition, the regime may encourage people to protest against a foreign enemy. For many decades, the authoritarian regimes in the Middle East had actively encouraged their citizens to protest against Israel, while brutally suppressing any other form of popular action at home. The usefulness of this diversionary tactic came to an end with the Arab Spring, when the regimes became the target of the protesters. These eruptions of popular anger in the Middle East were primarily spontaneous, largely unorganized, and invariably violent in nature, but mostly failing to achieve any positive outcome.

A diffusion of protest movements is necessary in order to keep them alive when the initial spark begins to sputter. As Tarrow argues, for the success of a protest, there is a need to transcend the "volcanic" stage of collective action.[36] People take part in protests in response to political opportunities and, subsequently through collective actions, create new ones. However, political opportunities draw people into collective action on the basis of trust and social networks through which social relations are based and organized. Social networks or ties play a critical role in the mobilization process of protest movements.[37] A protest receiving support from a dense and vibrant social structure is more likely to spread and be sustained, and successful protest mobilizations represent a "network of networks" in a society.[38] Robert Putnam defines social capital as "features of social organization, such as trust, norms, and networks, that can improve the efficiency of society by facilitating coordinated action."[39] Social capital promotes cooperation among people on common ventures and to take part in the political life of the community.[40] It supports the mobilization of a protest movement by building both bonds and bridges within the protesting groups and providing bridges to outside support groups. The drawback of a small group can be overcome through adaptable networking. Protests get larger support through the coordination of various groups of supporters. Though the Arab Spring protests erupted suddenly and received huge media attention internationally, the mobilizations were limited to a particular sectarian group and/or region and in most cases in the Middle East were put down by the authoritarian regimes. The restrictive sectarian network structure in the Middle East society did not allow the protests to mobilize successfully in the pursuit of a common interest.

Societies in the Middle East not only suffer from difficulties over networking due to sectarian, regional, and class differences, there is also a gradual decline of interpersonal trust hindering any successful social mobilization. The region has witnessed large-scale movement of skilled as well as unskilled workers in search for opportunities in other countries. Not only large economic migrants, some countries in the region also host a massive number of refugees, in some cases outnumbering the local population. With the help of an American sample, Putnam finds that the higher proportion of immigrants in a community lowers the trust not only between the migrants and host communities but also within them as well.[41] If Putnam's finding has universal applicability, then the migration-induced diversity in the Middle East reduces the social capital of the indigenous population and their ability to cooperate for a common cause.

REGION CAUGHT IN THE REALPOLITIK

In the beginning of the twentieth century, most parts of the Middle East were either clients or dependencies of one or other European countries. European colonial powers used the Middle East to make themselves rich.[42] Till the early 1930s, European companies had almost complete control of high-value oil production in the Middle East. In 1933, American oil companies got their major access to the region's oil fields in Saudi Arabia, and in the post–World War II period, their influence grew to greater heights.[43] These companies brought equipment and professional workforce from their home countries and took the major share of profits from their exploitation of the region's petroleum reserves.[44] The oil business even destroyed the traditional local economies, as in parts of Saudi Arabia agricultural fields were converted to build pipelines and pumping stations.[45] Even after withdrawing from its colonies in the 1950s, the United Kingdom continued to be one of the main international actors in the Middle East, and the Cold War raised the stakes for the superpowers to be interested in the region not only for economic gains but also for strategic purposes. Rather than directly involving armed conflicts, both the superpowers tried to empower regional proxies to protect their interests in the region.

The domination of the United States in the region came at the cost of the Soviet Union, when the Carter administration brokered the first Arab-Israeli peace deal in 1979. The overthrow of its strongest ally in the region, the Shah of Iran, enabled the United States to become the ultimate guardian of the region's oil flows. The decline in Soviet power and its ability to intervene in the 1980s made the United States the true hegemon of the Middle East.[46] Consolidation of power in the Middle East has proved costly for the United

States, as since the late 1970s, the region has been rocked by rebellion and violent wars. Security has remained elusive and has demanded more direct and costly forms of US interventions.[47] Due to expensive and painful wars, particularly in Iraq, there is a public desire to diminish America's role in the Middle East, if not end it altogether. To fill in the vacuum, there is an increasing presence of Russia and China in the region. Russia's bombing of opposition targets in Syria in the autumn of 2015 is a sign of the decline of the influence of the United States in the Middle East. However, securing the flow of affordable oil still remains as a cornerstone of America's Middle East policy. President George W. Bush, in his State of the Union Address to the nation on January 31, 2006, had explained the rationale of this policy: "Keeping America competitive requires affordable energy. And here we have a serious problem: America is addicted to oil, which is often imported from unstable parts of the world."

Europe's relationship with the countries of the Middle East has changed considerably since the colonial period. The United States has become the most influential world power and also the primary "security" provider for the Middle East. Countries in the Middle East consider the United States as a biased power, particularly in their opposition to Israel, but they lack unity and ability to oppose US involvement. Except the ruling regime in Syria, all others in the region have developed close working relations with Washington and cannot survive long without US support. But, at the same time, all these countries perceive the United States as a major threat to regional security, particularly due to its steadfast support to Israel and military intervention in Iraq.[48]

On many issues, the interests of the European Union and the United States in the Middle East largely converge. They desire and work toward keeping the countries of the Middle East as open market economies and also keep them out of Chinese and Russian influences. However, while the United States has been using more "hard power" and focusing on the regime security in the region, the European Union has adopted the strategy of using "soft power" and supporting policies aimed at human and social development. The European Union tries to bring peace and stability in the region by promoting economic development while simultaneously advocating in favor of human rights and democratization. This policy of "dualism" between the United States and the European Union over the Middle East has basically led to fragmentation of objectives and has failed to build a coherent strategy for a credible regional security framework. Neither the European Union nor the United States has been able to successfully support the building of strong state institutions in the region as use of hard power has not been followed up by a long-term peace-building strategy aimed at supporting and institutionalizing democracy. With the military interventions, while old state institutions have been dismantled, the international community has failed to create an effective alternative to fill the vacuum. The governance crisis has resulted in huge refugee movements, exposing the European Union's weaknesses of its foreign, security, and development aid policies in the region. The Middle East is very close to Europe geographically and culturally, and the European Union has a strong link to security and stability in this region. In terms of political and security cooperation, the European Union does not address the security interests of the Middle Eastern countries. The division of responsibility between the United States and the European Union has been detrimental to the security of the Middle East and also for the European Union and United States.

IDENTIFYING IMMEDIATE SECURITY RISKS

After an analysis of the emerging threats within the framework of the existing fault lines with the regional security architecture, what potential risks can be identified for the future? Further, how does this impact the security situation, in the region and beyond? Many predict, particularly after Kurds achieved regional autonomy in northern Iraq, the Sunni uprising in Iraq, and the rise of the ISIS, that the Arab and Middle Eastern states are on the way to collapse as the post–Ottoman order is falling apart.[49] The argument goes that after the collapse of the Ottoman Empire, the totalitarian regimes have been only able to maintain these countries with artificial boundaries by using oppressive measures. With the collapse of these regimes, the Middle East is facing chaos and this might lead to a redrawing of state boundaries. However, the states in the Middle East have survived despite their controversial origins and consolidation phases, and challenges from pan-Arabism, wars, internal armed conflicts, Cold War power politics, and serious economic maldevelopment. These states have survived by the oppressive regimes built up of internal and external security needs and military forces. What the analysts have overlooked while writing obituaries of the states in the Middle East is the possibility of new totalitarian regimes replacing the falling ones. Egypt has already witnessed this, and it will not be too far-fetched to predict similar scenarios developing in Iraq and Yemen. The international community is also averse to supporting dramatic changes to the present political map of Middle Eastern states.

Leaders might change, but artificial states and totalitarian regimes will most likely survive in the region. However, there is great opposition in the Middle East toward placing most resources on the security sectors while allocating fewer social and economic resources that have been unfairly distributed and shared among the common populations. In combination with high demographic transformation with high fertility rates, and an increasingly younger age structure, welfare needs increase dramatically in the Middle East. The decreasing availability of food and water, fluctuating global oil prices, growing threat of climate change, and increasing migrant population all make the task harder for the states. The combination of having regimes that are determined to stay in power and at the same time are unable to meet the development and economic needs of the people risk creating internal instability. This creates an insecure environment for the individual citizens, as well as for the security of the entire region. The eruption of the Arab Spring is a prime example of how social reaction follows when the states fail to provide the basic livelihood needs. Several non-oil-producing states have become so economically weak that they have accepted a great portion of the basic socioeconomic and social welfare distribution to be taken care of by the Islamic grassroots organization, that is, the Islamic sector of society. Though the Islamic fundamentalist sectors are perceived as a security threat vis-à-vis the state, necessity has led to a division of labor, where parts of the Islamic civil society sector provides basic welfare for people in most need.

This increasing withdrawal of the states from their social welfare responsibilities and ceding this area to religious groups is helping to strengthen fundamentalist forces at the grassroots level. This is increasingly becoming a serious policy challenge for the regimes, which cannot at the same time risk to prevent the Islamists, as that might lead to more protests. Thus, the Islamic movements are likely to continue to provide for the welfare of people in most need and the totalitarian regimes continue to hold power with the help of repressive tools. An increased support for Islamic movements and other oppositional groups will keep continuing to challenge the regimes and when democratic options will be available they will win elections but most likely will not get the approval of the international community to govern (Hamas won the elections in the Palestinian Authority in 2006, Muslim Brotherhood won the Egypt's Presidential election in 2012). Most of these Islamic movement groups have particular interests within their state, and the possibilities of them joining a pan–Islamic new caliphate across state borders are quite bleak. Hence, states, anxious, undemocratic, authoritarian but still having some political order, might continue to exist in the Middle East once the post–Arab Spring turmoil starts to subside. The most radical Islamists will continue to challenge the state, and this will create an insecure environment for the populations but not lead to a regime change. In the aftermath of the US invasion in Iraq and civil war in Syria and Yemen, with the increase in terrorist attacks inside the Middle East as well as in the West, and with the massive refugee movement to Europe, it seems that "back-to-the–usual" style of politics of maintaining regime stability will dominate the policy agenda of the international community.

A major challenge for the Middle Eastern states is that they are not homogenous but rather multireligious/sectarian states. The countries continue to struggle with a variety of state-building projects, with each state containing several different religious or sectarian groups. This problem will be further multiplied due to the impact of the increased numbers of refugees coming from war-torn Iraq, Yemen, and Syria to other countries in the region. The large population migration gradually challenges the existing demographic balance between different religious and sectarian groups, creating further political instability. There is also an overwhelming risk that Lebanon can return to a new internal war situation and the danger that the situation in Jordan can become further precarious. The Kurds in Iraq and Syria are doing their best to control their areas, preferably to become as independent as possible, but do thereby contribute to sectarian and ethnic politics, possibly resulting in further instability in the region. Overall, sectarian politics will not only create security dilemmas within the states, it will also further justify the continuation of repressive totalitarian regimes.

The Israeli-Palestinian conflict will continue to have adverse ramifications, not only to the security of the Middle East, but also for the international system. This long-running conflict has polarized the internal as well as external actors into complex hostility relations, and resolving this problem would remove one of the most important obstacles for resolving many other conflicts in the region as well. With the current stalemate, the reelection of a right-wing government in Israel, and the unwillingness of Hamas to recognize Israel's right to exist, conflict will not only continue but may escalate. New discoveries of huge gas fields in its Mediterranean coast provide more leeway to Israel to continue to maintain hard-line position vis-à-vis genuine Palestinian demands. Growing food and water crisis creates further economic difficulties for the population in occupied territories, resulting in further anger. Continued occasional violent escalations of this conflict will risk polarizing the regimes in the region on sectarian lines as well and will continue to fuel groups on all sides to enlarge the gulf between the Islamic world and the West.

REGION TO REGAIN THE INITIATIVE

It is clear that the regimes in the region in their effort to continue their hold on power have usually neglected sustainable economic development and favored short-term situational development. The resulting outcome of this approach has been unsustainable use and management, and in some cases, destruction of natural renewable and nonrenewable resources, which has contributed further to creating conflicts and insecurity in the society. In order to avoid these negative consequences, countries in the region need to prioritize good governance and regional cooperation. The challenges are as such that security has to be strengthened not only at the state level but also at the human and regional levels. This book has outlined a number of new and in many ways interlinked security challenges of water, food, energy, and migration. These are arguably some of the most important and pressing new security challenges. However, while these are important, we do not claim them to be all encompassing and there are other areas like health that could also in some cases merit a deeper and closer analysis.

The traditional view of security is not enough for the Middle East and there is a need for an analytical framework of security amenable to the twenty-first century, that is, one that moves beyond *state/regime security*, toward a broader and deeper analysis that also includes economic, societal, and environmental security issues. This integrated security structure, which brings together state security, human security, and regional security, can be better suited to provide sustainable security to this changing world and its emerging challenges. When the Middle East continues to face unusual transnational threats, mutual trust and cooperation between and among the countries of the region is required. Thus, the challenge is to forge a new sustainable security structure that is both effective and energetic in dealing with the challenges confronting the region.

States alone are not capable of solving many of the emerging problems that they face. An individual state in the Middle East cannot be fully secure with its agricultural production and water supply and cannot tackle fluctuating energy markets and increasing population movements in a globalized world. Moreover, the serious threat of climate change makes a strong case for increasing regional cooperation in the environment and development sectors. The crude power of a state is no longer enough to meet the newly emerging security challenges. State security or regime security is no longer a formula for prosperity and peace. The multidimensional nature of emerging threats demands that an integrated security approach be adopted.

Increased national agricultural production, while essential, is not always sufficient to provide food security. Adequate supply of food at the national level does not necessarily always guarantee that all people have enough to eat. There are always other matters involved, such as special access to food on the part of vulnerable people. Long-term food security in the region requires a comprehensive approach, which includes both sustainable agricultural productivity, agricultural trade (import), and guarantee of adequate and affordable nutritious food for all people. In the Middle East, numerous factors pose a challenge to the ability of large segments of the population to access adequate food, including the lack of income opportunities and absence of effective social safety nets. Thus, the Middle Eastern states should seriously rethink their strategy of achieving illusive self-sufficiency in food production with the highly unsustainable use of land and water resources to create effective institutions and infrastructure for better food supply and distribution.

All the countries in the Middle East are exposed to water scarcity. The adoption of a supply management strategy addressing only the water shortage in the region is not nearly sufficient. To meet future demands, there is a need to minimize water use, particularly in the agricultural sector. States in the region should opt for a planned allocation of agricultural activities to improve the productivity of scarce water. There is a need for putting institutions in place to restrict and regularize the water demand. As the region is heavily dependent on international rivers and aquifers, riparian states have to start establishing institutional cooperative arrangements to manage shared waters. Cooperation of water could possibly also help increase mutual trust and confidence among the riparian states of the basin.

The countries in the region maintain a strong dependence on fossil fuels to meet their energy demands. Increasing population, urbanization, and the increasing demands for more food, goods, and services have put enormous challenges to the energy supplies and energy infrastructure. As energy is the driver for development, sustainable energy is the incentive for sustainable development. The countries need to fast recognize the importance of a low carbon transition to abate global climate change, reduce poverty rates, and enhance efforts to reduce fossil fuel dependence. Moreover, all these will help the Gulf countries overcome the curse of resources, which has restricted their progress toward democratization for long.

The region also needs to adopt a positive approach to squarely face the enormous task of large-scale human migration. States need to be focused on preventing the causes of population displacement. The increasing numbers of population displacement can be addressed only in terms of setting up a comprehensive regional agenda to achieve human security. The focus should be to bring balance between human numbers and the available natural resources in an equitable way. The issue of population displacement cannot be confronted without energetic and earnest initiatives by both the migrant-producing and migrant-receiving countries in the region. To achieve this objective, countries should recognize the critical link between human security and migration and aggressively incorporate the migration variable in their state planning. At the same time, the region also needs to encourage the positive factors that result from migration.

To achieve working peace and stability in the Middle East, the states need to pursue a sustainable economic policy for growth and development, which not only will be sensitive to local needs and environment but will also take the support of the local resource base to promote cooperation in the long run. Human security should be the primary objective, and thus it is important to shift the referent object in the security discourse from the state to the individual. Promoting and supporting policies should not be limited to attain only "freedom from fear" but also "freedom from want." There is no doubt that policies toward "freedom from want" are equally important for the long-term security and stability of countries in the Middle East.

The continuing large-scale violence and bloodshed has given the Middle East a prominent place in the media discourse. However, it is not exactly a mysterious and dark region as often depicted to be. The people in the region like many other parts of the world struggle to get a living and hope and work for a better future. The politics of the region is not static, it is constantly evolving. There is an enlargement of spaces of political participation in many of these countries. However, democratization and the rule of law in the Middle East cannot be achieved through force or intervention, rather it should be envisaged in a way that enhances the potential for political participation and weakens the structural basis of authoritarianism.

NOTES

1. Anders Jägerskog, "Human Security – Problems, Opportunities and Policy Implications," *Conflict, Security and Development*, 4, 3 (2004): 309–12.

2. Jessica Touchman Mathews, "Redefining Security," *Foreign Affairs*, 68, 2, (1989); Richard Ullman, "Redefining Security," *International Security*, 8, 1 (1983): 129–53; Commission on Human Security, *Human Security Now: Protecting and Empowering People*. (New York: Commission on Human Security, 2003).

3. Barry Buzan, Ole Waever and Jaap de Wilde, *Security: A New Framework for Analysis* (Boulder, Colo. and London: Lynne Rienner, 1998).

4. It is understood that there are other areas that could also have been included in the analysis (e.g., health) from the perspective of a broadened security concept. However, the four areas that have been chosen for this book arguably represent the most pressing ones and have been increasingly seen as fast-emerging security challenges.

5. Ashok Swain, *Understanding Emerging Security Challenges: Threats and Opportunities* (London: Routledge, 2012).

6. Barry Buzan, *People, State and Fear* (Brighton: Harvester Wheatsheaf, 1983).

7. Ernst B. Haas, *Beyond The Nation-State* (Stanford: Stanford University Press, 1964); Robert O. Keohane, *After Hegemony: Cooperation and Discord in the World Political Economy* (Princeton: Princeton University Press, 1984); Thomas M. Franck, *The Power Of Legitimacy Among Nations* (Oxford: Oxford University Press, 1990); Barry Buzan and Lene Hansen, *The Evolution of International Security Studies* (Cambridge: Cambridge University Press, 2009); Joseph S. Nye Jr. and David A. Welch, *Understanding Global Conflict and Cooperation: An Introduction to Theory and History 9th Edn* (London: Pearson Longman, 2012).

8. Robert D. Putnam, *Democracies in Flux: The Evolution of Social Capital in Contemporary Society* (New York: Oxford University Press, 2004); David Halpern,

Social Capital (Cambridge: Polity, 2004); Ashok Swain, *Struggle Against the State: Social Network and Protest Mobilization in India* (Farnham, UK: Ashgate Publishing Limited, 2010); Elinor Ostrom and Toh-Kyeong Ahn, eds., *Foundations of Social Capital* (Cheltenham, UK: Edward Elgar, 2010).

9. Ken Conca and Geoff D. Dabelko, eds., *Environmental Peacemaking* (Baltimore: John Hopkins University Press, 2002).

10. Anders Jägerskog, "Functional Water Co-operation in the Jordan River Basin: Spillover or Spillback for Political Security," in *Facing Global Environmental Change: Environmental, Human, Energy, Food, Health and Water Security Concepts.* Hexagon Series on Human and Environmental Security and Peace, vol. 4, eds., Hans Günter Brauch, Ursula Oswald Spring, John Grin, Mesjasz Czeslaw, Patricia Kameri-Mbote, Navnita Chadha Behera, Béchir Chourou, Heinz Krummenacher (Berlin: Springer-Verlag, 2008), i. p.

11. Erik Berglöf and Shanta Devarajan, "Water for development: Fulfilling the promise," in Anders Jägerskog, Torkil J. Clausen, Torgny Holmgren and Karin Lexén, eds., *Water for Development; Charting a Water Wise Path*, SIWI Report Nr. 35, SIWI: Stockholm, 2015.

12. Jägerskog, "Functional Water Co-operation in the Jordan River Basin: Spillover or Spillback for Political Security."

13. J. A. Allan, *The Middle East Water Question: Hydropolitics and the Global Economy*, (London, I.B. Tauris, 2001).

14. Anders Jägerskog and Kyungmee Kim, "Land acquisition as a means to mitigate water scarcity and reduce conflict?," Accepted in *Hydrological Sciences Journal* (2015).

15. FAO *Global Food Losses and Waste – Extent, Causes and Prevention* (Rome: FAO, 2011).

16. Allan, *The Middle East Water Question: Hydropolitics and the Global Economy.*

17. IEA, *Regional Energy Efficiency Policy Recommendations: Arab-Southern and Eastern Mediterranean (SEMED) Region,* International Energy Agency. IEA, 2014.

18. A. Lindström, A. Hoffman, G. Olsson, "Shale Gas and Hydraulic Fracturing – Framing the Water Issue," S*IWI Report*, no 24, (Stockholm: SIWI, 2014).

19. Mary Kaldor, *New and Old Wars: Organized Violence in a Global Era*, 2nd Ed. (Oxford: Polity, 2006).

20. Joell Demmers, "New Wars and Diasporas: Suggestions for Research and Policy," *Journal of Peace, Conflict and Development*, 11 (2007).

21. Ashok Swain, Joakim Öjendal and Michael Schulz, *Security in the Middle East-Increasingly Multidimensional and Challenging,* A Study Commissioned by the Strategic Perspective Project within the Swedish Armed Forces Headquarters, Stockholm, August 2009.

22. Egypt has also historically been a key representative for Sunni Muslims with some of the most renowned Islamic scholars being based at Al-Azhar University. In addition, Iraq has, at certain time periods, aspired to be a leader of the Arab Muslim World.

23. Gause F. Gregory III, "Saudi Arabia in the New Middle East," *Council on Foreign Relations Special Report No. 63*, December 2011.

24. Yaroslav Trofimov, "Sunni-Shiite Conflict Reflects Modern Power Struggle, Not Theological Schism," *The Wall Street Journal*, May 14, 2015.

25. Hussein Mahdavy, "The Patterns and Problems of Economic Development in Rentier States: The Case of Iran," in Studies in Economic History of the Middle East, ed., M. A. Cook (London: Oxford University Press, 1970), 428–67; Hazem Beblawi, "The Rentier State in the Arab World," in The Rentier State, eds., Hazem Beblawi and Giacomo Luciani (New York: Croom Helm, 1987), 49–62; Jill Crystal, Oil and Politics in the Gulf: Rulers and Merchants in Kuwait and Qatar (New York: Cambridge University Press, 1990); F. Gregory Gause III, Oil Monarchies: Domestic Security Challenges in the Arab Gulf States (New York: Council on Foreign Relations Press, 1994); Kiren Aziz Chaudhry, "The Price of Wealth: Business and State in Labor Remittance and Oil Economies," International Organization, 43, 1, (1989): 101–45; Robert J. Barro, "Determinants of Democracy," Journal of Political Economy 107, 6 (1999): S158–83; Michael L. Ross, The Oil Curse: How Petroleum Wealth Shapes the Development of Nations (Princeton: Princeton University Press, 2012).

26. Bruce Bueno de Mesquita and Alastair Smith, "Leader Survival, Revolutions, and the Nature of Government Finance," American Political Science Review, 54, 4 (2010): 936–50.

27. Erwin Bulte, Richard Damania and Robert T. Deacon, "Resource Intensity, Institutions, and Development," World Development, 33, 7 (2005): 1029–44; Jonathan Isham, Michael Woolcock, Lant Pritchett and Gwen Busby, "The Varieties of the Rentier Experience: How Natural Resource Export Structures Affect the Political Economy of Growth," World Bank Economic Review 19, 2, (2005): 141–74; Mette Anthonsen, Åsa Löfgren, Klas Nilsson and Joakim Westerlund, "Effects of Rent Dependency on Quality of Government," Economics of Governance, 13, 2, (2012): 145–68.

28. Laila Alhamad, "Formal and Informal Venues of Engagement," in *Political Participation in the Middle East,* eds., Ellen Lust-Okar and Saloua Zerhouni (Boulder: Lynne Rienner Publishers, 2008), 33–47.

29. UNDP, *Towards Freedom in the Arab World* (New York: United Nations, 2004).

30. As outlined by Marwan Muasher at the Arab Summit on Sustainable Development in Manama, Bahrain, May 5, 2015.

31. UNDP, *Towards Freedom in the Arab World*, 21.

32. UNDP, *Towards Freedom in the Arab World*, 19.

33. Charles F. Andrain and David E. Apter, *Political Protest and Social Change: Analysing Politics* (London: Macmillan, 1995).

34. Ekkart Zimmermann, "Macro-comparative research on political protest," in *Handbook of Political Conflict: Theory and Research,* ed., T. R. Gurr (New York: Free Press), 167–237; Ted R. Gurr, "Why Minorities Rebel: A Global Analysis of Communal Mobilization and Conflict since 1945," *International Political Science Review/ Revue internationale de science politique*, 14, 2 (1993): 161–201.

35. Ronald A. Francisco, "The Relationship between Coercion and Protest: An Empirical Evaluation in Three Coercive States," *Journal of Conflict Resolution*, 39, 2 (1995): 263–82.

36. Sidney Tarrow, "Modular Collective Action and the Rise of the Social Movement: Why the French Revolution was not Enough," *Politics and Society*, 21, 1 (1993): 69–90.

37. Martien Briet, Bert Klandermans and Fredrik Kroon, "How Women Become Involved in the Women's Movement of the Netherlands," in *The Women Movements of the United States and Western Europe: Consciousness, Political Opportunities and Public Policy,* eds., Mary Fainsod Katzenstein and Carol McClurg Mueller (Philadelphia: Temple University Press, 1987), 44–63; Roger V. Gould, "Collective Action and Network Structure," *American Sociological Review*, 58, 2 (1993): 182–96; Doug McAdam, "Recruitment to High Risk Activism: The Case of Freedom Summer," *American Journal of Sociology*, 92, 1 (1986): 64–90.

38. Friedhelm Neidhardt and Dieter Rucht, "The Analysis of Social Movements: The State of the Art and Some Perspectives for Further Research," in *Research on Social Movements*, ed., D. Rucht (Frankfurt: Campus and Westview Press, 1991), 421–64.

39. Robert D. Putnam, *Making Democracy Work: Civic Traditions in Modern Italy* (Princeton, NJ: Princeton University Press, 1993), 167.

40. John J. Rodger, *From a Welfare State to a Welfare Society* (Houndmills, UK: Macmillan, 2000).

41. Robert D. Putnam, "E Pluribus Unum: Diversity and Community in the 21st Century," *Scandinavian Political Studies*, 30, 2 (2007): 137–74.

42. Eric Wolf, *Europe and the People without History* (Berkeley: University of California Press, 1982).

43. Gad G. Gilbar, *The Middle East Oil Decade: Essays in Political Economy* (London: Routledge, 1997).

44. Robert Vitalis, *America's Kingdom: Mythmaking on the Saudi Oil Frontier* (Pal Alto, CA: Stanford University Press, 2006).

45. Abdulrahman Munif, *Cities of Salt* (New York: Vintage International, 1989).

46. Mary Ann Tétreault, "International Relations," in *Understanding the Contemporary Middle East*, 3rd Edition, Jillian Schwedler and Deborah J. Gerner (Boulder, CO: Lynne Rienner Publishers, 2008): 137–75.

47. Toby Craig Jones, "America, Oil and War in the Middle East," *Journal of American History*, 99, 1, (2012): 208–18.

48. Report of the Defense Science Board Task Force on Strategic Communication, Washington DC, 2004.

49. Philip Gordon, "The Middle East is Falling Apart," *Politico*, June 4, 2015; Nafeez Ahmed, "Collapse of Saudi Arabia is Inevitable," *Middle East Eye*, September 28, 2015; Robert D. Kaplan, "The Ruins of Empire in the Middle East," *Foreign Policy*, May 25, 2015.

Index

Index

About the Authors

Ashok Swain is professor in the Department of Peace and Conflict Research and in the Department of Earth Sciences, CSD of Uppsala University, Sweden. He also serves as the director of the Research School for International Water Cooperation, a collaboration between Uppsala University and Stockholm International Water Institute (SIWI). He received his PhD from the Jawaharlal Nehru University, New Delhi, in 1991, and since then he has been teaching at the Uppsala University. He has been a MacArthur Fellow at the University of Chicago; visiting professor/fellows at UN Research Institute for Social Development, Geneva; University of the Witwatersrand; University of Science, Malaysia; University of British Columbia; University of Maryland; Stanford University; McGill University; and Tufts University. Ashok Swain has written extensively on emerging security challenges, international water sharing, and migration issues and democratic development.

Anders Jägerskog is counselor for regional water issues in the Middle East and North Africa for the Embassy of Sweden in Amman, Jordan. He is also associate professor at the School of Global Studies at Göteborg University as well as former head of the Transboundary Unit at the Stockholm International Water Institute (SIWI). He has worked at the secretariat for the Expert Group on Development Issues (EGDI) at the Swedish Ministry for Foreign Affairs, as senior program manager, water resources, at the Embassy of Sweden, Nairobi, as well as at the Stockholm International Peace Research Institute (SIPRI) with Middle Eastern security issues. The views expressed by Jägerskog do not necessarily reflect the views of the Swedish International Development Co-operation Agency or the Swedish Government.